International Retailing
Trends and Strategies

International Retailing
Trends and Strategies

Edited by
Peter J McGoldrick
and Gary Davies

PITMAN PUBLISHING
128 Long Acre, London WC2E 9AN

A Division of Pearson Professional Limited

First published in Great Britain in 1995

© Pearson Professional Limited 1995

ISBN 0 273 61183 6

British Library Cataloguing in Publication Data
A CIP catalogue record for this book can be obtained from the British Library

10 9 8 7 6 5 4 3 2

Typeset by 🝿 Tek-Art, Croydon, Surrey.
Printed and bound in Great Britain by Bell and Bain, Glasgow

The Publisher's policy is to use paper manufactured from sustainable forests.

CONTENTS

PREFACE

In the next millennium, we may well look back with nostalgia at the research and management effort that was exercised in the area of international retailing. As markets cease to be defined according to quirks of geography, history, language or culture, international retailing will surely become the norm rather than the exception. The early moves by retailers outside their home markets may seem as remote a memory as the voyages of the early explorers, high on hope but low on information. Like the early explorers, some found great wealth, while others lost everything and returned home empty handed.

So, if international retailing is only really an extension of retail marketing and retailing geography, why a book on the subject? The fact is that markets are still a long way from being homogenised. Even within the European Union, the competitive structures, infrastructures, legislative frameworks and economic environments are extremely diverse; then there are the cultures and the languages! Beyond the European Union, the problems of logistics and communications multiply, plus the complexities of tariffs and other barriers to free trade.

If multinational manufacturing companies have learnt to cope with this diversity and distance, why are they such problems for retailers? Unlike manufacturers, retailers cannot delegate their customer interface to others; they are the customer interface. The level of adaptation to local cultures and expectations must therefore be that much more precise. Unlike the multinational manufacturers, the international retailers cannot simply build their plants in the country/zone with the most favourable economic and political climate. Most of their property assets are their stores, which must be near to the potential customers. This often requires much adaptation to and compromise with the formats utilised in home markets.

One of the greatest gaps to be bridged in the internationalisation of retailing is that of information. It is probably true to say that a British retailer can apply more scientific analysis to a planned store opening in Scunthorpe than to one in Strasbourg or Singapore. Not that retail managers have failed to expend time and effort on the evaluation of international opportunities. At the present time, however, the supply of relevant and compatible information has not expanded fully to meet the needs of retailers.

The purpose of this book is to present a collection of contributions towards the better understanding of retail internationalisation. It is accepted that a great deal of work remains to be done; another purpose has been to identify major gaps in the research in this field. Most of the chapters originated at a seminar in Manchester sponsored largely by the Economic and Social Research Council. Following this seminar, each of the contributions has been revised and updated; further ones have been added.

The editors would like to thank all the contributors, who are listed on the pages following. They have persevered through a multiple review process, firstly for the seminar and then for the book chapters. Thanks are also due to Erica Betts who was responsible for co-ordinating the seminar and who has assisted greatly with the editing of this book. A great debt of gratitude is due to Mary O'Mahony who dealt with the correspondence in connection with the International Retailing seminar and book, and who has patiently interpreted my notes on chapters that I have edited or co-authored. Thanks are also due to Lynn Dalton for her work on the chapters edited or co-authored by Gary Davies.

The editors are grateful for the financial support for the ESRC, without which the seminar and this book would not have come about. Financial support for the seminar was also provided by the Manchester School of Management at UMIST and the Manchester Business School. The seminars benefited from the incisive review by Professor John Dawson, who brought into clear focus the extent and limitations of research to date in this field. Finally, and certainly not least, the editors are grateful for the patience and professionalism of the staff at Pitman Publishing, especially Angela Lewis, Simon Lake, Mark Allin and Julianne Mulholland.

Peter J McGoldrick
February, 1995

LIST OF CONTRIBUTORS

Nicholas Alexander

Senior Lecturer in Retailing
School of Commerce
Faculty of Business and Management
University of Ulster
Coleraine
Northern Ireland BT52 1SA

David Bennison

Department of Retailing and Marketing
Manchester Metropolitan University
Aytoun Building
Aytoun Street
Manchester M1 3GH

Debbie Blair

Manchester School of Management
PO Box 88
UMIST
Manchester M60 1QD

Steve Burt

Senior Lecturer
Institute for Retail Studies
University of Stirling
Stirling
Scotland FK9 4LA

Colin M Clarke-Hill

Senior Lecturer
School of Business
University of Huddersfield
Queensgate
Huddersfield HD1 3DH

Gary Davies

Post Office Counters Professor of Retailing
Manchester Business School
Booth Street West
Manchester M15 6PB

Keri Davies

Institute for Retail Studies
University of Stirling
Stirling
Scotland FK9 4LA

Hanne Gardner

Lecturer in Marketing
Department of Retailing and Marketing
Manchester Metropolitan University
Aytoun Building
Aytoun Street
Manchester M1 3GH

Hong Liu

Lecturer in Marketing
Manchester Business School
Booth Street West
Manchester M15 6PB

Angelo Manaresi

Dipartimento di Discipline Economico-
Aziendali
Università Degli Studi di Bologna
Piazza Scaravilli 2
40126 Bologna
Italy

Peter J McGoldrick

Littlewoods Professor of Retailing
Manchester School of Management and
Manchester Business School

Nitin Sanghavi

Senior Fellow in Retailing
Manchester Business School
Booth Street West
Manchester M15 6PB

Terry Robinson

Principal Lecturer in Marketing
Teesside Business School
University of Teesside
Middlesbrough TS1 3BA

André Tordjman

Professor of Marketing
Groupe HEC
78351 Jouy-en-Josas
Cédéx
Paris

Mark Uncles

Heinz Professor of Brand Management
Bradford Management Centre
University of Bradford
Emm Lane
Bradford BD9 4JL

Maureen Whitehead

Marks and Spencer Fellow in International
Retailing
Department of Retailing and Marketing
Manchester Metropolitan University
Aytoun Building
Aytoun Street
Manchester M1 3GH

CHAPTER 1

Introduction to international retailing

Peter J McGoldrick

INTRODUCTION

Most of the attention given to international retailing in recent years has focused upon the development of new markets (e.g. Alexander, 1994) or the 'invasion' of home markets (e.g., Duke, 1993). These two facets of internationalisation are understandable preoccupations, given their demands upon management time and their potential impacts upon balance sheets. The influence of internationalisation is, however, still more pervasive, as illustrated by Figure 1.1.

Well before the recent growth of international retailing activity, the flow of ideas and know-how has brought international influences to trading formats (e.g. Burt, 1994; Kacker, 1985). Complex networks of international alliances have also developed, furthering the spread of expertise and offering buying advantages for participants. The sourcing of products internationally – a well established practice in some sectors – is now spreading to virtually all sectors of retailing. These other important facets of internationalisation serve to lower psychological barriers, increase awareness of opportunities in other markets and increase international retail management expertise.

Each of these five facets is addressed within the chapters that follow. Firstly, a brief introduction is provided in section 1.1, summarising the basic frameworks that have developed to depict the internationalisation process. Section 1.2 outlines the structure of the book and the principal objectives of each chapter.

1.1 INTERNATIONALISATION OF RETAILING

1.1.1 Extent of retailer internationalisation

In spite of the attention given to international retailing in recent years, it is still the minority activity for the majority of retailers. Table 1.1 compares the relative importance of activities outside the home markets of 21 leading

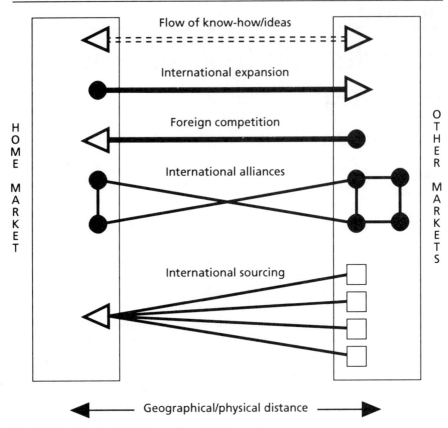

Fig.1.1 Facets of retail internationalisation

European retailers. In only four cases does the turnover derived outside the home market exceed 50 per cent of total turnover. In three cases, Dehaize, Ahold and Ikea, the high proportion is explained in part by the relatively modest size of the home markets (Belgium, Netherlands and Sweden). Tengelmann is the only one to derive more than 50 per cent outside the large German food market. Noticeably, Aldi, the subject of a great deal of media attention within its 'invaded' countries, derived only 20 per cent of its turnover from international operations.

The pace of retail internationalisation has undoubtedly quickened; Corporate Intelligence (1991) identified some 654 instances of market entry across 16 European countries during the 1980s, compared with 182 during the previous decade. In spite of this, most retailers still derive the greatest proportion of their turnover from domestic markets. Marks & Spencer is one of the most active amongst Britain's leading retailers, generating now around 14 per cent of turnover from international operations.

This implies that we are witnessing only the earlier stages of the movement towards internationalisation in retailing. There are still major problems

Table 1.1 International activities of European retailers

Company	Country	International turnover (million ecu)	per cent of total turnover	Main activity
Tengelmann	D	12,656.4	55.7	Food
Metro	D	6,036.1	35.0	Food/dept. store
Promodès	F	5,506.2	34.4	Food
Delhaize le Lion	B	5,283.0	72.4	Food
Ahold	NL	4,548.3	50.6	Food
Otto Versand	D	3,602.2	45.9	Mail order
Carrefour	F	3,414.7	31.1	Food
Vendex International	NL	2,808.7	35.3	Food/dept. store
Aldi	D	2,520.0	20.0	Food
Ikea	S	2,138.2	76.2	Furniture
Auchan	F	1,413.2	15.3	Food
J Sainsbury	UK	1,365.3	11.8	Food
Marks & Spencer	UK	1,055.5	14.0	Apparel/food
GUS	UK	1,013.6	26.9	Mail Order
Au Printemps	F	986.0	20.2	Dept. store
La Redoute	F	879.3	35.0	Mail order
Quelle	D	759.9	10.6	Mail order
Dixons	UK	508.4	30.6	Electrical
Docks de France	F	508.4	13.3	Food
Casino	F	449.3	6.1	Food
Ratners	UK	348.2	27.6	Jewellery

Source: Eurostat (1993).

which inhibit internationalisation, although many of these are diminishing. Reliable, comparative information on market conditions remains a major problem; retailers must often base location decisions abroad on far less sophisticated information than their location decisions at home. Trends in the development of internationalisation are the subject of Part One of this book.

1.1.2 Stimuli and obstacles to internationalisation

The factors that have pushed, pulled or in some way facilitated the movement towards greater retail internationalisation have been a major subject of investigation and discussion over the years (e.g. Hollander, 1969; Kacker, 1985; Corporate Intelligence, 1991; Williams, 1992; Alexander and

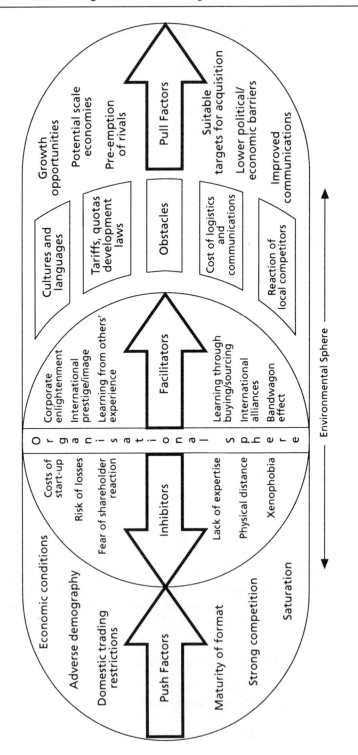

Fig. 1.2 Driving forces of internationalisation

Morlock, 1992). A number of ways of classifying these factors have come in and out of favour; an in-depth analysis of internationalisation motives is provided by Nicholas Alexander in Chapter 4.

The concept of 'push and pull' factors has drawn attention to the fact that retailers' international moves have often been motivated by difficulties within the home market rather than simply the attractions of the new market. Given the costs and risks usually involved in gaining initial experience in unfamiliar markets, there is some evidence that 'push' factors may be most significant at the early stages of internationalisation (e.g. McGoldrick and Fryer, 1993). The simple 'push–pull' dichotomy does, however, fail to distinguish between the factors that are primarily within the sphere of the organisation and those primarily within the broader environment.

Figure 1.2 makes this additional distinction, showing examples of each type of 'driving force'. Within this framework, three types of driving force are depicted, i.e., the 'push' and 'pull' forces within the environment and the various facilitators within the organisational sphere. The factors that inhibit internationalisation are also depicted as being either organisational or environmental obstacles.

Although this framework attempts to overcome some of the criticisms levelled at the earlier classifications of driving forces, it too is only a simplification of a complex network of forces. It is readily acknowledged that the interactions between organisation and environment are so pervasive as to make even this distinction problematical. It could be argued, for example, that perceptions within the organisation of the levels of distance, difficulty and risk will be more instrumental than the actual levels of these factors. In spite of these problems, it is considered helpful to distinguish between factors that can be controlled or influenced within the organisational sphere, in contrast with those which are external and elements of the geographical, political, economic or competitive environment. Further elaboration upon the individual issues is not appropriate at this stage, these being the subject of Part Two of this book.

1.1.3 Stages of internationalisation

The 'stages' concept has been applied to depict the typical movement by retailers towards internationalisation. Given the considerable risks and cost involved in expansion outside home markets, most have viewed the prospect with a degree of reluctance. The problems encountered by such flagship retailers as Printemps and Marks & Spencer, in their earliest developments, have contributed further to this reluctance. Treadgold (1990/91) used UK retailer Tesco as an example of the reluctant internationaliser. Although Tesco has subsequently acquired the French Catteau chain, this move was preceded by a great deal of financial and market analysis, all shrouded in great secrecy. In July 1994, the company also bought a 51.1 per cent stake in the Hungarian supermarket chain Global.

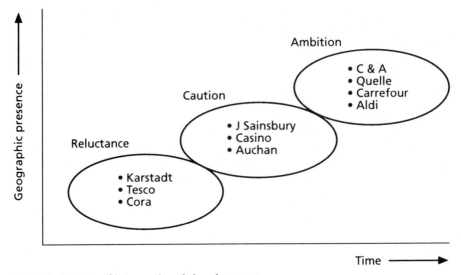

Fig. 1.3 Stages of international development
Source: Treadgold (1990/91).

This secrecy is typical of companies moving from reluctance to cautious expansion abroad. The stock market has shown adverse reactions to news of internationalisation, given the losses frequently incurred by retailers, at least in the short term. As well as seeking to reduce vulnerability at home, the secrecy is also designed to minimise the likelihood of rival bids for the international acquisition target.

Figure 1.3 illustrates the three typical stages, providing examples of each. In contrast with Tesco's recent moves, J Sainsbury has over twelve years of international trading experience. In 1983, a minority stake was obtained in Shaw's supermarkets, New England; the company was acquired by J Sainsbury in 1987 (Alexander, 1994). Aldi is cited as an example of a company at the 'ambition' stage, with a long history of international market entry (McGoldrick and Ali, 1994).

One may of course challenge the inference that companies necessarily proceed from stage to stage along the time axis. It could, for example, be pointed out that the early expansion of Marks & Spencer into Canada showed a great deal of ambition; many of their more recent international expansions, on the other hand, have demonstrated greater caution. Further discussion of Marks & Spencer's internationalisation is contained in Chapter 9.

1.1.4 International development positions

The internationalisation of retailing has produced very diverse styles of operation, ranging from global to multinational (Salmon and Tordjman, 1989; Treadgold, 1988). Global retailers such as Benetton vary their format very little across national boundaries, achieving the greatest economies of scale but showing the least local responsiveness (Treadgold, 1988). Multinationals, on the other hand, tend to develop or acquire a diversity of formats internationally, usually achieving rather lower benefits from integration. A middle course may be termed 'transnational' retailing (Treadgold 1990/91), whereby the company seeks to achieve global efficiency while responding to national needs, opportunities and constraints. Some of the more recent developments by Marks & Spencer could best be described as transnational, recognising that even the most successful retail formats within the domestic market may require adaptation to suit markets abroad.

Figure 1.4 illustrates these three major types of development position, providing examples of each. Companies within the 'multinational' category may operate as largely autonomous entities within each country. Before its demise, the retail assets of the Mountleigh Group included the Merry Hill shopping complex in the UK and the Galerias Preciados department stores in Spain. At the other extreme, Toys 'R' Us is frequently cited as the prime example of the global format. Indeed, their stores across the world are strikingly similar in terms of layout, products and services. Even Toys 'R' Us, however, was obliged to respond in France to the strong reactions of the hypermarkets, which were well able to compete on price and devote extensive space to toys during the peak selling season (Tordjman 1994). The concept of the 'category killer', as a vehicle for internationalisation, is explored further in Chapter 11.

The benefits of a strong format, sufficiently distinct to compete in many

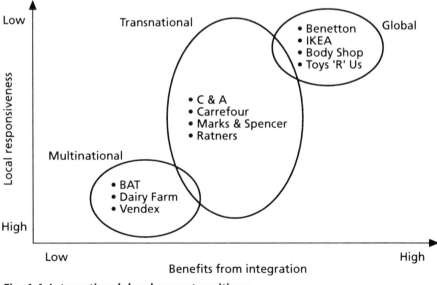

Fig. 1.4 International development positions
Source: Treadgold (1990/91).

different markets, are enormous. The 1990s are, however, seeing a shift away from uniformity, even within domestic retailing. Retailers are learning that no two markets are the same; why assume therefore that the same format is ideal for all markets? Micromarketing and more flexible systems have combined to allow diversity without chaos. Projecting this shift to an international scene, the 'transnational' position looks increasingly viable and attractive. While a retailer may wish to promote the same core values in all markets, the detailed characteristics of the stores, management and product range may differ considerably.

1.1.5 International entry strategies

Having identified the target market(s), a number of alternative entry strategies are available to the retailer. Broadly speaking, the retailer must select between high cost, high control options, such as acquisition, and low cost, low control options such as concessions. The main options are depicted in Figure 1.5 and are as follows:

- *Licensing:* requires the least capital investment and risk but offers the least control. Parents own no equity in the venture. Examples include the J C Penney Collection – stores in the Middle East licensed by the US parent and selling the retailer's private label goods.
- *Concessions:* again, a low risk, low cost option, involving the operation of 'shops within shops' in larger stores. Burton have used this strategy to test their formats in new markets, such as within Galerias Preciados department stores in Spain.

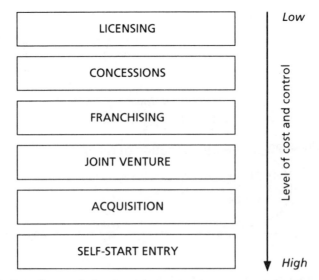

Fig. 1.5 Options for market entry

- *Franchising:* avoids much of the risk and demands upon capital, and is especially appropriate where a retailing concept can be readily exported. Notable examples include Italian manufacturer/franchiser Benetton, with over 6,000 outlets in over 80 countries.
- *Joint venture:* reducing time, cost and risk of entry by working with a partner already familiar with the market. In spite of their benefits at the outset, many joint ventures/partnerships have been terminated, having not met expectations (Burt, 1986).
- *Acquisition:* provides a quick entry route but at a cost, not least because companies available for acquisition may well be in financial difficulty. The approach has been used by many UK retailers, including the acquisition of Kings Super Markets and Brooks Brothers menswear in the USA by Marks & Spencer.
- *Self-start entry:* the chain being built up from scratch, or developed through organic growth from a very modest initial acquisition. Examples include Woolworths' early development in the UK and Laura Ashley in the USA.

Further discussion of these strategies is provided in Chapter 9, with regard to the internationalisation of Marks & Spencer.

Another approach to internationalisation, without necessarily operating stores outside the home markets, is to collaborate within one of the several retail/wholesale alliances. Cross-border alliances have become a major element of international retail co-operation and expansion in recent years. Treadgold (1990/91) examined four main types, namely, purchasing-led alliances, development alliances, skills-based alliances and multi-function alliances. Within this last category may be included the development of the European Retail Alliance (ERA) and Associated Marketing Services (AMS), linking retailers across Europe and opening opportunities for many forms of co-operation, including purchasing, sourcing, logistics, product development, promotion and political lobbying. These alliances are examined in detail within Chapter 7.

1.2 STRUCTURE OF THE BOOK

1.2.1 Trends in the internationalisation of retailing

In Chapter 2, André Tordjman sets the scene by presenting a wide-ranging review of retailing in Europe. In spite of the enormous diversity within European retailing, some convergent trends can be identified, notably towards greater segmentation, competition and concentration. Great differences, however, exist in the levels of development within the various countries, ranging from the 'traditional' retailing of Greece and Portugal to the 'advanced' retailing of Germany and the United Kingdom. The food and non-food retail sectors are examined in turn, highlighting the inter-country differences in the strength of each format. This underlines the importance of understanding the competitive context, both in terms of formats and organisation types, when entering new markets. The chapter concludes with an assessment of winning strategies and implications for manufacturers, retailers and consumers.

A longitudinal view of retail internationalisation is presented by Steve Burt in Chapter 3. A study of trends, both in retailer internationalisation and in the literature relating to this, shows evidence of evolution in the development of both theory and practice. While many of the early studies focused upon 'where', much interest is now focused upon 'why' and 'how'. Data sources are identified which enable the monitoring of international activity; these sources are analysed to depict trends from the 1960s to the 1990s. It is clear that the evolution of strategies for internationalisation has reflected the geographical spread of international activity. As retailers have shifted their attention beyond the geographically and/or culturally close markets, methods of entry which involve less cost and risk have gained in appeal.

1.2.2 Driving forces of internationalisation

The motives that have driven the process of retailer internationalisation are placed under scrutiny by Nicholas Alexander in Chapter 4. Various typologies of motives are summarised, notably the 'push and pull' classifications and the 'reactive vs proactive' approaches to internationalisation. He warns, however, of the dangers of accepting typologies of motives based upon a limited timespan. The balance of motives has shifted over time and, equally, the motives of individual organisations change and evolve. A critical view is taken of the emphasis given to 'push' factors, notably saturation, which is a problematic concept and difficult to define. The chapter highlights the importance of interpreting motives within specific organisational and competitive contexts.

A major but frequently neglected facet of retail internationalisation is that of international product sourcing. In Chapter 5, Hong Liu and Peter McGoldrick examine the factors that have stimulated, and those that have constrained, the shift of retail buying from domestic to international suppliers. Distinctions are drawn between the international sourcing activities of retailers, wholesalers and manufacturers. Individual companies tend to be reluctant to disclose proportions of goods sourced internationally but data on aggregate trade flows are discussed. Particular attention is given to the challenges of sourcing from developing countries and to the special characteristics of Japanese international sourcing. The chapter concludes with an examination of the stages and processes involved in sourcing internationally.

The importance of legislative environments, as driving forces for internationalisation, are addressed by Gary Davies and Maureen Whitehead in

Chapter 6. It is argued that, as an economy develops, there is a tendency for retailing to evolve towards fewer, larger outlets. This relationship is tested with comparable data on GNP and outlets per head of population; various forms of country-specific legislation can be identified which intervene in this relationship. The chapter highlights the disadvantages of entering markets with restrictive legislative environments. The need to assess the influence of current and likely future legislation upon the proposed international operation is stressed.

1.2.3 Strategies for internationalisation

The desire to develop international channels of supply motivated many retailers to establish or to join international alliances. Their role and functions now extend well beyond just the buying and sourcing role. In Chapter 7, Terry Robinson and Colin Clarke-Hill review the complex web of international alliances that has developed in Europe, focusing especially upon the networks within food retailing. They develop definitions of alliances and identify the retailers involved in two of the most significant types of alliance. The functions and workings of these alliances are examined, along with the advantages derived from alliance membership.

Franchising is the subject of Chapter 8, in which Angelo Manaresi and Mark Uncles review the benefits and potential problems of this method of entry. These benefits include the use of franchisees' capital and access to local business knowledge. Problems may, however, arise in the transfer of a format and management style into different cultural, lifestyle, business and legislative environments. The chapter focuses upon the management issues in franchise operation, notably the relationships between franchisors and franchisees. From a detailed study of such relationships in Britain and Italy, the authors report a surprising degree of similarity between the countries. It is concluded that retailers should not be discouraged from using the franchise method to enter markets perceived as being culturally different from the home market.

The problems of positioning a retail format within international markets are addressed by Peter McGoldrick and Debbie Blair in Chapter 9. Even the most successful of retail formats within home markets have sometimes encountered positioning problems when exported. In part, this stems from the lack of strength of the image, rather than problems in the quality or direction of the image. A framework for tracking image development within new markets is proposed; the major determinants of image within an international setting are also examined. Examples are drawn from a comparative study of the images of Marks & Spencer and C & A in two competitive contexts, one in France, one in the UK. The positioning of these two international retailers is compared in each case with that of the dominant local competitor.

Although more complex retail propositions can prove difficult to transfer across national boundaries, price is indeed an international language. In Chapter 10, Hanne Gardner and David Bennison examine the internationalisation of discount grocery operations. From a detailed study of discount operations in Denmark, the market and other environmental conditions that have nurtured the growth of discounting are analysed. In particular, limitations on hours of trading, large stores and forms of promotion limited the options for differentiation. The characteristics of the companies that have developed the 'hard discount' format are examined. The prospects and consequences of the format spreading within less constrained markets, including the UK, are discussed.

The 'category killer' is another format which has proved amenable to internationalisation. In Chapter 11, Gary Davies and Nitin Sanghavi explore what makes the category killer format distinctive. Is it price, choice, both or neither? They do this by examining one exponent of the format, the toy retailer Toys 'R' Us. They conclude that other product sectors are vulnerable to the entry of a category killer.

In Chapter 12, Keri Davies points to a serious gap in much of the literature on retail internationalisation. Most European markets have some barriers to retail entry in terms of land use and zoning regulations. In many other parts of the world the barriers are far more severe and often complex. The chapter analyses entry barriers in terms of inter-firm and inter-state interactions, as well as interactions between firms and state, home or foreign. The significance of the various agreements which have attempted to reduce barriers, either regionally or worldwide, are examined. Examples are drawn from the Pacific Asia region to illustrate the range of regulatory environments and issues that retailers may encounter when expanding into more distant markets.

In the final chapter Gary Davies reviews the stage that research into retail internationalisation has reached, in particular what gaps and opportunities remain for further research.

CONCLUSIONS

In spite of the attention given to international retail activities, it is clear that we are witnessing only the early stages of retail internationalisation. The number of retail companies for which international operations comprise the majority of turnover is still relatively small. Many major retailers do now have clear agendas for internationalisation, have learnt valuable lessons and have invested heavily in both managerial and physical assets.

Some retail formats have proved relatively amenable to 'export', notably the niche activities such as Benetton and 'category killers' such as Toys 'R' Us. In these cases, the retail proposition is sufficiently distinctive to survive/proposer in a number of different markets. That is not to say that the format is ideally positioned for each market; for some it is close to the ideal, for others it is between viable and ideal. Most retail formats have, however, proved difficult to export. Even the most successful of retail propositions within the home market typically require repositioning within a new market. While much is said on converging consumer tastes and global markets, the fact remains that the retail markets of, for example, the USA, France, Spain and Greece are enormously different.

This introduction has examined very briefly some of the research contributions in this field. As is typical within an emerging sub-discipline, much of the work is of a descriptive/classificatory nature. There have emerged some useful taxonomies of motives/driving forces for internationalisation, of entry strategies and of development positions. These have helped to provide a synthesis of the growing volume of case material that is available depicting entry to, or 'invasion' from, foreign markets.

As the subject matures, there is a pressing need for research into the 'hows' of international retailing. One of the greatest challenges facing retailers in this context is the thorough evaluation of international market opportunities. Compared with the vast weight of research devoted to the evaluation of domestic locations and market opportunities, relatively little help so far has been given to those wishing to internationalise. It is hoped that the chapters that follow will provide valuable guidelines for retailers, as well as helping to establish a research agenda for the future.

REVIEW QUESTIONS

1. What factors within the trading environment have encouraged retailers to consider internationalisation?

2. Discuss changes within the organisational sphere that may reduce the organisation's reluctance to internationalise.

3. Taking a retailer with considerable international experience, how well does the 'stages' model depict that retailer's international development?

4. Given examples of transnational, global and multinational retail development. Discuss the benefits of the transnational approach, vis-à-vis the global approach.

5. Why do some retailers prefer to enter markets through acquisition or self-start entry, when lower cost entry strategies are available?

REFERENCES

Alexander, N (1994) 'Sainsbury's move into New England', in McGoldrick, P J (ed.), *Cases in Retail Management*, Pitman Publishing, London, 185–193.

Alexander, N and Morlock, W (1992) 'Saturation and internationalisation', *International Journal of Retail & Distribution Management*, 20(3), 33–39.

Burt, S L (1986) 'The Carrefour Group – the first 25 years', *International Journal of Retailing*, 1(3), 54–78.

Burt, S L (1994) 'Carrefour: internationalising innovation', in McGoldrick, P J (ed.), *Cases in Retail Management*, Pitman Publishing, London, 154–164.

Corporate Intelligence (1991) *Cross-Border Retailing in Europe*, Corporate Intelligence Research Publication, London.

Duke, R C (1993) 'European new entry into UK grocery retailing', *International Journal of Retail & Distribution Management*, 21(1), 35–39.

Eurostat (1993) *Retailing in the European Single Market*, Eurostat, Luxembourg.

Hollander, S C (1969) 'The international shopkeepers', *MSU Business Topics*, 17(2), 13–28.

Kacker, M P (1985) *Transatlantic Trends in Retailing: Takeovers and Flow of Know-How*, Quorum Books, Westport, Conn.

McGoldrick, P J and Ali, S A (1994) 'Discount store patronage and the multi-attribute attitude model', *Proceedings of the Annual MEG Conference*, Ulster, 657–666.

McGoldrick, P J and Fryer, E (1993) 'Organisational culture and the internationalisation of retailing', *Proceedings of the 7th International Conference on Research in the Distributive Trades*, Stirling, 534–543.

Salmon, W J and Tordjman, A (1989) 'The internationalisation of retailing', *International Journal of Retailing*, 4(2), 3–16.

Tordjman, A (1994) 'Toys 'R' Us', in McGoldrick, P J (ed.), *Cases in Retail Management*, Pitman Publishing, London, 165–183.

Treadgold, A (1988) 'Retailing without frontiers', *Retail & Distribution Management*, 16(6), 8–12.

Treadgold, A (1990/91) 'The emerging internationalisation of retailing: present status and future challenges', *Irish Marketing Review*, 5(2), 11–27.

Williams, D E (1992) 'Retailing internationalisation: an empirical enquiry', *European Journal of Marketing*, 26(8/9), 8–24.

PART ONE

Trends in the internationalisation of retailing

CHAPTER 2

European retailing: convergences, differences and perspectives

André Tordjman

INTRODUCTION

In the course of the last 30 years, retailing in Europe has undergone profound transformations. Each country has adapted the nature and conditions of its commercial product range in order to meet with changes in the environment.

The traditional retailing industry is being replaced by organised and concentrated distribution, which contributes greatly towards European economic activity by the number of businesses (30 per cent of European businesses), by the employment (14 per cent of the working population) and by the services (13 per cent of added value) it embraces.

Convergent trends in environmental evolution have led to convergent swings towards structural changes in the European retailing market (section 2.1). However, substantial differences continue to survive, each country preserving its specificities, the fruits of its history and culture. The single European market is not therefore uniform and, compared to the manufacturing industry, remains localised (section 2.2).

In the future, the pace of evolution in the retailing industry should accelerate and the movements observed in the past should intensify. The most probable scenario indicates new trends which will affect the structure of retailing in Europe (section 2.3).

2.1 CONVERGENCES IN EUROPEAN RETAILING

The convergent evolutionary trends in the European retailing industry involve the sector and its concentration, retail formats and their organisation, operators and their strategies (Figure 2.1).

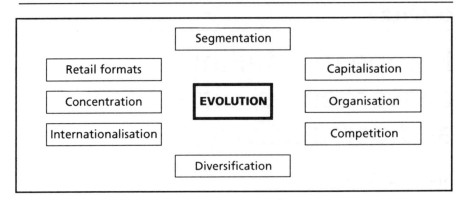

Fig. 2.1 Convergences in structural changes in European retailing (1962–1992)

2.1.1 Dominant retail formats

During the second half of the twentieth century, the hierarchy of retail formats has altered considerably. In particular, there has been:

- the loss in market share by department stores and variety stores;
- the growth of food retailing groups;
- the development of large non-food specialist stores;
- the emergence of discount stores.

Food retailers, leaders in all the countries of the European Union (with the exception of Spain and Ireland), held the top 15 positions in size of turnover in European retailing (Table 2.1). The domination of German, French and British groups and the strong presence of independent groups is particularly evident.

This evolution has been accompanied by an acceleration in the life-cycle of retail formats. It took 100 years for department stores to come to maturity, 40 for variety stores, 20 for hypermarkets, and 15 for large non-food specialised stores (Table 2.2).

However, the stage of development for each retail format differs from country to country. For example, hypermarkets have entered the maturity stage in France, Germany and Belgium, but are just being introduced in Italy and are in the growth stage in Spain. The hard discount store, already a mature concept in Germany and the Netherlands, is at present being developed in France.

2.1.2 Segmentation

The abundance of products, the segmentation of markets and the fragmentation of retail formats have all contributed to the creation of differentiated marketing strategies. Some firms practise mass marketing (hypermarkets, variety stores), whilst others opt for segmented marketing (specialists) or niche marketing (hyperspecialists).

Table 2.1 The fifteen leading enterprises in European retailing (1992)

Company	Country	Sector	Sales (million ecu)
1. Metro-Kaufhof	Switzerland/Germany	Multi-sector	23,100
2. Tengelmann	Germany	Grocery	22,400
3. Rewe	Germany	Grocery	17,800
4. Intermarché	France	Grocery	15,100
5. Leclerc	France	Grocery	15,000
6. Carrefour	France	Grocery	14,100
7. Edeka	Germany	Grocery	12,700
8. Sainsbury	UK	Grocery	12,100
9. Aldi	Germany	Grocery	12,000
10. Promodès	France	Grocery	10,700
11. Tesco	UK	Grocery	9,900
12. Auchan	France	Grocery	9,100
13. Co-operative Societies	UK	Grocery	8,900
14. Asko	Germany	Multi-sector	8,600
15. Ahold	Netherlands	Grocery	8,500

Source: Management Horizons (1992).

Table 2.2 Life-cycle of retail formats

Retail format	Maturity period	Number of years before reaching maturity
Department stores	1860–1960	100
Variety stores	1930–1970	40
Supermarkets	1950–1975	25
Hypermarkets	1965–1985	20
Large specialist stores	1980–1995(?)	15

Faced with consumers who are more demanding, more volatile and more eclectic, manufacturers have developed a range of products which is more abundant and innovative. The diversity of demand has led to the segmentation of supply, and the fragmentation of markets has led to a multiplicity of retail formats.

However, national retailers in Europe are relatively less segmented compared to those in the USA. It is true that, although the European market is larger than the US market, it is also more dispersed, limiting the potential for exploitation in each country.

2.1.3 Competition

The fragmentation of markets has contributed to expanding the competitive field of distribution companies. In addition to competition within types of retailing, there is now competition between different types: this development was observed in the USA in the 1980s, and is now spreading to Europe.

Relations between distributors and manufacturers have also evolved, and are tending to become confrontational in most European countries. Large national distribution groups are pitting themselves against the manufacturing multinationals, thus creating the conditions for bilateral oligopolies. This keen vertical competition reflects the shifting balance of power from the manufacturer to the retailer.

2.1.4 Concentration

In all the European countries, the tendency towards concentration is getting stronger. In 1991 the top five food retailing groups represented more than 45 per cent of the British market, 40 per cent of the French market, 12 per cent and 20 per cent of the Spanish and Italian markets respectively (Figure 2.2).

Concentration is most evident in the food sector and in Northern Europe, but it exists in all the European countries and is growing stronger in non-food retailing. With companies becoming larger in size and smaller in number, the catchment area of potential customers is expanding. In 1955, there

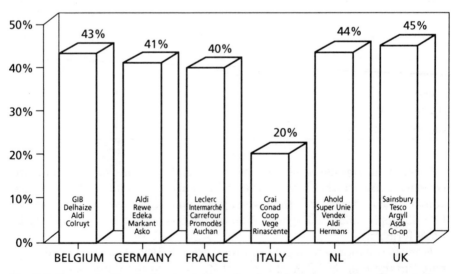

Fig. 2.2 Concentration in food retailing: food market share of top five retailers (1991)
Source: Secodip.

were 72 people per shop in the EEC, compared with 105 in 1991.

The process of concentration occurred in the 1980s at the buying level so that enterprises could negotiate better prices. In the 1990s, the trend continued at a store level as companies sought to reap the benefits of economies of scale. The takeovers of Nouvelles Galeries by Galeries Lafayette, Euromarché by Carrefour and Rallye by Casino are all examples of this phenomenon in France.

Concentration at a national level for mass markets (large-scale grocery stores and general non-food stores) has today reached international proportions for niche markets: the takeovers of Habitat by Ikea and of Darty by Kingfisher.

2.1.5 Diversification

In the period from 1975 to 1985, European retailing groups intensified their diversification activities in order to take advantage of market opportunities in specialised sectors created by new consumer demand (André Group), to spread risk by investing in formats which are more buoyant (Printemps), and to exploit know-how and transfer it to another sector (Auchan).

The diversification strategy, considered a major growth tactic in the 1980s, has now lost popularity amongst some retailers who prefer to concentrate their resources and focus their attention on their main activity. Argyll, for example, has ceased its activities in the industrial sector since 1987; Casino gave up its DIY stores in 1990 and 1991; Rallye sold Burton (clothing) in 1990 and Briker (DIY) in 1991.

However, although the extent of diversification varies from one enterprise to another, it remains an important activity, regardless of country, for the leading companies in the food retailing industry (Table 2.3).

Table 2.3 Importance of diversification activities for food retailers (1990)

Company	Country	% of turnover
Metro	Germany	50
Auchan	France	22
Casino	France	21
Intermarché	France	15
Tengelmann	Germany	15
Asda	United Kingdom	8

Source: Management Horizons (1992).

2.1.6 Internationalisation

Compared to production, the internationalisation of retailing remains partial and marginal. However, the movement towards internationalisation has accelerated and grown in scale. In 1992, there were more than 1,321 international establishments in the EC compared with 120 in 1970 (Figure 2.3). These operations concern both food and non-food retailing, general and

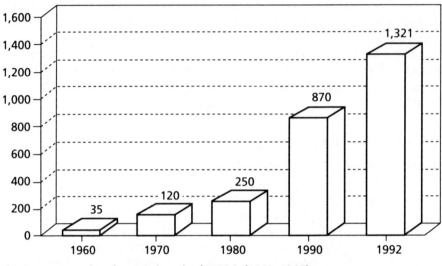

Fig. 2.3 International operations in the EEC (1960–1992)
Source: Corporate Intelligence Group.

Table 2.4 International operators and operations in Europe (1990)

Country	Number of operators	Number of operations		Total
		EC countries	Other Countries	
France	96	342	140	482
United Kingdom	89	267	156	423
Germany	46	189	135	324
Italy	26	70	48	118
Netherlands	23	91	28	119
Belgium	16	59	32	91
Spain	15	23	6	29
Denmark	11	23	19	42
Ireland	9	12	0	12
Portugal	7	14	1	15
Luxembourg	0	—	—	—
Greece	0	—	—	—
Total	338	1,090	565	1,655

Source: Corporate Intelligence Group (1991).

specialist retailing, large and small stores. However, the exported retail formats are most often the formats which remain dominant in their country of origin. Internationalisation of retailing occurs most often on a north/south and east/west basis. Thus, France, the United Kingdom and Germany represent two-thirds of international operations in Europe (Table 2.4).

Several factors may explain the growth of internationalisation in retailing. Firstly, there are *external factors* such as:

- the saturation of national markets, making it more expensive to gain a market share;
- constrictive legislation in some countries, which can make it necessary for firms to look beyond their country of origin if they wish to expand;
- falling transport costs, improving information systems and the opening of frontiers facilitating the exportation of sales formats and capital;
- the existence of international niche markets of customers with similar tastes in transcultural goods.

Next, there are *internal factors* such as:

- the search for a rate of growth and a profitability level higher than that which can be obtained in their country of origin;
- spreading risks geographically, operating in several countries with several formats;
- the belief that they possess exportable know-how;
- the will to increase power over international manufacturers in terms of both sales and negotiation.

Worldwide, international retailers in national retailing are still weak. However, in certain niches, they have strong positions (Ikea, Toys 'R' Us, Aldi), and in some countries they are even dominant (French hypermarket chains in Spain, or mail-order companies in Portugal).

2.1.7 Legislation

Compared to the USA, retailing in Europe is subject to rather stringent legislation. In order to protect the independent retailer in town centres, legislation primarily targets competition, new shops, and days and hours of opening. However, the way in which the law is applied often differs to the way in which the legislature intended, and it has not prevented the development of large-scale retailing.

Legislative conditions differ across Europe. In Spain, legislation is supple and liberal, which explains the rapid development of hypermarkets in the 1980s and large specialised stores in the 1990s. In Italy, where legislation is much more strict, the opening of department stores and hypermarkets has been limited.

Legislation can hamper the development of some forms of retailing (e.g. the Royer Law in France which applied to large stores), but it can also promote the growth of certain sales formulas. For example, the hard discount stores in Germany would not have had the success they know today if Article 11.3, restricting the opening of large stores on the outskirts of towns, had not existed.

2.1.8 Management and organisation

Although the principals of how to manage a retailing business are fundamentally the same as ever, the methods and tools used for doing so have changed a great deal. The technology of new information systems and systems for management control and decision making are necessary for the complex management of retailing companies. The development of bar-code scanning, the electronic exchange of information, methods of analysing direct product costs and the optimisation of sales space have all improved the standard of marketing information and reduced management and accounting costs.

2.1.9 Capitalisation

Retailing differs from other industries in that it remains family based, a characteristic which is very marked in certain companies: Metro, Tengelmann, Auchan, Aldi, C & A, Leclerc are private companies which have not been floated on the stock market, yet they all figure among the leading retailers in Europe. However, the development of these companies necessitates increasing amounts of investment (land, building, equipment) which raises the capital intensity of the companies (one English superstore represents the investment of 40 million ecu).

Sources of finance are private funds, stock markets, banks and suppliers. Depending upon the specific country, the importance of equity varies considerably. For example, equity represents 20 per cent of the overall total among the leaders in English food retailing, but only 5 per cent among the French leaders.

2.2 DIFFERENCES IN EUROPEAN RETAILING

Although there are many convergent trends in European retailing, there are also a great many differences. On the one hand, the stage of development of the commercial structure varies from one country to another, whilst on the other, the intensification of retailing formats differs between countries.

2.2.1 Levels of development in retailing

The contrasting structure of retailing in Europe reflects the different levels of organisation and concentration reached by the different countries. In the

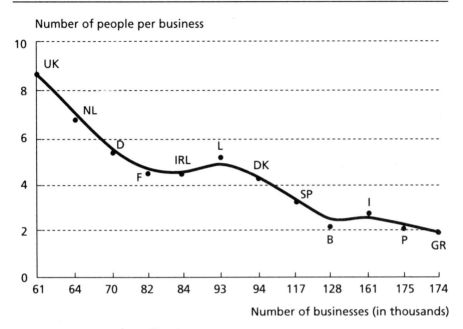

Number of people per business

Fig. 2.4 Structure of retailing in Europe
Source: Eurostat.

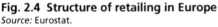

Traditional		Intermediary
Greece	Italy	
Portugal		Spain
Belgium France Netherlands Denmark	Germany	United Kingdom

Structured   *Advanced*

Fig. 2.5 Stages of retailing development

north, retailing is more industrialised whilst in the south it is more traditional. Thus in England there are 61 companies per 10,000 inhabitants with an average of 8.7 employees per business compared with 175 companies in Portugal employing only 2.1 people (Figure 2.4).

Without trying to judge the quality of retailing in each country, one can distinguish four stages of development (Figure 2.5).

Traditional retailing

In the 'traditional retailers' group can be found Greece and Portugal. The concentration of operators is weak, segmentation is nonexistent, and the level of integration of new technology is very low. These are often small-scale family retailing businesses, employing few people and with a low turnover: 114,000 ecu per enterprise in Greece and 116,000 ecu in Portugal, compared with 406,000 ecu on average for the twelve EC countries. It is also in these two countries that the productivity per person is the lowest: less than 60,000 ecu per employee.

Over the course of the last five years, the entry of foreign operators into the Greek and Portuguese markets has altered the retailing landscape. There are now hypermarkets, variety stores and non-food specialists which have stimulated competition and greatly modernised retailing in both countries.

Intermediary retailing

Retailing in Italy and Spain are in the process of transformation, being both modern and traditional. Most businesses are independent (117 and 162 businesses per 10,000 people respectively in Spain and Italy) with a turnover two times lower than the European average. However, there is a marked tendency towards concentration (particularly in the food sector) where the number of food retailing outlets per 1,000 people has dropped. In each country there were three outlets per 1,000 people in 1990 compared with four in 1970. The importance of wholesalers and voluntary chains is still very strong, particularly in Italy (192,000 wholesale businesses), explaining the weakness in the sector of integrated commerce.

In Spain between 1973 and 1991, 126 hypermarkets were built with a surface area of 915,000 m². These hypermarkets are essentially of French origin, with three companies dominating the market: Pryca (Carrefour), Continente (Promodès), and Al Campo (Auchan). In the non-food sector, large specialised stores have also entered the Spanish market: Burton, Mothercare, Ikea, Toys 'R' Us, Rodier, Marks & Spencer, Makro, Virgin, FNAC, etc.

However, foreign operators are not the only indicators of the dynamism of Spanish retailing: El Corte Inglés is the most successful chain of department stores in Europe, Mercadona has developed a thriving chain of supermarkets, and Cortefiel has exported its concept of a clothing store chain. The transformation of Spanish retailing has been swift, stimulated by the growth in demand, the dynamism of those involved and the liberal nature of legislation on building, opening hours and the establishment of foreign businesses.

In Italy, the development of large stores has been hindered by restrictive and protectionist legislation (the law of 1971). The application of this law was modified to become less strict in 1988, which has since accelerated the development of hypermarkets. However, the judicial framework and national lobbying in Italy provide very restricting conditions in comparison with the other European countries. This explains, in part, the gap between a large business, not yet fully established, and a small specialised business which is well developed. The tendency now, however, is towards international openings (in the form of associations) and the development of large-scale retailing formats. Thus transformation is in process.

Structured retailing

Retailing in the north of Europe is better structured, reflecting the level of economic development. In Denmark, Luxembourg, the Netherlands and France, enterprises are larger in size (4 to 6.5 employees per enterprise), and have a higher level of concentration and a greater level of productivity per employee (between 90,000 and 150,000 ecu according to country).

The commercial apparatus of these countries have the following characteristics in common:

- The number of national operators tends to decrease with such phenomena as concentration of sales and the growth of sales. There are half as many businesses per 10,000 people as in Greece or Portugal.
- Intertype and intratype competition has developed, giving the consumer more choice in a market which is becoming increasingly competitive.
- The mature relationship between suppliers and retailers (particularly in France) reflects the bilateral oligopolistic nature of operating conditions.
- New technology for stock control has been widely introduced, facilitating the implementation and execution of more and more elaborate competitive strategies.
- The internationalisation of concepts and ideas for finding growth opportunities abroad has led to new retailing formats being introduced, the effectiveness of which has already been proved.

Advanced retailing

Germany and the UK are the European countries in which retailing is the most advanced in terms of concentration, segmentation, capitalisation and integration.

In Germany and the UK respectively there are 63 and 56 retailing businesses per 10,000 inhabitants (98 being the European average). These enterprises employ 6.5 people in Germany and 9.5 in England, compared with an average of 4.1 in Europe. The turnover of these stores surpasses 800,000 ecu, eight times Greece or Portugal and twice the European average.

The German companies are the largest in Europe; the UK companies have the highest profit margins (6 per cent net for UK food groups, compared with 1.5 per cent for their French counterparts), although these margins have recently been eroded by increased price competition in the UK.

Segmentation is equally well developed in the grocery sector (particularly in Britain) with superstores being the most dominant format, but also with discount supermarkets (Kwik Save), qualitative supermarkets (Waitrose), hard discount stores (Aldi, Netto) and convenience stores (7 Eleven). In the non-food sector, large specialist stores are greatly developed in the UK (Kingfisher, Boots, Great Universal Stores).

German and UK businesses employ strong marketing techniques: strategies of differentiation, development of own brands (Marks & Spencer, Aldi) which represent 35 per cent of food sales in Germany and 41 per cent in Britain, and mastering of new technology (stock control, scanners and information systems).

In these two countries, the level of concentration is very high: the top five businesses represent 45 per cent of sales in the UK and 41 per cent in Germany.

German and UK retailers should not be seen as models, but their levels of organisation and maturity are the most advanced in Europe.

2.2.2 Penetration of retail formats: food

The economic importance of types of retailing varies from one country to another, and the dominant retail format is different in each country (Table 2.5). This can be explained by a number of factors linked to the cultural, judicial, demographic, sociological and economic environments but it may also be explained in part by the role played by local entrepreneurs who, at different times, have introduced specific concepts to their country. Thus, the early developments of superstores by Asda and some co-operatives did much to establish the strength of that format in the UK. Similarly, Carrefour helped establish hypermarkets in France, while Aldi developed strongly their hard discount format in Germany. Restrictions on a large-scale, out-of-town developments have contributed to the weakness of the superstore and hypermarket formats in Germany and Italy.

Food retailing in Europe has undergone a profound transformation over the last twenty years. The proportion of the household budget spent on food has fallen by 30 per cent in the last two decades: spending on food represented a third of household spending in 1970 and only a quarter in 1990. This phenomenon can be seen all across Europe and is more pronounced in the north than in the south (16 per cent in Germany compared with 26 per cent in Spain).

This relative fall in food spending has been accompanied by the loss of 400,000 grocery stores. This trend is again most advanced in the north of Europe: in 1990 there was one grocery store per 1,000 inhabitants in the UK and three in Italy, compared with 2.2 and 3.7 respectively in 1970. However, this reduction in the number of sales outlets is also becoming more evident in the south, and the next ten years will certainly be witness to a very definite reduction in the number of shops in the Mediterranean countries.

Table 2.5 Penetration of types of food retailing format

	France	UK	Spain	Germany	Italy
Strong	Hyper	Superstore	Hyper	Hard discount Hyper	Supermarket Independents
Medium	Supermarket	Hard discount	Independents Supermarket	Supermarket	—
Weak	Hard discount Superstore	Hyper	Hard discount	Superstore	Hyper Hard discount

On the other hand, the amount of sales space devoted to food products has vastly increased, rising from 8 to 18 million m² in France between 1966 and 1990, and from 5.2 million m² to 21.5 million m² in Germany between 1961 and 1990. This growth in sales area is common all over Europe and applies particularly to hypermarkets and supermarkets (+30 per cent between 1986 and 1990). This evolution explains the trend towards larger stores (Table 2.6).

Table 2.6 Sales area of hypermarkets and supermarkets (m² per inhabitant)

	Belgium	France	Germany	UK	Italy	NL	Spain	EC
1986	0.18	0.16	0.17	0.07	0.04	0.10	0.05	0.10
1990	0.24	0.20	0.20	0.10	0.05	0.12	0.08	0.13
Growth	33%	25%	18%	43%	25%	20%	60%	30%

Source: Secodip.

However, food retailing in Europe remains marked by differences in consumer behaviour, dominant retail formats, own brands, strategies and financial ratios.

Consumer behaviour

Nationally, food consumption differs noticeably: in the north of Europe people eat more potatoes and fatty products, whilst in the south they prefer cereals and oil. In France, 80 litres of mineral water are consumed per inhabitant compared with only 24 in Ireland, and 144 litres of beer in Germany compared with 23 in Italy.

A study carried out by Secodip reveals that, in choosing which shop to

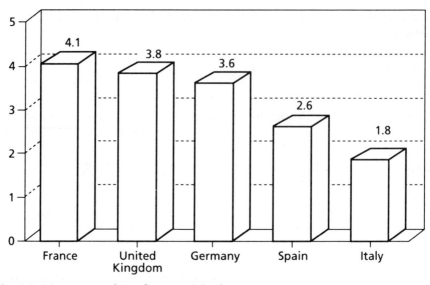

Fig. 2.6 Average number of stores visited
Source: Secodip.

frequent, the French consumer decides according to price, the British according to range and choice and the German according to proximity. The number of stores visited varies from 1.8 in Italy to 4.1 in France (Figure 2.6), reflecting the different retailing structures (many stores with a strong attraction) and the behaviour of consumers (decreasing loyalty depending on the promotions offered by retailers).

Retail formats

Food retailing in Europe offers a wide variety of retail formats, each responding to a specific position in the market (Figure 2.7). The supermarket remains the most homogeneous and developed format (Table 2.7), though it has been split up into various concepts: price oriented (hard discount, hypermarkets, discount supermarket) and service oriented (superstore, convenience store, quality supermarket).

Price-oriented formats

Price-oriented formats have had the most sustained growth. In Europe in 1990 there were about 10,000 hard discount stores and 2,400 hypermarkets, representing 4.5 and 13 million m² of sales area respectively.

Hard discount stores have a strong position in Germany where they hold 24 per cent of the food retailing market. They are also well established in Belgium, the Netherlands and Denmark. On the other hand, they have yet to develop in France, Spain and Italy, where their penetration is as yet weak.

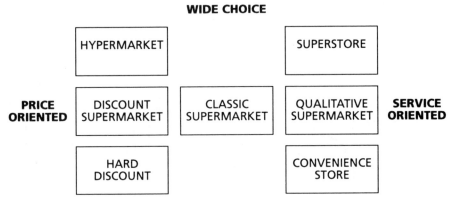

WIDE CHOICE

HYPERMARKET		SUPERSTORE

PRICE ORIENTED | DISCOUNT SUPERMARKET | CLASSIC SUPERMARKET | QUALITATIVE SUPERMARKET | **SERVICE ORIENTED**

HARD DISCOUNT		CONVENIENCE STORE

LIMITED CHOICE

Fig. 2.7 Positioning in food retailing formats

Table 2.7 Number of m² sales area for 1,000 inhabitants per food retailing format (1991)

Format	France	Germany	UK	Spain	Italy
Supermarkets	120	106	66	59	47
Hypermarkets	81	100	14	26	9
Hard discount	8	56	8	2	3
Superstore	—	4	32	—	9
Convenience store	18	65	89	28	81

Source: Author's estimates.

Hypermarkets have also undergone rapid and extensive expansion: in France in 1992 (30 years after their creation), there were 900 units holding a 26 per cent share of the market. In Spain there were 125 hypermarkets and in Portugal 13.

Service-oriented formats
Service-oriented formats have experienced a more limited and contrasted development than the price-oriented formats. The superstore, the large food store (3,500 m²) offering a large choice of products and services, has for the most part developed in Britain, where 800 shops captured 37 per cent of food spending in 1992.

Convenience stores, a more heterogeneous concept, are present all across Europe, but with forms of organisation which vary widely (service station, gourmet shop, specialist chains, etc.).

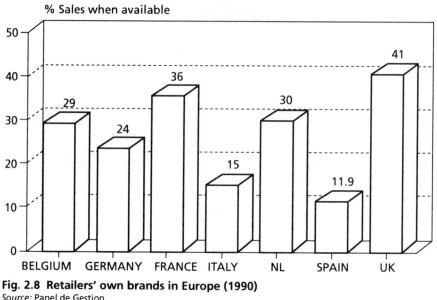

Fig. 2.8 Retailers' own brands in Europe (1990)
Source: Panel de Gestion.

Retailers' own brands

In 1991, retailers' brands represented 18 per cent of food sales in Europe. They are particularly well developed in northern Europe (Britain, the Netherlands, Germany and Belgium) and are growing fast in the south. In Spain, their market share has risen from 2.4 per cent in 1980 to 11.9 per cent in 1990 (Figure 2.8).

Among the main reasons for the adoption by retailers of an 'own brand' policy are a need for independence from national and international brands, a desire to increase profit and a need to be different to competitors and to inspire customer loyalty.

Strategies

European food retailing groups have opted for a variety of different strategies. Some have adopted a *mono-format strategy*, seeking to dominate a segment of the market by concentrating all their financial and human resources, marketing and business know-how on a single concept. Others have chosen to develop a *multi-format strategy*, penetrating the market via several different concepts, each being positioned in a specific segment (Tables 2.8 and 2.9).

Several food retailing companies have also tried to diversify into other sectors, even in different geographical areas, investing in markets where there are better growth opportunities (DIY, electrical goods, sport, gardening equipment) and regions where the retail format in question has a competitive advantage (Table 2.10).

Table 2.8 Mono-format strategies and food retailing companies

Company	Country	Retailing format
Aldi	Germany	Hard discount
Tesco	UK	Superstore
Mercadona	Spain	Supermarket
Ensselunga	Italy	Supermarket

Table 2.9 Multi-format strategies and food retailing companies

Company	Country	Retail format
Promodès	France	Hard discount, hypermarket, supermarket, convenience store
Argyll	UK	Hard discount, superstore, supermarket
Tengelmann	Germany	Hard discount, specialist, supermarket, hypermarket
Coop Italia	Italy	Hypermarket, supermarket, convenience store

Table 2.10 Extent of diversification

Company	Country of origin	Percentage of sales made outside the grocery sector
Metro	Germany	50
Auchan	France	22
Casino	France	25
Intermarché	France	15
Tengelmann	Germany	15

British companies tend to concentrate on their national market with a mono-format strategy (Tesco, Kwik Save); Belgian and Dutch companies, having taken into consideration the limitations of their national market have opted for a more international strategy (GIB, Vendex, Ahold). The French and German leaders have varied their approaches: Promodès has internationalised whilst still remaining in the food sector; Carrefour, Auchan, Metro and Tengelmann have both diversified and gone international. Intermarché and Massa remain national, but diversified. Aldi is international, but mono-format.

Table 2.11 briefly summarises some of these differences in strategy.

Table 2.11 Strategies of European food retailing companies

Strategies	National	International
Concentrated	Tesco, Kwik Save, Asda	Aldi, Promodès, Ahold
Diversified	Intermarché, Massa, Leclerc	Metro, Carrefour, Auchan, Tengelmann, GIB

Table 2.12 Profitability of leading European food retailers

	Turnover/m² (ecu)	Gross margin (% of turnover)	Net margin (% of turnover)	Credit supply period in days
France	8,800	16	2.0	58
UK	5,000	25	6.5	31
Spain	7,600	21	2.4	123
Germany	5,300	22	2.5	39
Italy	3,400	26	2.5	88

Sources: Management sample group, Secodip, author.

Table 2.13 The leading retailers in Europe according to profit

Company	Country	Sector	Profit (million ecu)
1. Sainsbury	UK	Grocery	880
2. Marks & Spencer	UK	Variety store	870
3. Tesco	UK	Grocery	760
4. Great Universal Stores	UK	Multi-sector	600
5. Boots Company	UK	Multi-sector	520
6. Argyll	UK	Grocery	500
7. Spar	Germany	Grocery	370
8. Kingfisher	UK	Multi-sector	315
9. Delhaise le Lion	Belgium	Grocery	310
10. Carrefour	France	Grocery	250

Source: Management Horizons (1992).

Profitability

In terms of profit, there are also clear differences between countries in Europe. The leading French food retailers have the highest levels of productivity per m² and the lowest gross margins; the German leaders have high margins which compensate for poor productivity; the UK leaders have high margins and high sales per m², but the shortest credit supply period (Table

2.12). Thus, although the French and German companies are the best in terms of size and turnover, the British companies occupy the six top positions in terms of profit (Table 2.13).

Non-food retailing in Europe covers a large variety of formats, sales areas and geographical implantations. It is possible to single out general retailers (department stores and variety stores), specialist retailers and non-store retailers. As in the case of food retailing, the strength of formats differs greatly between countries (Table 2.14).

Table 2.14 Penetration of types of non-food retailing format

	France	UK	Spain	Germany	Italy
Strong	Franchise Large specialised store	Variety store Specialist chains	Department store	Department store Mail order	Independents
Medium	Independents Mail order	Mail order Department store Franchise	Independents Franchise	Franchise	Variety store Franchise
Weak	Department store Variety store	Hypermarket	Variety store Mail order	Variety store	Department store Mail order

General retailing

Department stores and variety stores, despite a fall in their market share, continue to play a significant role in European retailing. Over the course of the last thirty years, their total sales area has doubled, rising from 3.9 million m^2 in 1962 to 7.7 million m^2 in 1990. However, during the last decade, a decline in selling area to the tune of 10 per cent has become apparent.

The position of department stores varies across Europe. Their market share is strongest in Germany (5.2 per cent) and weakest in Italy (0.3 per cent) (Table 2.15). Having suffered the competition offered by specialists in choice and discounters with price, department stores have sought to reposition themselves either by concentrating on fashion or household goods, in order to become specialists in the mid to top range of sectors. Figure 2.9

Table 2.15 Market share of department stores (1991)

	France *Declining*	UK *Stable*	Spain *Dynamic*	Germany *Leading*	Italy *Weak*
Spending per person (ecu)	73	118	147	248	11
Market share (%)	2.2	4.7	2.5	5.2	0.3

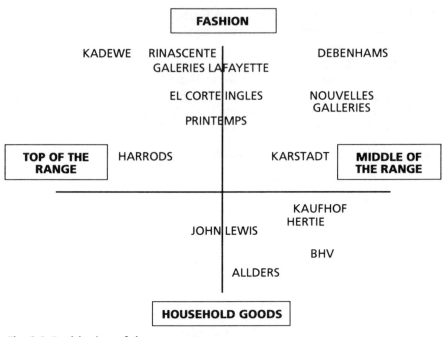

Fig. 2.9 Positioning of department stores

Table 2.16 Diversification by department stores

Supermarkets	GIB, Rinsacente, John Lewis
Hypermarkets	El Corte Inglés
Variety stores	Galeries Lafayette, Printemps, Kaufhof, Hertie
Specialist	Vendex, Printemps, Kaufhof, Hertie
Mail order	Printemps, Karstadt, Kaufhof

illustrates the positioning of some of Europe's leading department stores. By necessity (loss of market share) and by opportunity (financial resources) department stores have also been driven to diversify their activities (Table 2.16).

Variety stores have also suffered a decline across Europe, with the exception of the UK, where their share of the market remains significant at 6.2 per cent (Table 2.17). Their previous image having been taken over by discount stores, variety stores have evolved by concentrating on few product categories (Woolworth's), by repositioning their food section (Monoprix), and by developing their own brands (Marks & Spencer) (Figure 2.10).

In the future generalists will certainly have to withstand the blows of decreasing market share, strong competition, low productivity and insufficient service. Department stores will have to rethink their strategies for small town branches and concentrate their efforts on costs (logistics), the

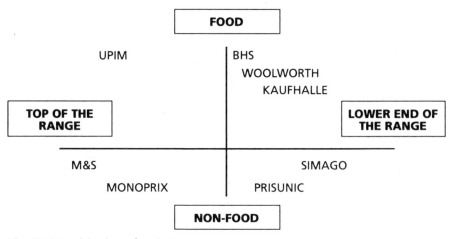

Fig. 2.10 Positioning of variety stores

Table 2.17 Market share of variety stores (1991)

	France *Declining stabilising*	UK *Powerful*	Spain *Marginal*	Germany *Weak*	Italy *Weak*
Market share (%)	2.1	6.2	0.4	1.1	1.5
Companies	Monoprix Prisunic	Marks & Spencer BhS Littlewoods	Simago	Kaufhalle Woolworth	UPIM Standa

development of own brands (marketing) and customer satisfaction (human resources). Variety stores will have to modify their original concept (variety) in order to concentrate on several ranges with a view to acquiring a strong position in each market by offering a dominant choice.

Speciality retailing

During the last twenty years, specialised retailing has undergone some significant structural changes. New specialists have developed in both large stores (B&Q, Ikea) and small stores (Tie Rack, Sweaterie). These different types of store tend to be situated on the outskirts of towns and in city centres respectively.

There are four distinct types of specialist:

- *Single-industry specialists:* C & A (clothing), Toys 'R' Us (toys), Ikea (furniture);

- *Single-product specialists:* Tie Rack (ties, scarves), Fil à Fil (shirts), Levi's (jeans);
- *Single-client specialists:* Prenatal (mother-to-be), Jacadi (infants' wear), Rondissimo (large sizes);
- *Single-theme specialists:* FNAC (leisure goods), Nature et Découverte (nature).

Some companies have opted for an own brand strategy at an international level; others have chosen to apply a multiple brand strategy at a national level. In some highly concentrated and international markets (toys), stores like Toys 'R' Us have succeeded in internationalising their concept in distributing manufacturers' brands (Figure 2.11).

The growth of specialists has been to the detriment of general retailers. However, the way in which they are organised differs from country to country. In Germany (Vendes, Katag, Ariston, Interfunk) and in the Netherlands (Beco, Samen Sterk, Hoogenbosh), the associative format is developing strongly. In the UK, the multi-brand chains are the most strongly developed (Boots, Kingfisher, WH Smith, Storehouse, etc.). In France, the franchise business has flourished (675 franchisers and 33,000 franchisees in 1991). In Italy, independent retailing is still very much in the majority, holding a 75 per cent share of the market. In Spain, there is a co-existence of traditional and modern specialist.

Specialist retailing should tend towards hyper-specialisation, vertical integration of operations and international concentration. The companies controlling specialist chains, such as Melville in the USA, André in France and Kingfisher in England, could evolve further. This strategy offers several

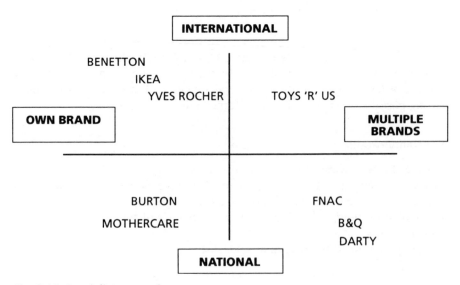

Fig. 2.11 Specialist strategies

advantages: it allows risk to be spread, profits to be made from the favourable tendencies of specialisation, benefits to be gained from economies of scale and resources to be diverted to sectors which warrant strategic priority.

Non-store retailing

The changes in population (working women, ageing population), technology (information technology, logistics), competition (difficulties reaching town centres, limited opening hours) all help to explain why non-store retailing (mail order, television shopping, minitel and telephone ordering, etc.) have developed. It is in the north of Europe – and most particularly in Germany with some large companies (Otto Verand, Quelle, Nekermann) – that mail order is the most strongly developed (4.3 per cent of total retailing turnover).

During the last decade, non-store retailing has developed sophisticated techniques for gaining clients and controlling orders. Companies have been employing international strategies (Otto Versand, Quelle, La Redoute) and have developed specialist catalogues. Compared to the USA, where the sector represents 10 per cent of retailing turnover, non-store retailing is still very marginal in Europe. However, in certain non-food sectors of the market (records, books, fabrics), the mail-order companies have a very strong position (Table 2.18).

Table 2.18 Market share of non-store retailing

	France	UK	Spain	Germany	Italy
	Dynamic	*Strong*	*Weak*	*Powerful*	*Weak*
Market share (%)	2.5	2.8	0.5	4.3	0.3
Companies	La Redoute	GUS		Otto Versand	Vestro
	3 Suisses	Empire Stores		Quelle	

2.3 PERSPECTIVES IN EUROPEAN RETAILING

2.3.1 Winning strategies

Amongst the growth strategies employed by retailing companies, the three most popular are as follows:

- *The intensification strategy.* Some companies have chosen to gain parts of the market by concentrating on their principal format in order to become a national, sometimes an international, leader: Aldi (hard discount), Marks & Spencer (variety store), Tesco (superstore), Otto Versand (mail order), Carrefour (hypermarket), C & A (clothing), Toys 'R' Us (toys), etc. Economies of scale gained in buying, marketing and logistics allow companies to dominate a market or a geographical sector.

- *The diversification strategy.* Other companies prefer to diversify their activities in order to take advantage of different markets, spread risk and exploit know-how. Auchan has diversified through internal growth into sport (Decathlon), clothing (Kiabi), DIY (Leroy Merlin), electrical goods (Boulanger), carpets (Saint Maclou), car equipment (Norauto) and cafeterias (Flunch). Kingfisher has employed a comparable strategy, but through external growth, i.e. by taking over companies which were already established: variety stores (Woolworth), DIY (B&Q), chemists (Superdrug), electrical goods (Comet) and car equipment (Charlie Brown).

- *The internationalisation strategy.* Finally, and not exclusive of the previous two strategies, internationalisation constitutes a further source of growth. Internationalisation strategies can be enacted in the form of investment (Kingfisher which partly owns Darty), alliances (ERA, AMS, BIGS), exportation of a concept adapted to the receiving market (Carrefour, Auchan, Promodès) or with a global approach (Toys 'R' Us, Benetton, Ikea).

The winning strategies for retailing formats evolve around two major axes: on the one hand, the domination by cost strategy resulting from economies made at different stages – logistics, marketing and management; on the other, the differentiation strategy based on the supply of products or services to meet the specific needs of the consumer. The strategies may have a strong international dimension or a varied level of national concentration (Table 2.19).

Table 2.19 Winning strategies in retail formats

Strategies	Food	Non-food
Cost	Hyper Hard discount	Large specialised store
Differentiation	Superstore Convenience store	Specialist

The retail formats which are likely to undergo the most progress in Europe are as follows.

- The *hard discount* format may gain a stronger position in the food and stock-up buying sector and could, at the end of the century, be responsible for 5 to 10 per cent of food sales, depending on the country. Only those companies which manage to combine the best expertise at the buying and logistic levels will be able to withstand the onslaught of the discount stores.

- *Hypermarkets*, battling against the competition offered by discount stores and large specialised stores, will seek to improve their productivity by investing in logistics and information systems. They will develop ranges with higher added value and own brands in order to find a means of differentiation and increasing margins. In the non-food sector, some hypermarkets will offer a wider but shallower range of products (the leading products in each category); others will prefer to offer a narrow choice of ranges, but with a depth of choice in each range offered, making it a dominant retailer for the product concerned. Finally, some companies may be tempted to become warehouse stores or price clubs.

  In Spain, Greece, Portugal and Italy hypermarkets will continue to grow whilst in France their market share will stabilise.
- *Superstores* and *convenience stores* should make progress, especially in countries where their development is at present limited (France, Germany, Belgium). However, they will only be able to win the market for last-minute buys and pleasure shopping, and their economic role will be very modest.
- *Large specialised non-food stores*, combining the advantages of choice and low prices, should make strong progress in the north and later the south of Europe. The sectors in which growth should be the strongest are: sport, toys, DIY, electrical goods, office equipment and household goods.
- *Hyperspecialists*, concentrating on a theme (nature, security), a product category, a clientele (age, style, size) or a service, will develop primarily in countries where retailing is already well structured. For the most part, the companies which will operate in these sectors will be international operators practising global strategies.

These trends will affect the retail formats and not the companies. There will always be companies which flourish using outdated concepts and companies that flounder despite the use of strong new formulas.

2.3.2 The future scenario

The next ten years should confirm the trends observed in the course of the last three decades. European retailing will thus move towards concentration, internationalisation and segmentation. Competition will be more aggressive, leaving room only for the development of formats which hold a strong position with regard to price (hard discount, warehouse), choice (large specialised stores) and service (convenience store, independent retailer).

The pace of evolution in retailing should accelerate, though at a different rate in each country. In the south of Europe, changes should be rapid, and the gap between the north and the south should diminish. In the north of Europe, retailing will strengthen its level of industrialisation.

Although it would be a little ambitious to try to present a scenario for the evolution of retailing over the next ten years – the relationship between the different environmental variants being so complex – a certain number of projections can be made.

Less growth, more segmentation

The stagnation of the population (+6 per cent between 1970 and 1990 compared with +1.5 per cent between 1990 and 2010) and its ageing, the low rise in wages and changes in the nature of consumption will lead to slower growth.

On the other hand, the fragmentation of markets, the diversity of types of consumption, the variety of retailing formats and the proliferation of different products will tend to promote the segmentation of sales formats. Segmentation is already a reality in European non-food retailing, even if its presence remains modest in comparison with the USA. On the contrary, in coming years the food retailing industry should witness increased forms of segmentation revolving around three groups: traditional supermarkets (conventional), quality supermarkets (extended formats) and discounters (economy formats). This segmented analysis of food stores will not depend on the classical criteria of sociological, demographic and economic profiles or lifestyles, but on the type of shopping trip and the attributes of the store (Table 2.20). Five principal types of shopping trip are distinguishable:

- *Routine shopping trip:* representing household provisions bought for a period ranging from 3–7 days;
- *Stock-up shopping trip:* corresponding to products required for long-term conservation or frequent use;
- *Fill-in shopping trip:* unavailable goods for which convenience stores are essential;
- *Same-day shopping trip:* products consumed the same day, such as meat, fish and ready-prepared meals;
- *Adventure shopping trip:* products sought in order to bring pleasure.

Table 2.20 Importance of store attributes by type of purchase

	Routine	*Stock up*	*Fill in*	*Same day*	*Adventure*
Price	=	+	–	–	–
Convenience	+	–	+	=	–
Importance of choice	+	+	–	=	+
Quality of choice	+	+	–	+	+
Service	=	–	–	+	+
Atmosphere	=	–	–	=	+

Key: High +, Medium =, Low –
Source: Food Marketing Institute.

Each consumer requires each type of purchase and expresses these desires alternately in different stores. Hence, the importance of price, assortment (quantity), convenience, service and atmosphere varies according to the type of store. It is likely that formats focusing on a specific type of purchase will develop to the detriment of traditional supermarkets.

Fewer national operators, more international operators

The attempt to find a critical size should lead to concentration and it can be estimated that 50 per cent of the European food retailing market will belong to 50 groups. In those countries where concentration is already high (the UK, France and Germany), this change will be made as a result of the buying of companies. The less concentrated southern European countries should undergo an acceleration in progress, bringing them more into line with their northern counterparts.

However, the globalisation of markets, the saturation of national retailing markets and the identification of niche markets will encourage international operators. This movement towards internationalisation will be accompanied by a tendency towards international concentration for two main reasons: on the one hand, the difficulty in winning over competitive parts of the market will encourage expansion into less aggressive markets; on the other hand, distributors will be able to set up negotiations with manufacturers on an international level as a result of such movements towards the exportation of concepts and capital.

Fewer shops, more sales area

Like the more advanced countries of northern Europe, the Mediterranean countries will undergo a reduction in the number of sales outlets. In Spain, the number of sales outlets fell from 580,000 in 1980 to 523,000 in 1988. It is in the grocery sector that this fall has been the most pronounced: 200,000 shops in 1988 compared with 282,000 in 1980. In Italy the same trend has been observed, though to lesser degree (due to legislation): there were 300,000 food retailing outlets in 1990 compared with 341,000 in 1982.

However, actual sales area continues to grow in almost all areas of retailing. Manufacturers are creating an ever larger range of products and brands; general retailers are increasing the size of their shops in order to be able to offer as full a range as possible to ward off competition; specialists are expanding so as to be able to offer the customer an exhaustive choice of products and thus continue to dominate the general retailer.

Less stock, more customer service

Techniques which have led on from the information scanner, such as just-in-time, management of products by category, Direct Product Profitability

(DPP) and space management, will help to reduce the amount of stock held in-store and increase the rate of turnover.

Faced with a more comprehensive product range and better service, customers will become more selective. They will become more demanding, optimising purchases by frequenting several shops in order to get the best value. They will be less loyal and will visit in turn a hard discount store, a superstore, a department store, a specialist, a large out-of-town store and a city centre store, buying national brands and retailers' own brands, etc.

Fewer independent retailers, more affiliations

Although the independent retailers will continue to thrive, their number will fall due to the trend towards affiliations and associations. Franchises, central buying groups and independent groupings will develop as a form of competition for the large retailing companies.

Lower turnover per square metre, greater margin differentials

More intense competition, low population growth, limited economic expansion and the increase in retailing areas will lead to a decline in the productivity per square metre of shops. In the USA, weekly sales per square foot were \$111 in 1971 compared with \$72 in 1991. During this same period, the average size of supermarkets rose from 3,400 m² to 4,200 m², the number of products from 13,000 to 30,000, and gross margins from 19.3 per cent to 23 per cent (Figure 2.12). In France and in Germany the same trend can already be seen in all retail formats (Table 2.21).

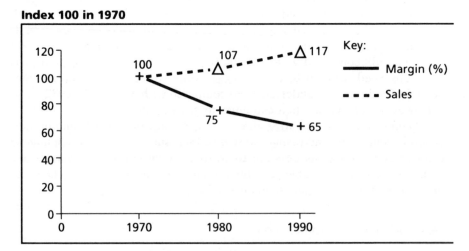

Index 100 in 1970

Fig. 2.12 Evolution of supermarkets in the USA
Source: FMI.

Table 2.21 Evaluation of sales in m² in Germany

Retail formats	Sales area (million m²)		Sales per m² (fixed price 1988 DM)	
	1968	1988	1968	1988
Hypermarkets	1.16	8.10	9,830	7,900
Department stores	2.02	36.0	11,680	7,360
Specialists	28.9	55.8	7,890	6,930
Total	32.08	67.5	8,190	7,070

Source: Batzer (1991).

The fall in productivity will lead some European operators to adapt their offers towards products with higher added value which generate larger margins. Department stores and variety stores adopted this approach in the 1980s. This rise in margin due to different offers but unchanged sales formats will create market opportunities for newcomers offering low prices. This phenomenon exists today in the form of the Price Club in the USA and hard discount in Europe. Thus, the difference in margin between discount stores and service oriented stores will rise, giving the consumer a larger and more varied choice. The wheel of retailing will continue to turn: yesterday's new entrants will see their formulas lose their edge, and give way to new discounters.

2.3.3 Conclusions and consequences

Manufacturers will have to face up to competition from integrated retailers, reorganise their commercial structures and be prepared to operate internationally. In effect, the price consciousness of the consumer on the one hand and the improved quality of retailers' own brands on the other will increase awareness of the price differential. The question will be how much more the customer is willing to pay for a leading brand rather than a retailer's own brand. If the price difference is too high, one can expect a transfer of customer loyalty in favour of good quality retail brands.

Retailers will have to analyse threats and opportunities beyond national frontiers and meet training needs for high level managers. They will have to improve their management methods in order to increase their margins and compensate for low productivity of sales per m². The globalisation of retailing will have consequences for the independent retailer, which will be very much affected by the evolution in retailing and should concentrate on improving the offer they give the customer. The most dynamic independents will seek to co-operate together in order to withstand the pressure of competition from multinational companies. Others will resort to legislation, which will maintain traditional barriers against new entrants and put up

		1960	**1970**	**1980**	**1990**
CONSUMER		Buys what he finds	Buys what he wants	Buys what he needs	Buys what he likes
	ISSUE	PRODUCT	PRICE	CHOICE	VALUE
		Little information Little choice	Accustomed to brands	Better informed	More selective
MANUFACTURER		Limited range of products	Large range of products	International concentration	International organisation
	PRODUCT	LOCAL	NATIONAL	INTERNATIONAL	GLOBAL
RETAILER		High margin	Concentration Low margin	Saturated markets Diversified Large specialised stores	International specialist chains
		Family business Department stores	Supermarket Hypermarket	International hypermarket	International hypermarket
	COMPETITION	LOCAL	REGIONAL	NATIONAL	INTERNATIONAL

Cost	Choice	International

Non-food supermarket

International non-food supermarket

Fig. 2.13 Historic perspective

fresh ones. European governments, though all the while supporting the single market, should take into consideration internal pressure.

Consumers will have a new supply of products and services and will have access to a greater range of choice. Power will change hands: as we can see from Figure 2.13, in 1960 it was in the hands of the manufacturer, today it is in those of the retailer, and by the year 2000 it will be in those of the consumer.

REVIEW QUESTIONS

1. Illustrate how the duration of the retail format life-cycle has differed between countries.

2. In northern Europe, concentration is most evident within the food sector. Why has the food sector been especially conducive to higher levels of concentration?

3. What are the principal external and internal factors that explain the growth of retailer internationalisation?

4. Some European countries have four times more stores (when expressed as a ratio of population) than the United Kingdom. Explain this difference.

5. What are the distinguishing characteristics of countries with (a) traditional, (b) intermediary, (c) structured, and (d) advanced retailing?

6. Explain why the superstore is a dominant format in UK food retailing, the hypermarket is strong in France and Spain, whereas the hard discounter prevails in Germany.

7. The variety store format is considerably stronger in the UK than elsewhere in Europe. Why?

8. How do you account for the differences in the levels of penetration of non-store retailing across Europe? Do you anticipate greater differences or more convergence in the future?

9. What fundamental strategies seem most likely to prevail within European retailing over the next ten years?

10. You are advising a US manufacturer which is considering expansion into Europe. Taking a product sector of your choice, summarise the most relevant implications of the current and future changes in European retailing.

REFERENCES

Bartos, R (1977) 'The moving target: the impact of women's employment on consumer behaviour', *Journal of Marketing*, 41(3), 31–37.

Batzer, E (1991) *Der Handel in der Bundesrepublik Deutschland*, IFO-Institut für Wirschaftsforschung e.V. München.

Belay, J (1986) 'Trends in the consumption environment in Europe', in *Retail Strategies for Profit and Growth*, ESOMAR Seminar Proceedings, 1-12, ESOMAR, Amsterdam.

Blackwell, R D and Talarzyk, W W (1983) 'Life-style retailing: competitive strategies for the 1980s', *Journal of Retailing*, 59(4), 7–27.

Brosslin, C (1979) *La Marque de Distributeur*, Entreprise Moderne, Paris.

Burt, S (1989) 'Trends and management issues in European retailing', *International Journal of Retailing*, 4(4), 1–97.

Burt, S (1991) 'Trends in the internationalization of grocery retailing: the European experience', *International Review of Retail, Distribution and Consumer Research*, 1(4), 487–515.

Burt, S and Dawson, J A (1990) 'From small shop to hypermarket', in D Pinder (ed.) *Western Europe: Challenge and Change*, Bellhaven, London.

Cathelat, B (1985) *Styles de Vie*. Editions d'Organisation, Paris.

Cisneros, G and Martinez, L (1989) 'Segmentation by lifestyle of the consumers in Barcelona's Metropolitan area', in *Adding Value to Retail Offerings*, ESOMAR Seminar Proceedings, 49–60 ESOMAR, Amsterdam.

Colla, E (ed.) (1990) *Le vendite a distanza, I casi Italia, Europa*, USA, Etas, Milan.

Colla, E (1992) *Gli ipermarcati sviluppo e maturita delle grandi superfici di vendita in Italia e in Europa*, Etas, Milan.

Commission of European Communities (1985) *Measures taken in the Field of Commerce by the Member States of the European Communities*, Studies Collection, Commerce and Distribution Series, 10.

Cook, D and Walters, D (1991) *Retail Marketing: Theory and Practice*, Prentice Hall, Hemel Hempstead.

Corporate Intelligence (1991) *Cross-Border Retailing in Europe*, Corporate Intelligence Research Publications, London.

Davies, G and Brooks, J (1989) *Positioning Strategy in Retailing*, Paul Chapman, London.

Dawson, J A (1982) *Commercial Distribution in Europe*, Croom Helm, London.

Dawson, J A (1991) *Le commerce de détail Européen: Evolution et perspectives*, Presses du Management, Paris.

Dawson, J A, Shaw, S A, Burt, S L and Rana, J (1986) *Distributor Brand Packaged Groceries in the European Community*, Commission of the European Communities, FAST Occasional Papers, 104.

Distributive Trades EDC (1973) *The Distributive Trades in the Common Market*, HMSO, London.

Dominioni, L C, Danderighi, L and Zaninotto, E (1992) *Le Forme di Impresa nel Commercio Europeo*, EGEA, Milano.

Ducrocq, C (1991) *Concurrence et Stratégies dans la Distribution*, Vulbert, Paris.

Dupuis, M (1991) *Marketing International de la Distribution*, Editions d'organisation, Paris.

Europanel and CCA (1989) 'Euro-Styles : Eine Europaweite Landkarte mit 16 sozio-kulturellen Typen', *Marketing Journal*, 89(2), 106–111.

Eurostat (1993) *Retailing in the Single European Market*, Eurostat, Luxembourg.

Fielding, A J (1982) 'Counter urbanisation in Western Europe', *Progress in Planning*, 17, 1–52.

Filser, M (1987) 'Les options stratégiques de la firme de distribution', *Revue Française du Marketing*, 115, 37–48.

Filser, M (1990) *L'enjeu stratégique du marché unique pour les firmes de distribution*, Cahier 9005, CREGO-IAE Université de Bourgone.

Françoise, P and Leunis, J (1991) 'Public policy and the establishment of large stores in Belgium', *International Review of Retail, Distribution and Consumer Research*, 1(4), 469–486.

Gardner, H and Bennison, D (1993) *The Internationalisation of Discount Grocery Operations : the Danish Experience*, ESRC Seminar, UMIST, Manchester.

Hamill, J and Crosbie, J (1990) 'British retail acquisitions in the USA', *International Journal of Retail and Distribution Management*, 18(5), 15–20.

Harding, S and Phillips D (1986) *Contrasting values in Western Europe: Unity, Diversity and Change*, Macmillan, London.

Homma, N and Ueltzhoffer J (1990) 'The internationalisation of every-day-life research: markets and milieus', *Marketing and Research Today*, 18(4), 197–207.

Hollander, S (1970) *Multinational Retailing*, Michigan State University, East Lansing.

Jefferys, J B (1985) 'Multinational retailing: are the food chains different?', in Kacker M P *Transatlantic Trends in Retailing: Takeovers and Flow of Know-How*, Quorum Books, Westport, Conn. 14–144.

Jefferys, J B and Knee, D (1962) *Retailing in Europe*, Macmillan, London.

Kacker, M P (1985) *Transatlantic Trends in Retailing*, Quorum Books, Westport, Conn.

Kapfere (1991) *Les Marques: Capital de l'Entreprise*, Editions d'Organisation, Paris.

Laulajainen, R (1992) 'Louis Vuitton Malletier: a truly global retailer', *Annals of the Association of Economic Geographers*, 38(2), 55–70.

Linda, R (1983) *Le distribuzione commerciale in Europa*, Etas, Milan.

Lugli, G (1988) 'DPC/DPP: un nuovostrumento per gestir il rapporto tra industria e distribuzione ne grocery', *Commercio*, 28, 59–64.

Lugli, G (1989) 'Sviluppo multinazionale delle Aziende Commercial: opportunità e minacce per la destribuzione Italiana', *Commercio*, 32, 7–13.

Management Horizons (1992) *Europe's Leading Retailers*, Management Horizons, London.

Martenson, R (1985) *Innovation in Multinational Retailing*, University of Göteborg, Göteborg.

Martenson, R (1992) *The Future Role of Brands on the European Grocery Market*, Soderburg Research Institute of Commerce, Göteborg.

Mendelsohn, M (ed.) (1992) *Franchising in Europe*, Cassell, London.

Messerlin, P (1982) *La Révolution Commerciale*, Bonnel, Paris.

Molle, P (1992) *Le Commerce et la Distribution en Europe*, Editions Liaisons, Paris.

Ochel, W and Wegner, M (1987) *Service Economies in Europe*, Frances Pinter, London.

OECD (1973) *The Distribution Sector*, OECD, Paris.

Pasdermadjian, H (1961) *Le Grand Magasin: Son Origine – Son Evolution – Son Avenir*, Dunod, Paris.

Salmon, W and Tordjman A (1989) 'The internationalisation of retailing', *International Journal of Retailing*, 4(2), 3–16.

Segal-Horn, S and Davison, H (1990) *Global markets, the global consumer and international retailing*, Working Paper SWP41, Cranfield School of Management, Cranfield.

Sybrandy, A and Tuninga, R S J (1991) 'A comparative study of distribution system structure: Australia, the Netherlands and West Germany', *Journal of Macromarketing*, 11(2), 42–55.

Thompson, K (1992) 'The serpent in the supermarket's paradise', *European Management Journal*, 10(1), 112–118.

Tordjman, A (1983) *Stratégies de Concurrence dans le Commerce*, Editions d'Organisation, Paris.

Tordjman, A (1988) *Le Commerce de Detail Américain*, Editions d'Organisation, Paris.

Tordjman, A (1988) 'The French hypermarket: could it be developed in the States?', *Retail and Distribution Management*, 16(4), 14–16.

Treadgold, A (1988) 'Retailing without frontiers', *Retail and Distribution Management*, 16(6), 8–12.

Treadgold, A (1989a) 'Pan-European retail businesses: emerging structure', *European Business Review*, 89(4).

Treadgold, A and Davies, R L (1988) *The Internationalisation of Retailing*, Longman, Harlow.

Villermet J-M (1991) *Naissance de l'Hypermarché*, Armand Colin, Paris.

Waldman, C (1978) *Strategies of International Mass Retailers*, Praeger, New York.

Sources

Major trade journals

Convenience Store News
Discount Merchandiser
Discount Store
Distribución Actualidad
Distribution d'Aujourd'hui
DIY Superstore
Drugstore News
Dynamik im Handel
Euro-food
Frozen Food International
Grocery Bulletin of the Institute of Grocery Distribution

International Trends in Retailing
Largo Consumo
Lebensmittel Praxis
Libre Service Actualites
Loeb Retail Letter
Pointes de Vente
Private Label in Europe
Progressive Grocer
Retail Europe
Retail Week
Stores
Supermarket News

Reports

BAG
Bernard Julhiet
Bishop Williard
Comptes Commerciaux de la Nation (INSEE)
Corporate Intelligence Group
Distribución Actualidad
Economist Intelligence Unit, Marketing in Europe
Euromonitor, Retail Business International
Eurostaf
Eurostat
Fairchild Publications
Food Marketing Institute
Handel Aktuell '92
IFO Institut

Institut de la Commerce et de la Consommation
Management Horizons
Marketing Logistics
Mintel, Retail Intelligence
Neilsen
NRMA Publications
Oxford Institute of Retail Management
Panel de Gestion
PRESCEPTA
Secodip
Syndicate de la vente par correspondance
Verdict

CHAPTER 3

Retail internationalisation: evolution of theory and practice

Steve Burt

INTRODUCTION

Monitoring retail internationalisation has become a popular pastime for academics and other industry commentators over the past few years. Improvements in databases, or perhaps more accurately access to a wider range of databases and sources of information, have facilitated this process. Like most industry-based studies of internationalisation, the common pattern is for researchers to establish a picture of the volume, type and nature of activity before moving on to provide views on the motives and processes involved. The work of Hollander (1970) is seen by many as a starting point for the study of retail internationalisation, attempting as his study does to provide as comprehensive a view of the scale and nature of internationalisation as possible.

Hollander approaches the subject from a broad retail sector or institutional perspective, a line of enquiry followed by others such as Waldman's (1978a) study of French mass retailers, Burt's (1991) survey of European grocery retailing, and the more limited observations on Japanese department store internationalisation presented by Davies and Jones (1993). These reviews of activity are complemented by studies of the international development of specific retail concepts in new, usually underdeveloped, retail environments. Most focus on the supermarket (Goldman, 1974, 1981; Kaynak, 1985; Conners et al, 1985; Alawi, 1986), although more recent retail innovations such as the convenience store (Ho and Sin, 1987) have also been considered.

Often case studies of the internationalisation of a retail concept are provided through analysis of the activities of a specific company. Studies falling into this category include those of Kaynak (1980) who explored the early internationalisation of Migros' supermarkets in Turkey, Truitt (1984) who illustrated the spread of the mass merchandise store via the activities of Sears, Roebuck and Co in South America, the study of the discount store activities of Albert Gubay undertaken by Lord *et al* (1988) and Martenson's (1981, 1985, 1988) work on Ikea, the large non-food store specialist.

3.1 FROM DIRECTION TO PROCESS

3.1.1 The geographical dimension

Not surprisingly, the geographical dimension of retail internationalisation provides a major focus for existing studies. With the emphasis on either inward or outward investment from a defined market, many examples can be found of studies monitoring specific geographical flows. Trends in transatlantic activity are reviewed from an American perspective by Kacker (1985, 1990) and Exstein and Weitzman (1991), whilst UK studies of the same flows are provided by Hamill and Crosbie (1990) and Wrigley (1989). Within Europe, Bruins (1989) explores retail internationalisation in the Netherlands and Blümle and Briw (1990) do likewise for Switzerland, whilst further afield Davies (1993) examines patterns of Japanese outward investment. Other academic surveys of the internationalisation of the United Kingdom retail companies, in addition to the transatlantic activities noted above, include those of Jackson (1976), Burt and Dawson (1989) and Burt (1993) which consider outward investment, and those of Mitton (1987, 1988) which look at flows into the UK.

A combination of the sectoral/institution and geographical approaches has seen a number of company-based studies such as those authored by Laulajainen (1991a, 1991b, 1992) on Hennes and Mauritz, Toys 'R' Us and Ikea, and Louis Vuitton respectively, Bunce (1989) on Laura Ashley and Treadgold (1991) again featuring Laura Ashley and Dixons. No matter what the starting point, a common theme in much of the work monitoring retail internationalisation is the innovative nature of the retail concept to the host market.

3.1.2 The strategic dimension

Studies monitoring the volume, type and nature of retail internationalisation are less well matched by those explaining the processes involved. Academic papers in this area tend to focus on two themes – the motives stimulating international activity and the managerial mechanisms involved. Research on motives has on the whole concentrated on external environmental influences and borrows heavily on well recognised push and pull factors. Yoshino (1966) provides a relatively early view of the key factors, many of which are echoed later in the work of Treadgold and Davies (1988), Alexander (1990), Pellegrini (1992) and Williams (1992a, 1992b). Often the observed motives are specifically linked to discrete geographical flows, such as transatlantic activity (Wrigley, 1989).

Work published in the 1970s (Hollander, 1970, Waldman, 1978a, 1978b) identified common market entry strategies and key managerial success factors; it only appears to be in the late 1980s that management issues and processes were again addressed. The clear emphasis upon geographical flows and entry mechanisms in the studies which monitor internationalisation means that these factors are often emphasised in work attempting to explain the management processes involved. Treadgold (1988), for example, develops a typology based upon these factors which consists of four clusters – cautious internationalists, emboldened internationalists, aggressive internationalists and world powers (Figure 3.1). Companies in each of these clusters exhibit different managerial approaches to internationalisation. The vast majority of the academic literature on retail internationalisation deals implicitly with retail operations, although Kacker (1988) deals with the role of flows of know-how, and Burt (1991) and Dawson (1993, 1994) highlight the implications of defining retail internationalisation in such a narrow way upon a clear understanding of the full internationalisation process.

The emphasis upon the internationalisation of retail operations in the literature focuses attention upon managerial control, particularly in respect to the viability of a standardised or global approach to international markets. This debate, echoing that found in the international marketing literature, focuses attention upon the characteristics of the retail business and what is on offer to the international consumer. The Salmon and Tordjman (1989) approach identifies three basic strategies, including a sleeping partner investment strategy. The main thrust of their paper, however, deals with the global approach to retail internationalisation namely 'the faithful replication of a concept abroad ... as if their targeted market was homogeneous, thereby ignoring all national or regional differences' and the alternative multinational approach whereby 'retailers consider their subsidiaries to be a portfolio of geographically dispersed retail businesses, for each of which they adapt their standard formula to fit the local market conditions'. The choice of approach has implications for the degree of management control required within the company.

The studies examining managerial issues suggest a link between the nature of the retail operation, in terms of management structures and control mechanisms, and the approach to international markets; few commentators, however, go beyond these links. To date, surprisingly few authors attempt to understand retail internationalisation in the context of other theoretical models of business internationalisation. Pellegrini (1992) and Dawson (1994) introduce Dunning's (1981) eclectic paradigm for direct foreign investment to the debate. This framework, with its three main tenets of ownership specific advantages, location specific advantages and internalisation factors, is on the surface attractive. It appears to deal with issues highlighted by existing studies, namely sources of competitive advantage, the geographical dimension and market entry/control issues. For example, Williams (1991) emphasises the importance of differential firm advantage as

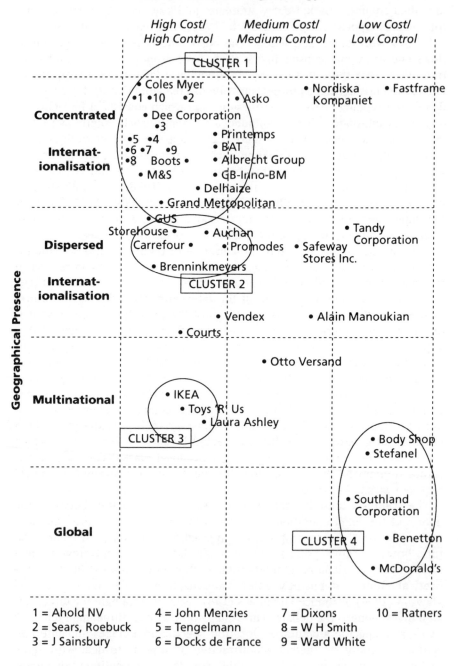

Entry and Operating Strategy

| | *High Cost/*
High Control | *Medium Cost/*
Medium Control | *Low Cost/*
Low Control |

CLUSTER 1

Concentrated

**Internat-
ionalisation**

• Coles Myer
•1 •10 •2   • Asko
• Dee Corporation
•3
• Printemps
•5 •4
•6 •7 •9   • BAT
•8 Boots •   • Albrecht Group
• M&S   • GB-Inno-BM
• Delhaize
• Grand Metropolitan

• Nordiska   • Fastframe
Kompaniet

Dispersed

**Internat-
ionalisation**

• GUS
Storehouse •   • Auchan
Carrefour •   •Promodes   • Safeway
• Brenninkmeyers   Stores Inc.

• Tandy
Corporation

CLUSTER 2

• Vendex   • Alain Manoukian
• Courts

Multinational

• Otto Versand

• IKEA
• Toys 'R' Us
• Laura Ashley

CLUSTER 3

• Body Shop
• Stefanel

Global

• Southland
Corporation

CLUSTER 4   • Benetton

• McDonald's

Geographical Presence

1 = Ahold NV	4 = John Menzies	7 = Dixons	10 = Ratners
2 = Sears, Roebuck	5 = Tengelmann	8 = W H Smith	
3 = J Sainsbury	6 = Docks de France	9 = Ward White	

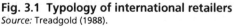

Fig. 3.1 Typology of international retailers
Source: Treadgold (1988).

a factor in the internationalisation process and highlights four potential sources – retail marketing skills and expertise, large-scale retailing, distinct retail concept and a strong retail brand – whilst the subjects of geographical spread (location-specific advantages) and method of investment (internalisation measures) have been considered earlier. However, further investigation leads both Pellegrini and Dawson to conclude that inherent differences between retailing and manufacturing may limit the applicability of the framework. We are left with the broad conclusion that a clear understanding of what is being internationalised in a retail context is an important part of the equation.

3.1.3 The time dimension

A further factor which may contribute to our understanding of retail internationalisation is the time dimension. All the studies reviewed above have implicitly such a dimension, either by their nature as longitudinal studies or in the context within which they have been undertaken. We are fond of stating that retailing is a dynamic and rapidly changing industrial sector – yet the extent to which we consider changes over time between and in studies is less clear. Kacker (1985) identifies time-specific issues as important in the influx of British investment into the United States, and similarly Hallsworth (1992) emphasises that contingency and contextual factors are not static.

One of the few studies to introduce a fairly straightforward time dimension is that of Treadgold (1990/91), which argues that retailers travel through a learning curve over time as they move through stages termed reluctance, caution and ambition. As early as 1970, Hollander admits to surprise at the 'scope, magnitude and diversity' of retail internationalisation; most previous UK studies concentrate on activities taking place from the mid-1980s onwards. A broader temporal perspective may, however, contribute to the debate as changes in geographical direction, entry method and management behaviour may provide clues to factors influencing the process. This is the premise upon which this chapter is based.

3.2 MONITORING RETAIL INTERNATIONALISATION

3.2.1 Data sources

The monitoring of retail internationalisation over a significant time period requires access to a range of data sources. Reports from commercial agencies such as the Corporate Intelligence Group (1992) and regular fact sheets from the Oxford Institute of Retail Management (OXRIM) provide a base source, whilst the monitoring of recent events is possible through the trade press – particularly in the case of the UK since the launch of *Retail Week*. Historical data may be obtained from long-established event monitoring newsletters such as the International Association of Department Stores' *Retail Newsletter* (a source extensively used by Hollander (1970)) Management Horizons' *Retail International/Retail Europe* and the CWS *Retail Review*, company reports and archives and academic articles and theses. From these various sources datasets can be generated.

The multitude of sources inevitably leads to variations in the nature and quality of the data available. In the case of the dataset used for this chapter the following details were recorded since 1960:

- date of activity;
- company and product sector involved;
- country of destination;
- market entry method.

Each entry to the dataset was recorded as an 'action'. An action is regarded as any form of operational investment undertaken by British companies in retailing overseas. These operational investments were recorded as entry mechanisms – acquisition, minority acquisition (less than 50 per cent), increased shareholdings, internal growth (store openings and concessions/shop-in-shop), joint ventures, franchises. These categories are commonly regarded as the main entry methods employed in international retailing – for example, see Dawson (1994).

3.2.2 International activity

On this basis for the period January 1960 to January 1994, a total of 798 actions involving British companies investing abroad in retailing were recorded by the year of entry. A further 120 actions could be dated by the decades of 1960–69, 1970–79 and 1980–89, mainly from Corporate Intelligence Group data, and a further 142 actions were identified but could not be related to either a single year or decade during the 1960–94 period. In total therefore 1,060 actions were recorded over the study period, 918 of which could be dated by decade.

Although 1960 is taken as a starting point for this analysis, the first issue to establish is that the internationalisation of British retailing is not new. Hollander (1970) refers to a number of early forays into foreign markets at the end of the nineteenth century – particularly the exploits of Liptons who were represented in France, Ireland, Germany, Turkey, Sweden, Denmark, India, Ceylon, South Africa, Australia and the USA before the turn of the century. Other early pre-war movers still trading include Mappin & Webb, Burberry, Harrods, WH Smith, Church & Co and Dunhill. If one charts the individual dated actions (798) from 1960 one can observe a steady flow of activity over the past 33 years. Figure 3.2 clearly identifies a steady rise in volume over this period plus two peaks of activity in the early 1970s and late 1980s. The cyclical nature of this investment would appear to mirror general economic trends over the study period. The dent in economic

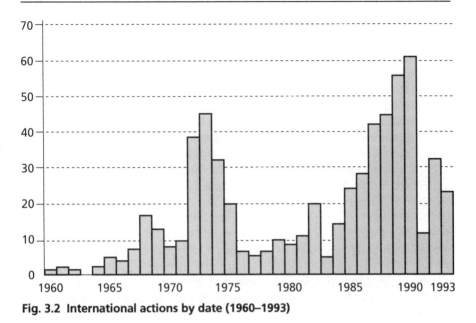

Fig. 3.2 International actions by date (1960–1993)

activity and confidence caused by the 1973 oil crisis is evident as is the credit driven retail boom of the Thatcher years. The strong growth in international investment during the 1980s reflects corporate confidence during the so-called 'golden age' (Wrigley, 1989) of British retailing when companies could (or felt they could) do no wrong.

The increased volume of activity observed over the period may reflect a number of factors raised in the existing literature. Internationalisation is regarded as a high-risk venture, so firms may only move overseas once experience in domestic markets or low-risk overseas markets is gained – in essence the argument of Treadgold's (1990/91) learning curve. Common push and pull factors, as defined in the literature, would also imply a growing interest in internationalisation over time, for example as existing markets become more saturated and opportunities overseas become more visible. Similarly, the importance of enabling factors derived from the widespread adoption and use of information technology will grow over time. One should also consider that the growth shown in Figure 3.2 merely reflects the increase in sources of information available from the mid-1980s, and the general attention given to internationalisation in the trade press which allows international activity to be recorded at a level of detail not possible in earlier years.

3.3 MARKET ENTRY MECHANISMS

The growing interest of UK retailers in international expansion is clear. Although motives and management processes are difficult to identify and as rationalisation of activity after the event is fraught with problems, changes in the mechanisms of investment and destination provide some proxy indication of growing confidence, experience and changing processes. By their very nature different market entry mechanisms involve different levels of risk, investment and management skills. The advantages and disadvantages of the most common market entry mechanisms are outlined in Table 3.1. Changes in the nature of entry mechanism over time therefore can provide some clue to understanding the trends in activity.

The dataset allows identification of entry method for the 'decade-based' data of 918 actions (Table 3.2). Although the choice of decades imposes a somewhat artificial time frame on the dataset, it does provide a maximum number of entries to be assessed. Of the activity monitored over the 1960–1993 period, internal growth is seen to be the major entry mechanism accounting for 41.3 per cent (379) of recorded actions. Acquisition is the second most preferred entry method with 23.7 per cent (218) of actions, rising to 28.6 per cent (263) if the sub-groups of minority shareholding and raised shareholding are included, followed by franchising with 21 per cent (193) of actions. Joint venture activity with 8.6 per cent (79) of actions is relatively unimportant.

The acceptance of franchising as a viable management control method in more recent years has had a significant impact upon activity. If one examines changes in the relative importance of entry methods over decades (Table 3.2), it is clear that whilst internal growth remains the preferred entry method, franchising becomes a significant alternative during the 1980s and appears to be equally popular so far in the 1990s. Although, as will be shown below, franchising is closely associated with a limited number of very internationally active companies, it is noticeable that it is becoming a more viable entry mechanism and is one which widens the scope and range of international activities.

In addition to the global picture, changes in the volume of activity and the entry method show some relationship to the sector and company involved. Categorising retail companies is a difficult exercise, particularly with the degree of segmentation in some product markets and the continued appearance of retail innovations which cross traditional definitional boundaries. Taking the dataset in its three forms – known actions, decade-based actions and all actions – specific sectors/categories of retailing dominate (Table 3.3). The clothing sector is responsible for by far the greatest proportion of the actions recorded, at whatever level of detail, accounting for around 28 per cent of actions. A 'new' category, that of bodycare, is the next most dominant source of actions followed by (perhaps surprisingly) TV rental, furniture, variety stores and footwear. In all, these six categories account for around 55 per cent of the recorded actions over the 1960–1993 period.

Table 3.1 Common market entry mechanisms in international retailing

Mechanism	Advantages	Disadvantages
Internal expansion	Can be undertaken by any size of firm. Experimental openings are possible with modest risk and often modest cost. Ability to adapt operation with each subsequent opening. Exit is easy (at least in early stages). Allows rapid prototyping.	Takes a long time to establish a substantial presence. May be seen by top management as a minor diversion. Requirement to undertake full locational assessment. More difficult if host market is distant from home market. Requires firm to become familiar with host country property market. Lack of suitable sites of host country.
Merger or takeover	Substantial market presence quickly achieved. Management already in place. Cash flow is immediate. Possibility of technology transfer to home firm. May be used as a way to obtain locations quickly for conversion to the chosen format.	Difficult to exit if mistake is made. Evaluation of takeover target is difficult and takes time. Suitable firms may not be available. Substantial top management commitment necessary. Management of acquired firm may be unsuited to new operation.
Franchise type agreements	Rapid expansion of presence possible. Low cost to franchiser. Marginal markets can be addressed. Local management may be used. Wide range of forms of agreement available. Use locally competitive marketing policy.	Possibly complex legal requirements. Necessary to recruit suitable franchisees. Difficult to control foreign franchisees. May become locked into an unsatisfactory relationship.
Joint ventures	Possible to link with firm already in market. Help available to climb learning curve and to overcome non-tariff barriers. Possible to move later either to exit or make full entry into the market. Share entry costs with other entrant.	Necessary to share benefits. Difficulties in finding a suitable partner.
Non-controlling interest	Find out about market with minimal risk. Allows those who know the market to manage the operation.	Passive position. Investment made over which little influence.

Source: Dawson (1994).

Table 3.2 Activity by decade

Entry mechanism	Decade data set		1960–69		1970–79		1980–89		1990–93	
	No.	%	No.	%	No.	%	No.	%	No.	%
Acquisition	218	23.7	12	20.3	62	27.3	120	28.7	24	11.2
Minority acquisition	19	2.1	2	3.4	5	2.2	8	1.9	4	1.8
Raise shareholding	26	2.8	1	1.7	10	4.4	13	3.1	2	0.9
Internal growth	379	41.3	29	49.4	113	49.8	147	35.2	90	42.1
Joint venture	79	8.6	12	20.3	18	7.9	22	5.3	27	12.6
Franchise	193	21.0	3	5.1	19	8.4	104	24.9	67	31.3
Unknown	4	0.4	—	0	—	0	4	0.9	—	0
Total	918	100	59	100	227	100	418	100	214	100

Table 3.3 Activity by sector

Sector	Total dataset	Decade dataset	Dated dataset
Clothing	299	260	214
Bodycare	87	77	66
TV rental	57	55	50
Furniture	49	40	33
Variety store	49	47	43
Footwear	45	41	35
Leading six sectors	586	520	441
(% of total)	55.2%	56.6%	55.3%
Total	1060	918	798

For the decade-based data set it is possible to identify preferred entry mechanisms within each sector (Figure 3.3). Clear preferences are evident in some cases. Companies in the clothing sector have made the vast majority of their excursions abroad via internal growth (69.2 per cent), whilst bodycare and variety store retailers show a clear preference for franchising (80.5 per cent and 61.7 per cent respectively). The dominance of a single entry mechanism is less clear in other sectors, although 52.5 per cent of actions undertaken by furniture retailers are internal growth, and 41.5 per cent of

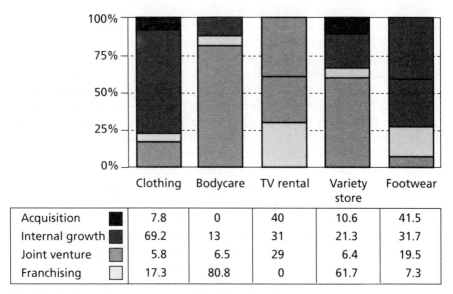

		Clothing	Bodycare	TV rental	Variety store	Footwear
Acquisition	■	7.8	0	40	10.6	41.5
Internal growth	■	69.2	13	31	21.3	31.7
Joint venture	▨	5.8	6.5	29	6.4	19.5
Franchising	☐	17.3	80.8	0	61.7	7.3

Fig. 3.3 Preferred sector entry methods by decade

footwear actions are via acquisition. The actions of TV rental companies are more evenly spread across different mechanisms, although a relatively high proportion of actions are via joint venture agreements (29 per cent). The apparent differences in preferred entry mechanisms imply that sector-specific features have an important role to play in understanding retail internationalisation.

3.4 GEOGRAPHICAL TRENDS

Changes in the destination of investment similarly provides further clues as to the internationalisation process. The existing literature argues that part of the risk of moving overseas is tempered by moving initially to geographically or culturally close markets. A sequential move from low to high-risk destinations is therefore expected. Previous studies examining internationalisation over a significant study period (Burt 1991, 1993) provide some evidence of this. In the UK case this implies an initial preference for culturally close markets such as the USA, Ireland and Canada, and geographically close markets such as northern Europe, with a slow dispersion of activity to more culturally and geographically distant markets over time. Such views are intuitively attractive and fit with some of the general literature on business internationalisation, which deals with risk reduction and the role of psychic distance, and a stages approach to market expansion.

In all, 80 different countries can be identified as the recipients of UK retail internationalisation over the 1960–1993 period. These 80 countries can be associated with 1,047 actions (the remaining 13 actions being attributed to regions rather than countries). The most popular individual destination for investment was by far the United States, which received 164 actions, 147 of which could be dated by decade, followed by France with 91 (85) actions, the Netherlands with 83 (76) and Germany with 78 (71). Although a potentially arbitrary exercise, if one assigns countries into geographical regional 'clusters' an aggregate picture of development may be identified. Table 3.4 relates these clusters to the number of actions per country within the cluster. From this exercise, four sub-groups of clusters may be identified which appear to exhibit different levels of attraction and which, one could argue, represent different perceptions of risk.

The clear attraction of an Atlantic cluster, comprising the USA, Canada and the Republic of Ireland, and a North European cluster of France, the Netherlands, Germany, Belgium, Denmark and Luxembourg is shown by the high average number of actions per cluster. The next most attractive grouping includes a Scandinavian and a Central European (essentially Austria and Switzerland) cluster, which attract a level of interest a little above the overall average for the clusters. The Southern Europe and Far Eastern clusters form a third group which have a level of investment below the average but clearly greater than the remaining group of clusters. At a

Table 3.4 Destination of international activity by geographic clusters

Cluster	Number of countries	Actions	Actions per country
Total	80	1,047	13.3
Atlantic	3	274	91.3
N Europe	6	333	55.5
Other Europe	2	41	20.5
Scandinavia	3	47	15.7
S Europe	9	107	11.9
Far East	11	124	11.3
Pacific	5	40	8.0
East Europe	6	15	2.5
Middle East	11	26	2.4
Caribbean	10	16	1.6
Other	14	24	1.7

very general level one could equate the four groupings to broad perceptions of risk based upon the relative cultural and geographical distance from the UK. The Atlantic/Northern European grouping represent known developed retail markets which are either geographically or culturally close to Britain, whilst at the other extreme a grouping comprising Eastern Europe, Pacific, Caribbean, Middle Eastern and Southern American/other country clusters perhaps represent the most risky markets given their geographical and cultural distance from Britain and the potential returns from investing in these markets.

A further caveat to this scheme is provided through an assessment of changing destinations over time. The decade data set is the largest available for this approach (Table 3.5) and shows that five regional clusters account for over 80 per cent of activity over the 1960–93 period. This shows the consistent importance of the geographically or culturally close Northern European and Atlantic markets throughout the study period, although with different periods of relative ascendancy. The Northern European markets are dominant during the 1970s whilst the Atlantic markets – particularly the USA – are the prime target of investment in the 1980s. Other tentative patterns show the emergence of relatively new markets of interest – namely the Far East and Southern Europe – which as we enter the 1990s appear to be of particular interest. In contrast, the significance of the Scandinavian markets appears to be on the wane from the 1980s.

This temporal pattern in destination again provides some support for the literature on internationalisation as investment appears to switch from perceived lower risk areas to higher risk areas. This is reinforced by the

Table 3.5 Major destination (regional clusters) by decade

Major regional cluster	Total data set No.	%	Decade data set No.	%	1960s No.	%	1970s No.	%	1980s No.	%	1990–93 No.	%
N Europe	333	31.4	300	32.7	19	32.2	103	45.4	112	26.8	66	30.8
Atlantic	274	25.8	238	25.9	17	28.8	53	23.3	139	33.3	29	13.6
Far East	124	11.7	110	12.0	4	6.8	23	10.1	38	9.1	45	21.0
S Europe	107	10.1	94	10.2	3	5.1	10	4.4	44	10.5	37	17.3
Scandinavia	47	4.4	43	4.7	5	8.4	19	8.4	18	4.3	1	0.5
Total	1,060	100	918	100	59	100	227	100	418	100	214	100

Table 3.6 Major destinations (country) by decade

1960–93		1970s		1980s		1990–93	
USA	147	Netherlands	29	USA	100	France	26
France	85	France	23	Netherlands	36	Spain	22
Netherlands	76	Germany	23	France	32	USA	21
Germany	71	USA	20	Germany	21	Germany	19
Ireland	50	Canada	17	Ireland	21	Japan	19
Japan	49	Belgium	16	Spain	20	Netherlands	9
Canada	41	Ireland	16	Japan	18	Belgium	7
Total (7)	519		144		248		123
Total (all)	918		227		418		214
% of total	56.5%		63.4%		59.3%		57.5%

ment of individual country destinations in the 1970s, 1980s and so far in the 1990s (Table 3.6). Signs of market spreading are evident from the fact that the seven most popular destinations in each decade are accounting for a declining number of the total actions. In the 1970s, all of the leading seven destinations are from the 'low risk' Atlantic/North Europe grouping, with the Netherlands which has long been seen as the retail market most similar in nature to the UK as the first destination, closely followed by France and Germany. The USA dominates investment during the 1980s, but more significantly for the future Spain and Japan – perhaps previously seen as higher risk or more closed markets – appear in the list of leading destinations. This trend, particularly in the case of Spain, appears to be being sustained at the start of the current decade.

3.5 SECTORAL TRENDS

Differences in approach to international markets witnessed by differences in entry mechanisms imply that sectoral characteristics may provide a further input to understanding the internationalisation process. This leads us back to the debate underpinning the Salmon and Tordjman (1989) article which implies that the nature of the sector or individual company characteristics will influence the approach taken to internationalisation. The six sectors identified above account for 55 per cent of recorded actions, but each sector has different characteristics. The number of companies involved and their corresponding commitment, measured by the number of actions, varies by sector. The average number of actions per company within a sector provides one indication of the level of activity (Table 3.7) and clearly reflects the influence of entry method on the spread of activity. Those sectors favouring

Table 3.7 Intensity of activity by sector

Sector	Total actions	Number of companies	Action per company	Number of companies <3 actions	>10 actions
Clothing	299	60	4.98	36	9
Bodycare	87	5	17.40	2	2
TV rental	57	8	7.13	1	1
Furniture	49	7	7.00	3	2
Variety store	49	3	16.33	1	2
Footwear	45	10	4.50	5	1

Source: Total dataset.

franchising provide a high average number of actions per company, whilst the lowest ratios are found in those sectors were internal growth dominates. Within each sector experienced or committed internationalists appear to exist, and their behaviour may both reflect or dictate sector norms.

Internal growth as an entry mechanism is preferred by both the clothing and the furniture sectors. However, on examining the two sectors different features become apparent. In the case of clothing, which dominates the data set with 299 actions, a total of 60 different companies or strategic business units can be identified. Clothing is a particularly difficult sector to monitor, given the large number of companies involved, the degree of segmentation of trading formats and the heavy use of in-store concessions. Of the companies and actions identified, 60 per cent of companies have been involved in three or less actions, with 30 per cent involved in a single action. On the basis of the total number of actions observed, Laura Ashley is by some way the most active international clothing retailer, followed at some distance by Jaeger, Austin Reed, Tie Rack, Sock Shop and Aquascutum.

These companies represent a range of experiences. Laura Ashley, Jaeger, Austin Reed and Acquascutum, all of which could be said to retail a typical 'British' style of clothing, began their international activity in the early 1970s, and in Austin Reed's case the 1960s. By 1975, Laura Ashley had entered eight markets, Austin Reed nine and Aquascutum six. These typically focused on western Europe (including the Scandinavian markets owing to the UK's membership of EFTA), with the obligatory foray into the USA and Japan, and generally involved internal growth mechanisms. Laura Ashley has latterly, in the 1980s and 1990s, expanded further afield with the use of franchising – for example, into Sweden, Greece, Norway, Italy, Denmark, Finland and Austria in the 1980s, and Hong Kong, Singapore, Portugal and Taiwan in the 1990s. Tie Rack and Sock Shop are more representative of the product-niche 1980s players, moving overseas from 1987 using a combination of internal growth and franchising. The chequered history of both these companies has seen a series of market entry, exit and re-entry moves in their short periods of international involvement. However classified, all of these active clothing companies could be argued to have a very clear niche offer, whether based upon 'Britishness' or product expertise.

The furniture sector, which also favours internal growth, involved eight companies, with Courts and Habitat dominating activity, each with fifteen actions from the total of 49 observed. The next major player, with nine actions, was GUS during the 1970s, largely through the Cavendish chain. Other internationalists in this sector include Conran, MFI, Waring & Gillow and Maples. Although for most companies small numbers limit the identification of clear trends, internal growth appears to be a consistently popular mechanism throughout the study period. Company preferences show through, with GUS and Waring & Gillow responsible for most of the acquisition activity, whilst Courts has expanded in the Caribbean and Far East almost exclusively via store openings, with the exception of an acquisition in Trinidad in 1990 (Table 3.8).

Table 3.8 The internationalisation of Courts

Year	Destination	Method
1965	Barbados	Internal growth
1969	Australia	Internal growth
1971	Fiji	Internal growth
1974	Singapore	Internal growth
1981	St Lucia	Internal growth
1983	Papua New Guinea	Internal growth
1985	Antigua	Internal growth
	Mauritius	Internal growth
1987	Grenada	Internal growth
	Malaysia	Internal growth
1990	Trinidad	Acquisition
1992	Jamaica	Internal growth
	Dominica	Internal growth
Other undated	USA	Internal growth
	Hong Kong	Internal growth

The international expansion of Courts appears to go completely against the expected pattern as espoused in some of the literature. Psychologically or geographically close markets have been ignored as expansion has concentrated on distant markets. Courts point out that they now have a store open in some part of the world for 24 hours a day. The importance of this expansion to the company is reflected in the financial contribution of the overseas activities, which accounted for 57 per cent of turnover and 85 per cent of operating profit in the 1994 financial year. Habitat appears to have pursued a more conventional approach of opening stores in geographically and culturally close markets in the 1970s, before moving to more peripheral European and Far Eastern markets in the 1980s. Internal growth is a feature of both the 1970s and the 1980s, but a switch to franchising occurred in the case of the Belgian and Dutch operations in 1988, an approach also used further afield in Singapore, Hong Kong, Martinique and Portugal.

Franchising is the dominant entry mechanism for bodycare retailers and variety store retailers – two contrasting types of retailer in terms of length of time in the marketplace, store size, and product range. Bodycare retailing is epitomised by the Body Shop which, together with Nectar, account for 92 per cent of the 87 observed actions. This sector is a further example of 1980s niche retailing – although Body Shop first ventured abroad to Belgium in 1978. The scope of franchising to allow rapid and geographically diverse international moves is clearly evidenced by the Body Shop (Table 3.9), which is now represented in over 45 countries. A more recent entrant to the international market is Nectar, which began to franchise internationally within Europe in the mid-1980s to Sweden (1986), Canada, Ireland, Italy, Portugal, Spain and Switzerland (1987), before moving into some Far Eastern markets at the start of the 1990s. One feature of the use of franchising as a means of expansion is the potential for multi-market entry within a single year.

Variety store retailing as a concept based in large store mass-market retailing is almost the antithesis of the bodycare sector in every respect. The international activity in this sector is dominated by the activities of Marks & Spencer, with 29 of the observed 49 actions, and BhS, with 19 actions, plus Littlewoods' entry into Russia in the 1990s. Despite opening a store in Ireland in 1977, it was another ten years before BhS made a major overseas commitment, which then occurred exclusively through franchising, predominantly in the Middle East with operations in Dubai, Abu Dhabi, Kuwait, Bahrain, Qatar, Egypt and Oman, and the Mediterranean (Malta, Cyprus, Gibraltar and Turkey). Marks & Spencer has pursued a range of entry mechanisms from joint ventures in Canada, licensing agreements in Japan and store openings in Europe during the 1970s, to a greater emphasis on franchising in the 1990s, which has seen entry into Greece, Hungary, Thailand, Austria, Malaysia and Turkey.

Finally, acquisition is a relatively important mechanism in the footwear sector, which exhibits a range of entry mechanisms. Although ten different companies are involved, the British Shoe Corporation was responsible for 12 of the 45 actions, and Church & Co for a further 10. Following the acquisition of Hartt in Canada during 1964, Church & Co appeared to prefer expansion by internal growth, particularly in the early 1970s, when the majority of their European moves (Netherlands, Sweden, Denmark,

Table 3.9 The internalisation of the Body Shop

Year	Destination	(City)
1978	Belgium	(Brussels)
1979	Sweden	(Stockholm)
	Greece	(Athens)
	Austria	(Vienna)
1980	Canada	(Toronto)
	Iceland	(Reykjavik)
1981	Denmark	(Copenhagen)
	Finland	(Tampere)
	Ireland	(Dublin)
1982	Holland	(Leiden)
	France	(Paris)
1983	Australia	(Melbourne)
	Cyprus	(Limassol)
	Germany	(Cologne)
	Singapore	
	Switzerland	(Zurich)
	UAE	(Dubai)
1984	Hong Kong	(Kowloon)
	Italy	(Catania)
	Malaysia	(Kuala Lumpur)
1985	Bahamas	(Nassau)
	Bahrain	(Meenoma)
	Norway	(Oslo)
1986	Kuwait	(Safat)
	Oman	(Muscat)
	Portugal	(Lisbon)
	Spain	(Madrid)
1987	Antigua	(St John)
	Qatar	
	Saudi Arabia	
	Malta	(Sliema)
	Bermuda	(Hamilton)
1988	USA	(New York)
	Gibraltar	
	Taiwan	(Taipei)
1989	New Zealand	(Welligton)
	Caymen Islands	
1990	Indonesia	
	Japan	(Tokyo)
1991	Luxembourg	
1992	—	
1993	Brunei	
	Macao	
	Mexico	
	Thailand	

Source: Annual Reports.

Belgium and France) took place. The British Shoe Corporation has been involved in a number of American and Dutch acquisitions mainly in the 1980s, with internal growth and joint venturing used in the Netherlands, Belgium and Germany in the late 1980s/early 1990s.

Other companies, with fewer recorded actions, all seem to show a trend towards acquisition: Rayne buying out the Delman joint venture (USA) in 1968; K Shoes acquiring Hess Modelschoisel and Chaussures Moderne de Bock (both Netherlands) in 1972, George Oliver acquiring the Arizona Shoe Corporation (USA) in 1985 and Benson Shoe acquiring John Taylor (Ireland) in 1986. The acquisition method was particularly favoured by C&J Clark, which acquired France Arno and Footrest (Australia) in the 1970s and the American chains Bostonian, Big Sky and Hanover in the 1980s.

CONCLUSIONS

A longitudinal analysis of the broad trends in retail internationalisation over a 33 year period provides some insight into the process and highlights issues for future research. The internationalisation of retail operations is a well established strategic option for companies. Although this review does not assess the scale of investment nor its importance to the company concerned, the number of companies involved and the range of markets receiving investment has steadily grown. Changes in the volume, destination and nature of activity over time reinforce a view that the context of the move appears to be important. The prevailing environmental influences, management perceptions and attitudes should be borne in mind when commenting on broad trends.

At a macro (industry) level, the general issues arising from the literature with respect to control mechanisms and the geographical dimension to investment would appear to be supported by the UK experience. UK investment tends towards entry mechanisms which provide high levels of control, such as internal growth and acquisition, and activity seems to be primarily directed towards markets which can be perceived as less risky – namely North America or Northern Europe. Over time, evidence suggests that other mechanisms such as franchising have been adopted and the spread of investment has widened to encompass 'less familiar' markets in the Far East and elsewhere. This combination of mechanism and destination to manage risk is a familiar view from the existing literature.

Although a macro approach allows such parallels with generalisations from the existing literature to be made, when the process is considered at the level of the sector or firm, such generalisations become more difficult. Within a sector there is a suggestion that 'uniqueness' or 'innovation' – whether in the retail offer *per se* or in the context of the destination market – underpins the most active retail internationalists. This suggests that a clear understanding of the company and the host market context is crucial in assessing internationalisation. Similarly, although market entry preferences may be observed within specific sectors, often the corporate preferences of active or dominant companies can skew the overall picture. This reinforces a feeling that a greater understanding of the process at the level of the firm is required. We are well aware of the volume and direction of British retailer internationalisation, it is now time to explore the processes involved in more detail.

REVIEW QUESTIONS

1. What dimensions of the retail internationalisation process have been explored by academics?

2. How important is the nature of the retail sector to the internationalisation process?

3. What effect has franchising had on patterns of British retailer internationalisation?

4. Which destinations are likely to be the most popular in the 1990s?

5. Explain the different patterns of retail internationalisation exhibited by clothing and furniture retailers.

6. Given the patterns of retail internationalisation observed for some sectors, how would you expect British food retailers to internationalise?

REFERENCES

Alawi, H M A (1986) 'Saudi Arabia: making sense of self-service', *International Marketing Review*, Spring, 21–38.

Alexander, N (1990) 'Retailers and international markets: motives for expansion', *International Marketing Review*, 7(4), 75–85.

Blümle, E B and Briw, A (1990) 'Internationalisierung des Einzelhandels. Eine explorative studie über die Schweiz', in Tommsdorff, V (ed.) *Handelsforschung 1990 – Internalisierung im Handel*, Gabler, Wiesbaden, 83–94.

Bruins, A (1989) *Handelen Over de Grenzen*, EIM, Zoetermeer.

Bunce, M L (1989) 'The international approach of Laura Ashley', in ESOMAR Proceedings, *Adding Value to Retail Offerings*, 24–6 April 1989, Edinburgh, 101–106.

Burt, S L (1991) 'Trends in the internationalisation of grocery retailing', *The International Review of Retail, Distribution and Consumer Research*, 1(4), 487–515.

Burt, S L (1993) 'Temporal trends in the internationalisation of British retailing', *International Review of Retail, Distribution and Consumer Research*, 3(4), 391–410.

Burt, S L and Dawson, J A (1989) 'L'Internazionalizzazione del Commercio al Dettaglio Inglese', *Commercio*, 35, 137–57.

Connors, S B, Samli, A C and Kaynak, E (1985) 'Transfer of food retail technology into less developed countries', in Samli, A C (ed.), *Technology Transfer*, Quorum Westport, Connecticut, 27–44.

Corporate Intelligence Group (1992) *Cross-Border Retailing in Europe,* Corporate Intelligence Group, London.

Davies, B K (1993) 'The international activities of Japanese retailers', in Burt, S L and Sparks, L (ed.) *Proceedings of the 7th International Conference on Research in the Distributive Trades,* Institute for Retail Studies, University of Stirling, 574–583.

Davies, B J and Jones, P (1993) 'The international activity of Japanese department stores', *The Service Industries Journal,* 13(1), 126–132.

Dawson, J A (1993) *The Internationalisation of Retailing,* University of Edinburgh, Working Paper 93/2.

Dawson, J A (1994) 'Internationalisation of retail operations', *Journal of Marketing Management,* 10, 267–282.

Dunning, J H (1981) *International Production and the Multinational Enterprise,* Allen & Unwin, London.

Exstein, M B and Weitzman, F I (1991) 'Foreign investment in US retailing: an optimistic overview', *Retail Control,* January, 9–14.

Goldman, A (1974) 'Growth of large food stores in developing countries', *Journal of Retailing,* 57(2), 5–29.

Goldman, A (1981) 'Transfer of retailing technology into the less developed countries: the supermarket case', *Journal of Retailing,* 57(2), 5–29.

Hallsworth, A G (1992) 'Retail internationalisation: contingency and context?', *European Journal of Marketing,* 26(8/9), 25–34.

Hamill, J and Crosbie, J (1990) 'British retail acquisitions in the US', *International Journal of Retail and Distribution Management,* 18(5), 15–20.

Ho, S C and Sin, Y M (1987) 'International transfer of retail technology: the successful case of convenience stores in Hong Kong', *International Journal of Retailing,* 2(3), 36–48.

Hollander, S C (1970) *Multinational Retailing,* MSU International Business and Economic Studies, MSU, East Lansing.

Jackson, G I (1976) 'British retailer expansion into Europe', unpublished PhD thesis, UMIST, Manchester.

Kacker, M P (1985) *Transatlantic Trends in Retailing,* Quorum, Westport, Connecticut.

Kacker, M P (1988) 'International flow of retailing know-how: bridging the technology gap in distribution', *Journal of Retailing,* 64(1), 41–67.

Kacker, M P (1990) 'The lure of US retailing to the foreign acquirer', *Mergers and Acquisitions,* 25(1), 63–68.

Kaynak, E (1980) 'Transfer of supermarketing technology from developed to less developed countries: the case of Migros-Turk', *Finnish Journal of Business Economics,* 29(1).

Kaynak, E (1985) 'Global spread of supermarkets: some experience from Turkey', in Kaynak, E (ed.) *Global Perspective in Marketing,* Praeger, New York.

Laulajainen, R (1991a) 'International expansion of an apparel retailer – Hennes and Mauritz of Sweden', *Zeitschrift für Wirtschaftsgeographie,* 35(1), 1–15.

Laulajainen, R (1991b) 'Two retailers go global: the geographical dimension', *International Review of Retail, Distribution and Consumer Research,* 1(5), 607–626.

Laulajainen, R (1992) 'Louis Vuitton Malletier. A truly global retailer', *Article of the Japan Association of Economic Geographers,* 38(2), 55–70.

Lord, D, Morgan, W, Parker, A and Sparks, L (1988) 'Retailing on three continents – the discount food store operations of Albert Gubay', *International Journal of Retailing,* 3(3), 1–54.

Martenson, R (1981) *Innovation in Multinational Retailing,* University of Göteborg, Göteborg.

Martenson, R (1985) 'Cross cultural analysis in global marketing: a European case', in Shaw, S, Sparks, L and Kaynak, E (eds.), *Marketing in the 1990s and Beyond, Proceedings of the Second World Marketing Congress, Volume II,* University of Stirling, 694–709.

Martenson, R (1988) 'Cross-cultural similarities and differences in multinational retailing', in Kaynak, E (ed.), *Transnational Retailing,* de Gruyter, 21–22, Berlin.

Mitton, A E (1987) 'Foreign retail companies operating in the UK', *Retail and Distribution Management,* 15(1), 29–31.

Mitton, A E (1988) 'Foreign investment in UK retail trades', in West, A (ed.) *Handbook of Retailing*, Gower, Aldershot, 63–72.

Pellegrini, L (1992) 'The internationalisation of retailing and 1992 Europe', *Journal of Marketing Channels*, 1(2), 3–27.

Salmon, W J and Tordjman, A (1989) 'The internationalisation of retailing', *International Journal of Retailing*, 4(2), 3–16.

Treadgold, A (1988) 'Retailing without frontiers', *Retail and Distribution Management*, 16(6), 8–12.

Treadgold, A (1990/91) 'The emerging internationalisation of retailing: present status and future strategies', *Irish Marketing Review*, 5(2), 11–27.

Treadgold, A (1991) 'Dixons and Laura Ashley: different routes to international growth', *International Journal of Retail and Distribution Management*, 19(4), 13–19.

Treadgold, A and Davies, R L (1988) *The Internationalisation of Retailing*, Longman, London.

Truitt, N S (1984) 'Mass merchandising and economic development: Sears, Roebuck and Co in Mexico and Peru', in Shelp, R K, Stephenson, J C, Truitt, N S and Wasow, B, *Service Industries and Economic Development*, Praeger, New York, 49–113.

Waldman, C (1978a) *Strategies of International Mass Retailers*, Praeger, New York.

Waldman, C (1978b) 'La Stratégie Internationale des Sociétés Francaise de Distribution', *Revue Francaise de Gestion*, November/December, 76–87.

Williams, D E (1991) 'Differential firm advantages and retailer internationalisation', *International Journal of Retail and Distribution Management*, 19(4), 3–12.

Williams, D E (1992a) 'Motives for retailer internationalisation: their impact, structure and implications', *Journal of Marketing Management*, 8, 269–285.

Williams, D E (1992b) 'Retailer internationalisation: an empirical inquiry', *European Journal of Marketing*, 25(8/9), 8–24.

Wrigley, N (1989) 'The lure of the USA: further reflections on the internationalisation of British grocery retailing capital', *Environment and Planning A*, 21, 283–288.

Yoshino, M Y (1966) 'International opportunities for Américan retailers', *Journal of Retailing*, 42 (Fall), 1–10.

PART TWO

Driving forces of internationalisation

CHAPTER 4

Internationalisation: interpreting the motives

Nicholas Alexander

INTRODUCTION

International retailing has attracted considerable research interest in recent years. The motives behind internationalisation have been identified through observation and empirical research. However, research efforts, far from providing a coherent, definitive answer, have only highlighted methodological issues and the complexity of a dynamic process of development, which is not easily explained by research focusing upon a particular point in time. Therefore, the research itself must be considered if an attempt is to be made to understand not only the time-specific influences on internationalising retail operations, but also the context in which researchers have interpreted international development. This chapter discusses the implications of these issues for the study of international retailing, and addresses issues which need to be considered in future research activity.

While it is acknowledged that retailers have had operations in foreign markets for a considerable period of time, it is also acknowledged that, in the last thirty years, there have been major developments in international retailing. By the mid-1960s, there were an increasing number of retailers who could be said to have reached national coverage and hence saturation. In consequence, an increasing number of retailers who had achieved such market development at home began to look at opportunities in other markets, notably in the USA. The development stimulated interest and comment; parallels were drawn with the growth opportunities and trading conditions in the internationalising retailer's home market. Subsequently, a particular emphasis was placed on saturation and the negative factors stimulating internationalisation. While the pull factors of the new market were not ignored, the push factors of the home market were invested with considerable significance and emphasised in the literature. The pull factors were often perceived as the reasons for choosing one market over another, rather than the reason for internationalisation.

By the 1980s, a combination of economic, social, political and retail-specific conditions, together with the themes raised by academic thought and research, combined to suggest to researchers that limited opportunities at home were the prime reason for retail internationalisation. The literature reflects the preoccupations of the intellectual and commercial agenda of the period prior to, or at the time of, output. However, recent research would now appear to suggest that this preoccupation with, or emphasis on, the domestic market is not entirely appropriate. Empirical research has shown the importance of proactive, rather than reactive, responses to retail growth and internationalisation. Retailers, the research suggests, are identifying opportunities first and internationalising accordingly. They are not simply waiting for limited opportunities at home to stimulate an attempt to regain impressive growth rates by expanding abroad.

Caution, however, must be exercised in concluding that proactive internationalisation has, in reality, characterised international retailing and will continue to do so. What the research does is first to redress the balance between the two themes of reactive and proactive internationalisation, and second to provide an interpretation of retailers' professed motives at the end of the 1980s and in the first half of the 1990s. The second point raises two further issues, one of the long-term development of retail operations in both the domestic and international marketplace, the other of research methodology.

4.1 THE STUDY OF INTERNATIONALISATION MOTIVES

4.1.1 Research activity

There has been a considerable amount of academic interest in the area of international retailing in recent years. Only a few years ago, researchers in this area were faced with a paucity of information and analysis. This is no longer the case. Research has now not only highlighted a fascinating and important area of study, but has begun to address a number of lacunae within retail studies. While there remains a considerable amount of work to be done, there is now a literature available on the subject which represents a corpus of knowledge.

The study of international retailing has, therefore, reached a stage where it is appropriate to look back at the literature and attempt to extract themes and to question certain assumptions. However, research has ventured into numerous areas and it would not be feasible within the confines of this chapter to do justice to even a fraction of those different areas of study. This chapter addresses one central issue in the literature, namely the motivations behind internationalisation. Consideration is consequently given to the agenda that has emerged, and how certain assumptions have been, or are in danger of being made, which will affect future research.

4.1.2 A long-term perspective

While it is recognised that retailers were operating across state boundaries before the last two or three decades, there is a degree of equivocation surrounding this issue. By suggesting a dichotomy between earlier and more recent developments in internationalisation, the literature has presented recent developments as a single process and thereby implied uniqueness. The uniqueness of the event, and, by inference, the common causes of this new development, have thereby invested the process with a unity; in consequence, insufficient consideration has been given to the changing conditions which have affected recent international activity. That is, a norm is implied by the uniqueness of the event, when that uniqueness is by no means proven, both with reference to itself but also its context.

The literature notes, '… during the past three decades, retailers have increasingly concerned themselves with the international market …' (Salmon and Tordjman, 1989: 3), or 'over the last 20 or so years an increasing number of retailers have been active in developing an international presence' (Treadgold, 1988: 8). These are accurate statements, but they have unfortunately led to the interpretation that 'cross-frontier retailing is not … a wholly new phenomenon' and the recent 'wave of internationalisation is unique in its scale, geographical orientation and motivations from early efforts to develop an international presence' (Treadgold, 1988: 8).

These conclusions raise important issues. First, by describing the process as not 'wholly' new, the process is defined by conditions at a point in time. That is, international actions before a relatively recent point in time may be considered to be merely precursors to current activity. If international activity is interpreted as a phenomenon of the last 20–30 years from the perspective of the last ten years, then there is a danger certain assumptions will be made which are not entirely appropriate. The danger is that past activity will be continually replaced in the minds of observers with contemporary developments. A clear danger inherent in this is that internationalisation will always be a product of recent years, and that idiosyncrasies of recent activity will define and explain the activity. Contemporary activity, however, may not be representative of sustained international operations, particularly in a context where a considerable number of retailers are developing international interests. Retailers, even large retailers, withdraw from foreign markets.

A brief survey of European retailing at the end of the 1980s would reveal a surprisingly limited number of US operations. The US impact on European retailing, however, has been considerable and of fundamental importance to the growth of international retail activity (Alexander, 1992). The new US international retailers – those of the early 1990s – are different to those of previous decades or waves of development. The danger of taking a snapshot in time is shown by a recent commercially oriented report on international retailing, which, while a valuable contribution to data available in this area, noted: 'It is clear ... that cross-border retailing in Europe is overwhelmingly a phenomenon of the 1980s and of the late 1980s in particular' (CIG, 1991: 3). This observation was based on data relating to foreign retailers operating in European markets in the early 1990s and their decade of entry. Retailers who entered European markets in the 1950s, for example, but had later withdrawn from those markets, were not recorded. The report was correct in one sense, and did acknowledge the existence of earlier international activity, but how many of the internationalising retailers of the late 1980s will still have operations, or indeed the same, foreign operations in thirty years' time? If the number of international operators does rise dramatically, will the same statement appear as valid in another decade? Will it not be clear that cross-border retailing is overwhelmingly a phenomenon of the 1990s, and of the late 1990s in particular?

Second, in what way is international activity of the 1960s through to the 1990s unique, both in terms of what has gone before and in terms of itself? What evidence is there to invest the process with a unity? Is it possible to say that the motivations behind recent activity are different from those of earlier periods? Are not the motivations within different companies going to be very diverse in all periods? Is it possible to say that the geographic orientation of those companies who have recently internationalised is unique? Is it even possible to say that the scale is unique? What scale is implied? Is the turnover of international retailers to domestic operators being compared, or the impact on the host environments – retail structures and consumer markets – being compared? Does not the impact of Woolworths' operation on UK retailing rank high on the latter scale?

The events of the more recent past, while noteworthy and the main theme of this chapter, should not be perceived as fundamentally unique, nor a single development. By investing them with a unique quality, they take on a significance and their causes are interpreted without the appreciation of other contexts and other phases of development. These in themselves shed light on the process of, and motives behind, internationalisation, and the framework within which managers must operate in the international environment.

How should recent developments be placed in context? International retail activity is a long-established element within the retail environment and has been present within modern retailing as it emerged in the second half of the nineteenth century. Therefore, international retail activity is not a product of recent conditions. Nevertheless, it is possible to say that a new phase of international retailing began to emerge by the end of the 1960s. As Burt's (1991, 1993) research has shown, this increase in activity stalled in the mid-1970s but gathered pace in the early to mid-1980s.

This new wave of international activity represented a response to new stimuli from the international environment and from within retail operations. Indeed, given previous international retail activity, it may be more appropriate to view this wave of activity as a renaissance of international retailing. Therefore, different motivations behind, or reasons for, international activity may be more relevant in one period than another. Without this assumption, it is possible to misinterpret important issues such as the motivation behind contemporary, and future, international retail activity, the focus of this chapter.

4.2 KEY MOTIVATIONS

Hollander (1970), with the publication of his work on international retailing in 1970, may claim to be a pioneer in the study of international retailing. Hollander's work was a ground-breaking exercise, and many of the questions he raised remain to be answered, or indeed to be discussed in sufficient depth. Hollander recognised that there were a number of fundamental reasons why retailers internationalise.

4.2.1 Hollander's legacy

The first and second reasons for internationalisation listed below, while significant, do not have an important place in the recent literature. However, they are worthy of note, because they indicate conditions perceived as important when Hollander analysed the international environment and the underlying reasons for expansion which are present, but not always overtly stated, when internationalisation occurs. The first reason emphasises the problems of political stability within the global environment.

First, operations in more than one state may be the product of 'inadvertent internationalization' (Hollander, 1970: 102). In the context of the early 1990s, centripetal rather than centrifugal political forces may appear to be more important and influential in the markets into which European retailers have expanded. Integration in Europe and the closer economic ties between the USA, Canada and Mexico support this belief. As Treadgold has noted, 'political and perceptual barriers between countries are throughout the world being lowered' (Treadgold, 1990: 4). From Hollander's perspective of the late 1960s and early 1970s, different forces were significant in the international arena. Decolonisation and post-colonial developments had only recently, as Hollander described it, 'altered the flags that fly over the branches of many international retailers' (Hollander, 1970: 102).

Political stability is a crucial factor in considering international operations. Dawson (1993) notes the retrenchment of Julius Meinl, the Austrian grocery operation, after 1945 as a result of the political changes in Eastern European countries such as Czechoslovakia and Hungary. However, Julius Meinl also offers a good European example of how political change may lead not only to withdrawal from international operations, but may also lead to inadvertent internationalisation. The establishment of new states in Eastern Europe after the 1914–18 war made Meinl an inadvertent international operation in markets which had previously been part of the Austro-Hungarian Empire. On the basis of recent developments, Meinl would appear to be a resilient international operation. The company, through franchise and joint venture operations, established outlets in Hungary in 1990, and in Poland, along with the former Czechoslovakia, USSR and Yugoslavia in 1991 (CIG, 1991). However, as Kmart discovered, political fragmentation is a recurrent theme within Eastern Europe, when, less than a year after entering the Czechoslovakian market, the independent Czech and Slovak Republics were established (Loker *et al*, 1994).

The recent turmoil in Eastern European markets underlines the contemporary relevance of Hollander's (1970) observation. In the majority of cases during the early 1990s, retailers have not been greatly affected by the political turmoil which has established new state boundaries. Equally, the disintegration of political entities in Eastern Europe and the strengthening of international organisations such as the EU and NAFTA underlines the fact that national political developments will directly affect international retailers. They make their task in some cases simpler, in others more difficult or even impossible.

Second, Hollander (1970) noted the importance of 'non-commercial motives'. 'Social, political, personal, and ethical' (Hollander, 1970: 103) factors are important here, and are factors which have led to retailers advising on the development of supply or supporting that supply in underdeveloped markets.

UK retailers' involvement with the distribution problems in the former USSR indicates the continuing relevance of humanitarian and political action in this respect. The establishment of high profile retail or service operations (McGoldrick and Holden, 1993), in countries such as the former USSR may in part be interpreted as support for developing systems and the proselytising of the message of free enterprise. Other ethically motivated reasons for retailers becoming involved internationally may also be observed in the commercial setting of the early 1990s. The Body Shop's 'trade not aid policy' is an example of this.

Third, Hollander (1970: 105) notes commercial objectives 'are as varied as nonprofit ones'. These may be subdivided.

- Trade with the country of destination whether in the form of imports from or exports to a non-domestic market may, he observes, lead retailers to develop international operations. This will depend on the nature of the company that possesses international outlets. Integrated manufacturing and retailing operations, and the trading companies noted by Hollander, will be particularly relevant in this context.
- Retailers may expand defensively, so that a move into a new market by a retailer acting defensively will seek to preclude the expansion of other operations within the international arena into that market. This prevents such potential competitors using the newly addressed market as a base

for operations in the defensive retailer's home market. Hollander (1970) cites the example of Swedish firms expanding into Denmark to restrict German operations expanding in Denmark, then using their Danish operations as a base for expansion in Sweden. On a wider scale this argument may be extended; that is, international growth leads to the development of economically powerful operations, which are thereby better able to survive in a global environment in which international operators are increasingly important players.

- Operations in non-domestic markets are a means by which market knowledge may be acquired. This may occur through the establishment of solely owned operations in new markets but, as recent international activity has shown, retailers have used methods such as franchise operations and minority holdings to gain an understanding of non-domestic markets. Marks & Spencer has used franchising in less familiar markets, and Sainsbury's cautious acquisition of Shaws in New England – acquisition of a minority holding followed, after a learning period, by outright acquisition – illustrates that small-scale development, or limited commitment development, as part of a learning exercise retains its importance. Hollander (1970) noted US interest in the Spanish market in the 1960s, which was perceived as offering a base for further European expansion when Spain joined the European Community.

Another important aspect of this process is the opportunities international retailers have of becoming familiar with new operating techniques and technological innovation within a new market. Kacker (1988) has indicated how retailers' domestic operations may benefit from a flow of 'know-how' as a result of either direct investment or joint operations in non-domestic markets. This flow of knowledge may also occur through buying alliances. Strategic or buying alliances are a form of international activity, and may be placed in a hierarchy of international activity (Robinson and Clarke-Hill, 1994).

Fourth, Hollander (1970) also notes the importance of government regulation and taxation policy on the process of internationalisation. Government decisions, in both the country of origin and the country of destination, will affect development. Hollander observes the impetus US retailers have been given by anti-trust restrictions and suggests this may become the case in the UK. This is an interesting prediction in the light of Kacker's (1985, 1986) analysis of European expansion in North America in the late 1970s and early 1980s, which Kacker suggests was heavily influenced by the unfavourable regulatory and tax environment of the European markets.

Fifth, regardless of these other factors, Hollander (1970: 109) observes: 'In the main, sizeable foreign retail operations are usually mounted in the hopes of capitalizing upon existing or potential sales opportunities.' It is the attraction of similar levels of economic development and high consumer incomes which prove attractive to internationalising retailers. The attractiveness of these markets may be predicated on the fact that, while economically attractive and developed, the market does not contain indigenous retailers who have adopted new formats or created a more efficient retail distribution structure, in which case international operations may contribute to the development of that structure, while gaining significant competitive advantages in the process. Similarly, the seeking of new markets may also be a result of the saturation of home markets (Hollander, 1970). Hollander saw this as a factor which supported international moves.

The reasons for internationalisation recognized by Hollander (1970) and discussed above provide a useful framework for the internationalisation process, but further work needs to be carried out to elaborate, develop and test his conclusions. In recent years, two fundamental motivating factors behind internationalisation, inherent within Hollander's analysis, effectively established the parameters for the discussion of internationalisation in the 1980s. These may be classified as reactive and proactive motivations (Williams, 1992a). However, before these responses are considered, the push and pull factors, which describe international market conditions, and the place of push and pull factors in the interpretation of the motives which lie behind international activity, should be considered.

4.2.2 Push and pull

Where there exist limited opportunities at home 'it is reasonable to expect', as Morganosky (1993: 527) has noted, that retailers will seek 'expansion opportunities in international markets'. This 'reasonable expectation' or assumption underlies analysis of the motivations for internationalisation when categorised in terms of push and pull factors. In turn, such an assumption is fundamental to an interpretation which sees internationalisation as a reactive response to the competitive environment, and qualifies an interpretation which sees internationalisation as a product of retailers' proactive response to international opportunities.

Push and pull factors discussed in the international retailing literature (Kacker, 1985; Treadgold and Davies, 1988; Treadgold, 1989; Alexander, 1990; CIG, 1991; McGoldrick and Fryer, 1993) provide a useful basis for analysis, and have formed a basis for further research and theoretical development (see Table 4.1). Push factors may be described simply as those issues which encourage internationalisation, or even make it imperative, as a result of environmental or company-specific conditions in the domestic market. Pull factors are essentially attractive conditions which draw retailers into new markets.

Push factors are, therefore, characterised by unattractive trading conditions. Environmental factors such as poor economic conditions, negative demographic trends and regulatory constraints are commonly referred to in this context. Company-specific issues, such as the stage of the retailer's development, are also commonly seen as instrumental in prompting interna-

Table 4.1 Push and pull factors

Push:
- unstable political structure
- unstable economy
- mature domestic market
- format saturation
- small domestic market
- restrictive regulatory environment, e.g. planning
- hostile competitive environment
- poor economic conditions, e.g. low growth
- negative social environment, e.g. low population growth
- unfavourable operating environment
- operating costs, e.g. labour, distribution
- consumer credit restrictions

Pull:
- stable political structure
- stable economy
- underdeveloped retail structure
- large market
- relaxed regulatory environment
- good economic conditions, e.g. high growth
- positive social environment, e.g. high population growth
- favourable operating environment
- favourable exchange rates
- low share prices
- property investment potential
- niche opportunities
- attractive socio-cultural fabric
- innovative retail culture
- company-owned facilities/operations
- company ethos
- 'me too' expansion

Sources: Kacker (1985); Treadgold and Davies (1988); Treadgold (1989); Alexander (1990); CIG (1991); McGoldrick and Fryer (1993).

tional action. Where, for example, they are characterised by issues such as limited growth opportunities, they will be interpreted as pushing retailers out of the home market. Conversely, pull factors will include opportunities for faster growth in new markets, perhaps as a result of an undeveloped retail structure in the new market, or niche opportunities. Retailers may be encouraged, hence pulled, across frontiers as a result of the ethos of the company and as a result of 'me too' international actions.

Push and pull factors should be viewed as relative rather than absolute. Kacker (1985) has convincingly argued that the push factors within the European environment of the 1970s encouraged internationalisation whilst pull factors from the US encouraged investment within that market. The US market, with relatively attractive social, economic and regulatory

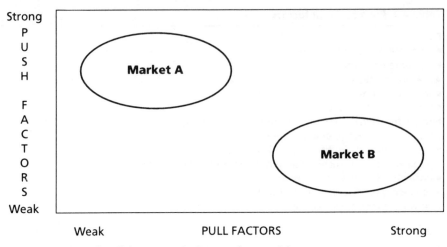

Fig. 4.1 Push and pull factors: relative market positions

conditions, pulled European retailers into North America, while unhealthy operating conditions and limited commercial opportunities at home prompted expansion outside the home market. Figure 4.1 depicts the conditions within two markets A and B. Retailers in market A will be subject to intense push factors and will view market B as an attractive target for growth. Retailers in market B, however, have growth opportunities available to them at home and will not be inclined to expand into market A. Figure 4.1 depicts the relative position of the European – market A – and US – market B – conditions from the mid-1970s to the early 1980s. European retailers were moving into the US market at this time. In the early 1990s, different conditions have encouraged US retail expansion in Europe, and, to some extent, prompted a re-evaluation of European opportunities by some European retailers (OXIRM, 1994; Reynolds, 1994; Alexander, 1994a).

How conditions are balanced within an environment and within a retail organization will determine whether the retailer is seen as reactive or proactive within the global environment. Therefore, while the identification of push and pull factors is a good starting point for the analysis of markets, retailers' positions within that market and in terms of their organisational development, a different approach is needed to interpret retailers' responses to domestic and international conditions and opportunities.

4.2.3 Reactive

This response is essentially negative, springing as it does from a lack of opportunity. Reactive internationalisation is the result of limited opportunity in the home market, that is 'restriction and saturation within purely domestic markets' (Hollander, 1970: 110).

Saturation has become an important theme of the international retail debate. There is an inherent logic in the supposition that retailers will seek to satisfy demand in their familiar home market before they launch an international operation on essentially unfamiliar territory. As retail markets are developed, indeed modernised, through the growth of large retail enterprises, then retailers will have less opportunity for expansion. Some retailers will reach this point of development sooner than others, depending on the nature of their business and the sectors in which they operate.

In respect of saturation, Hollander used as an example Debenhams' announcement in 1958 that it planned to internationalise in the Australian market, because the company 'had reached the virtual limits of its possible domestic growth with a store in every major British city' (Hollander, 1970: 111). Debenhams' justification for internationalisation, and in this instance description of saturation, raises the issue of what is saturation? Saturation, a word frequently employed in the debate on retail internationalisation, is not well defined. Saturation, with its hydrological associations (Treadgold and Reynolds, 1989), is problematic in the retail context. While useful as a colourful metaphor, on closer examination it becomes somewhat cumbersome and misleading. Saturation may be used to describe a number of conditions pertinent to both an individual firm and, for example, the format used by that firm, which is also exploited by other retailers in a particular market. Thus Sainsbury, Tesco and Safeway may be described on their own terms in respect of saturation, while the superstore format and saturation may be differently described and evaluated. Debenhams clearly had a definite if less than sophisticated answer in 1958. Debenhams' approach is clearly defined in terms of the company's market opportunities within a state. This market-based approach, however, is not the only basis for identifying effective saturation.

Regulatory environments, where the interests of the small retailer have been protected, have proved a check to large businesses in small markets such as the Netherlands and Belgium, but also larger markets such as France and Japan. The activities of the Monopolies and Mergers Commission (MMC), with reports on the subject of the proposed Dee and Booker McConnell merger and discounts to retailers in 1985 and 1981 respectively, have helped define this issue in the UK (MMC, 1981, 1985). Perhaps media concern for the profit margins of grocery operations helped to define this issue in the early 1990s. Different report outcomes and political agendas have a major influence. Regulation is effectively an artificial level of saturation which a change of administration, or an administration's thinking, will alter. However, it is a factor in the internationalisation process which has been emphasised particularly in respect of European expansion in North America.

Kacker (1985), in his study of European retail penetration of the US market, identified an unattractive operating environment at home as an important motive behind internationalisation. Therefore, accepting Kacker's (1985) analysis, reactive internationalisation is the result of not only market saturation, such as that recognised by Debenhams in 1958 and other retailers before and since, but also of regulation and hence of the business environment which is created by that regulation.

These are negative factors. They produce reaction to the problem once encountered. They suggest a preference for domestic market expansion which, when no longer available, will result in reluctant internationalisation.

4.2.4 Proactive

Internationalisation has not, however, merely been the result of lack of opportunities at home. Retailers have actively sought expansion across borders in recognition of the fact their market segment is thereby served. Retailers of luxury goods have long been able to justify international operations. Names such as Mappin & Webb, Cartier and Dunhill have retailed in major centres around the world during the twentieth century (Hollander, 1970). They have either accessed the cosmopolitan market and expatriates, or attracted customers eager to buy into their foreign cultural offering.

Operations such as Woolworths in the early twentieth century, or McDonald's more recently, have utilised a distinct format and operating style to access markets on a less exclusive level. These are retailers who have reacted to the socio-economic development of the non-domestic markets. These retailers are the early representatives of those successful operations with outlets across the globe and appeal to a global market segment. They are companies that have adapted to 'global realities' (Levitt, 1983). High levels of internationalisation, however, could not be realised until international markets offered attractive operating environments. US retailing has provided European retailers with innovative examples of retail operations either operating in the US market or European markets. US retailing has exported ideas and operators. For operators to penetrate the European market, there clearly had to be suitable market conditions, measured by incomes, urbanisation and a growth in consumption (Hollander, 1970).

Woolworths was not operating at the luxury end of the market when the company expanded into the UK, nor serving customers who had first experienced their retail outlets in Paris or New York. What Woolworths did was to observe a need for the company's merchandise, price and service option in the newly urbanised markets of the industrial world. Woolworths introduced its operation into the UK at the same time as Marks & Spencer was expanding south from their northern base. Two operations with similar operating principles, one domestic, one international, were both recognising the same market need.

This proactive approach to retailing – the identification of opportunities abroad – does not have to occur after saturation at home. Indeed, it may be argued that the more aggressive international operations have not waited for saturation at home before they have ventured abroad and begun to learn lessons in the foreign market.

4.3 INTERPRETATION OF THE MOTIVES

4.3.1 A traditional interpretation

Within modern retailing, that is retailing as it developed at the end of the nineteenth century, there has always been an international element. Retail units owned by a single retailer have traded, separated by state boundaries, throughout the period. Those international retailers, however, did not operate in the context of saturated home markets, as saturation is commonly recognised and experienced by large retailers.

There were, throughout the period prior to the early 1960s, opportunities for most retailers at home, opportunities that did not require them to operate outside their home markets. It has even been suggested that the recent retraction in US international retailing is a result of the large home market (Treadgold, 1988). Yet the US provided a significant number of early international operators. The size of retail operations was, when compared to the size of manufacturing operations, small and localised in nature. Urbanisation, population growth and economic development were providing retailers with new opportunities at home.

By the late 1960s, and certainly the 1970s, both the organisational and environmental assumptions of previous decades were less valid. The number of retailers capable of internationalisation had grown; the same organisations' position in the home market had become more problematic as traditional expansion routes became restricted. The environment was also changing, offering new challenges undoubtedly, but in essence redefining the market and market requirements.

By the 1960s and 1970s, there were an increasing number of retailers who could be said to have reached national coverage and hence a form of saturation. In consequence, an increasing number of retailers who had achieved such market development at home began to look at the opportunities in other markets. In the context of European retailing, the US market played an important role in this respect.

European retailer expansion in the US stimulated interest and comment, and parallels were drawn with the growth opportunities and trading conditions in the European home markets from which these retailers had emerged. This led Kacker, writing in the US, to suggest that, 'A dominant position in a domestic market with a large market share' (Kacker, 1985: 69) encouraged international expansion by European retailers. The picture painted by Kacker was one of limited opportunities in the European market because of expansion of what were by this time large retail operations and the regulatory environment. He compared the European environment with that of the US, where there was 'a vast landscape and an economy that valued free enterprise and equality of opportunity' (Kacker, 1985: 72). This theme was taken up and developed by other writers, notably Treadgold, who suggested that for many retailers who have expanded internationally the 'principal motivation' was 'the limited opportunities for sustained domestic growth' (Treadgold, 1988: 8). This established the proposition that international retail expansion will be pursued, and therefore dominated, by retailers of a certain size who have exhausted opportunities at home, and that the reasons for increased internationalisation will be the growth in the numbers of retailers reaching saturation in their domestic market (Treadgold, 1988).

This model of internationalisation was considered appropriate to markets other than the US. Treadgold drew a comparison between the markets of Northern Europe and the markets of Southern Europe. The latter being 'relatively under developed' (Treadgold, 1990: 7) would contrast with the developed, concentrated markets of the north of Europe from which retailers would expand. Opportunities in the new markets, and particularly the US market, led Treadgold (1988) to support Kacker's contention that the US market was particularly attractive to firms undertaking internationalisation: not only were restrictions in the European market and opportunities in the US market encouraging European expansion, they were also encouraging divestment by US retailers in foreign markets. The argument that internationalisation is pointless where more attractive options exist at home, where by inference saturation has not been reached, thus became well established.

A perception of saturation in the domestic market has led retailers to consider foreign investment, but whether this motive should be perceived as the primary motive behind the process is not proven. Indeed, the assumption that saturation has been reached is flawed by the very term itself. Emphasis, however, has been placed on saturation and the negative factors behind internationalisation in the literature. The push factors of the home market were seen as the motivations behind internationalisation, and while the pull factors of the new market were not ignored, they assumed the role of reasons for choosing one market over another. The pull factors attained a subordinate status relative to the push factors, which were seen as 'the principle motivating factor' (Treadgold, 1990: 5). This suggests that internationalisation is the secondary option, which is considered only in the context of the relative absence of growth opportunities at home.

Consequent to developments in the 10 or 15 years before these writers set pen to paper, there was some justification for their conclusions. National retailers, justified in perceiving limited options at home – whether because of diminishing market opportunities at home or regulatory restrictions – turned to foreign markets as a means by which to sustain their growth through geographic expansion. Therefore, the 'traditional' (Williams, 1992a) view of retail internationalisation was as much a product of the stage in the historical development of retailing within national markets, and particularly European markets, as it was a product of interpretations of the development. These interpretations, while valid observations, either did not consider or were unable to consider, because of the time of writing, developments in the late 1980s and early 1990s. In consequence, there

emerged in the 1980s a school of thought which placed considerable emphasis on the role of saturation as a motivating factor. There was much justification for this interpretation in the light of previous scholarship and scholastic
preoccupation in the area of retail studies.

In UK retail research, the development of large retail operations has been
a fundamental theme. Jefferys' (1954) work is an early example of this. The
Monopolies Commission, through its investigations into retailing, gave large
retailers reasons for concern when they came to consider the regulatory
implications of merger or acquisition in the home market. Similarly, intellectual and political conditions in the UK since the mid-1960s supported the
view of any retailer who maintained that opportunities in the home market
were narrowing and that expansion should be sought elsewhere. This was an
argument which would clearly have a particular validity in the context of
family-owned operations, where the opportunity to spread financial risk
would have been of considerable advantage. Certainly within the UK, and
Kacker (1985) suggests elsewhere in Europe, political groups well disposed
to larger business enterprises were not in the ascendency during this period
of retail internationalisation.

Consequently, by the 1980s, a combination of retail-specific, wider economic, social, political and intellectual conditions, together with the themes
raised by academic thought and research, combined to suggest to writers on
retail internationalisation that limited opportunities at home were a prime
reason for retail internationalisation. The literature reflects the preoccupations of the intellectual and commercial agenda of the period prior to, or at
the time of, the research activity on which interpretations were based.
However, recent research would now appear to suggest that this preoccupation with, or emphasis on, the limitations of the domestic market is not
appropriate.

4.3.2 Proaction revisited

This emphasis placed on reactive internationalisation is not entirely satisfactory as an explanation for retail expansion. Empirical research carried out in
the late 1980s (Alexander, 1990; Williams, 1992a) indicated the importance
of proactive rather than reactive responses to retail growth and internationalisation. Retailers, the research suggested, identified opportunities first and
internationalised accordingly. They were not waiting for limited opportunities at home to stimulate a panic-stricken attempt to retain or regain impressive growth rates by expanding abroad. Neither were they primarily
concerned by such issues as favourable tax regimes, share prices and site
acquisition conditions in the market of destination.

The results of both Alexander's (1990) and Williams's (1992a) surveys
showed that retailers are more likely to stress the importance of niche
opportunities, growth prospects and the size of non-domestic markets along
with the retail formula – format and merchandise – they have to offer a new

market. They are less likely to identify a saturated domestic market with increased competition and excessive restrictions as the motive for internationalisation. Thus, retailers emphasised the value they perceived in their own operations and their operations' relative worth in the market of destination. Their retail format, product lines or innovative formulae were considered to have had a major role in their internationalisation process. Therefore, they looked to markets of which they had some knowledge and which possessed characteristics which would facilitate the exploitation of their operation. Saturation in the domestic market, whether perceived as limited growth opportunities or restrictions in the environment, was not collectively described as fundamental to the decision to internationalise.

Figure 4.2 depicts diagrammatically the positions adopted by the two 'schools' of thought. In the diagram, saturation in the market of origin and the global relevance of the retailer's operation are used to indicate the emphasis of these two 'schools' of thought. The issue is an extremely complex one, and reducing it to two such measures is a simplification of the arguments. However, they both lie at the heart of the issue and represent key elements. In Table 4.2, quotations illustrative of the positions taken up in the literature are presented. These quotations are representative of the thrust of the arguments found in these papers but should be interpreted in the light of qualifications which the authors make. Essentially, these statements indicate primary positions.

Williams concluded that reactive motives are 'not the major reason behind the recent internationalisation of UK retailers' (Williams, 1992a: 278). On this basis, it is possible to say that 'the UK multinational retailer places far greater emphasis on opportunities in new markets than on the

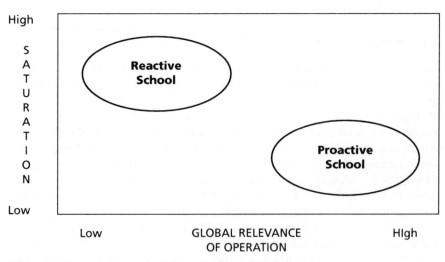

Fig. 4.2 Interpretations of motives for internationalisation
Source: Alexander (1994b).

Table 4.2 Schools of thought

Reactive

'For many ... retailers ... the principal motivation for expanding internationally has been the limited opportunities for sustained domestic growth.' (Treadgold, 1988: 8.)

'Retailing firms in Italy, Belgium and the United Kingdom experienced a great deal of legal harassment because the government favored the growth of small, independent stores. And local zoning boards were a stumbling block in the expansion of many large retail companies, which were left with no alternative but to seek other avenues for growth opportunities. To quote Dr. Dreesmann: "The driving force to internationalization during the last ten years has been the declining prospects in Europe." ' (Kacker, 1985: 62)

Proactive

'... the major motives behind the RI of UK-based international retailers originate from a perceived internationally appealing and innovative offering and growth oriented and proactive motives.' (Williams, 1992a: 279)

'... the UK multinational retailer places far greater emphasis on opportunities in new markets than on the lack of opportunities in home markets when international expansion is considered.' (Alexander, 1990: 84)

lack of opportunities in home markets when international expansion is considered' (Alexander, 1990: 84). Rather than exploit marginal opportunities in their domestic markets, retailers are prepared to cross international boundaries to reach the most appropriate markets. How we define those marginal opportunities, as has already been acknowledged, is not an easy task. The answer will in itself affect the identification of reactive internationalisation. Williams (1992a) points out that the issue of limited domestic growth opportunities stimulating internationalisation is complex.

4.3.3 Reconciling the interpretations

Caution, however, must be exercised in concluding that proactive internationalisation has, in reality, characterised international retailing and will continue to do so. Limited domestic opportunities should not now be considered as necessarily of secondary importance. What the empirical research does is first to redress the balance between the two themes of reactive and proactive internationalisation; second, to provide an interpretation of retailers' professed motives at the end of the 1980s. The second point raises two issues, one of time, the other methodology.

Both Alexander's and Williams's research was carried out in the late 1980s. The impact of marketing on retailing and retailers increased during the 1980s (Piercy and Alexander, 1988). Retailers in the domestic market were developing a more proactive role, not least as they assumed the responsibilities gained from their increased and increasing influence within the distribution channel. If retailers were more proactive on a domestic level, then concomitantly, why not on an international level?

Lifestyle retailers, some of whom achieved recognition by Treadgold (1988) as global retailers, may be considered examples of retailers who have had the opportunity to internationalise on a proactive basis. These are retailers who appeal to Levitt's (1983) global consumer. Whether from shared fashion tastes (Benetton), philosophical or ethical values (Body Shop), or through the exploitation of a consumer desire to share the consumer service dream of other nations (McDonald's), some retailers have expanded globally, with relative disregard for state boundaries.

Nevertheless, the empirical results must be placed in context; it is not enough to say that internationalisation has been proactive. UK retailers, in the commercial and socio-economic environment of the 1980s, were eager to exploit opportunities where and when they occurred and not just to make knee-jerk responses to restrictions in the domestic market. However, further work by Williams (1994) in North America and Alexander (1994a) in the UK indicates that geographical and temporal considerations do not necessarily alter earlier conclusions.

Methodologically, as Williams notes, empirical research has added to knowledge. Williams is less than flattering about preceding research which did not follow an empirical approach remarking: 'most research and comment is largely fragmented and non-analytical descriptive and prescriptive accounts, which lack an empirical base' (Williams, 1992a: 270). However, there are further methodological refinements to be made. Retailers will be inclined to stress the positive and reluctant to admit opportunities have narrowed so considerably at home they have been forced to internationalise (Alexander and Morlock, 1992). It is not the corporate image many would wish to promote. The empirical research carried out, while valid, must be further developed, and it should not be inappropriately interpreted. On the basis of the research carried out, methodological refinements are necessary; not least, the importance of time-specific motivations must be considered.

While the empirical research has, and will, continue to throw light on the issue of retail internationalisation, care must be taken before a period of proactive interpretation replaces one of reactive interpretation. Indeed, there is no reason why it should be assumed that one motivation or identifiable group of motivations should be considered dominant and the norm over time. It is perhaps more appropriate to take the approach that internationalisation is not a new unitary process, but a long-established element within retailing. It has been stimulated by a variety of motives, groupings of which have been of greater significance at different times. If it is accepted that the empirical and the non-empirical have both identified accurately motivations and developments, then it would be appropriate to suggest that one theme has predominance over another at different times.

However, even within one organisation, the motives behind internationisation will not be clear cut. Williams quite rightly looks also to the firms' internal strengths and weaknesses, which create 'obstacle' and 'differential firm advantages' (Williams, 1992b). Internal conditions will impact on the motivations behind internationalisation. The organisational culture is an important and fertile area for investigation as McGoldrick and Fryer (1993) have recognised. There is, therefore, a need for a research agenda which does not generalise 'across and vacuously abstract from time and place' (Vink, 1992: 222). Nor is it appropriate that a positivist approach should be adopted to interpret the process of internationalisation, even if such an approach does fit, as Carr has remarked, 'perfectly with the empiricist tradition which was the dominant strain in British philosophy from Locke to Bertrand Russell' (Carr, 1964: 9). It is not enough to identify and categorise; interpretation is also needed. This is perhaps the greatest danger of the observational approach. The facts do not merely speak for themselves. Ultimately, an approach should be adopted which, while maintaining as a specific aim the identification of general trends, recognises that discontinuities are not easily explained by normative judgements. Furthermore, such discontinuities may hold more important lessons and indicate less easily identifiable critical issues than periods of 'normal development'.

A study of the process as it is affected by environmental constraints will also provide an insight into the less than satisfactory terminology which is currently employed. International, multinational and cross-border retailing are difficult terms in themselves, which imply recognition of characteristics of the process of internationalisation but ignore differences within state boundaries or the domestic market (Hollander, 1970; Alexander, 1990; Brown and Burt, 1992). Similarly, saturation is a term which may be observed on different levels – the market, the format and the company.

CONCLUSIONS

The process of internationalisation is a complex one, and there is a danger of oversimplification. Williams (1992b: 21) has found '"push" and "pull" ... active–passive and proactive–reactive dichotomies' unsatisfactory. He prefers to use four motivational dimensions of 'proactive and growth-oriented', 'limited domestic growth opportunities', 'internationally appealing/ innovative retail offer' and 'passive motives'.

Williams (1992b) notes that the first of these motivational orientations – proactive and growth-oriented – is similar to the proactive motives in international business studies. It may also be seen as recognition of pull factors identified in other research. Similarly, the second category of motives – limited domestic growth opportunities – resembles the negative reactive or push factors identified elsewhere. Likewise, internationally appealing retail operations are also associated with proactive internationalisation, while passive motives for internationalisation are essentially reactive in nature.

These motives may be useful replacements for the previous schema or sub-categories of well recognised basic motivations. Whichever they are, they represent movement in the right direction by attempting to explain more exactly this multi-faceted issue, recognising the complexity of the issue under consideration.

The issue of retail internationalisation needs to be addressed in far greater detail. The components of responses to the international option need specific study. The responses themselves need to be tested and critically evaluated.

The vocabulary of internationalisation needs further attention for this will determine the research itself. What is meant by internationalisation and saturation? What is the domestic market? Is expansion within the EU internationalisation, as it has previously been understood, given the context of the Single European Market, or is it cross-cultural retailing? If it is, where are, and what determines, the cultural boundaries?

Disinvestment needs to be considered in greater depth. Hence, the periodisation of the international process should be considered as a method of testing the response of retailers to changing conditions. Has the recent wave of international activity been essentially a European wave which has followed a US wave, and is it to be followed by a Japanese wave?

Research must identify the process as a process, neither merely as the observed responses of a group of firms nor the views of executives at any one point in time. The process – that is, connected actions which create change – should be identified and studied as a facet of the retail marketplace, determined and defined by its cross-border and cross-cultural aspects. It should be studied essentially as a management process which deals with challenges of product delivery within a dynamic and heterogeneous market context.

REVIEW QUESTIONS

1. How relevant are Hollander's reasons for retail internationalisation in the global environment of the 1990s?

2. Push and pull factors have been used to explain the reasons for international retail activity. With reference to an international retailer you have studied, which factors have proved most important?

3. What are the fundamental differences between reactive and proactive interpretations of retail internationalisation?

4. Are retailers from the food sector and the clothing sector likely to be motivated by the same considerations when developing international operations?

5. What factors are likely to motivate retailers to expand into the markets of Eastern Europe and the former Soviet Union?

6. Give examples of retailer internationalisation that may have been motivated by the desire to pre-empt internationalisation from another country. Are such tactical moves likely to be more or less important in the future?

REFERENCES

Alexander, N (1990) 'Retailers and international markets: motives for expansion', *International Marketing Review*, 7(4), 75–85.

Alexander, N (1992) '"First with the most": marketing and retailing the American Dream', *The Americanisation of Culture and the End of History*, Conference Paper, American Studies Centre, University of Wales, Swansea, 15–18 September.

Alexander, N (1994a) 'NAFTA and the EU: UK retailers' strategic response', *Recent Advances in Retailing and Services Science Conference*, Banff, Alberta, Canada, 7–10 May.

Alexander, N (1994b) 'UK retailers' motives for operating in the Single European Market', *Marketing Unity in Diversity*, Marketing Education Group Conference, 4–6 July, 1994.

Alexander, N and Morlock, W (1992) 'Saturation and internationalization: the future of grocery retailing in the UK', *International Journal of Retail and Distribution Management*, 20(3), 33–39.

Brown, S and Burt, S (1992) 'Conclusion – retail internationalisation: past imperfect, future imperative', *European Journal of Marketing*, 26(8/9), 80–84.

Burt, S (1991) 'Trends in the internationalization of grocery retailing: the European experience', *International Review of Retail, Distribution and Consumer Research*, 1(4), 487–516.

Burt, S (1993) 'Temporal trends in the internationalization of British retailing', *International Review of Retail, Distribution and Consumer Research*, 3(4), 391–410.

Carr, E (1964) *What is History?* The George Macaulay Trevelyan Lectures delivered in the University of Cambridge, January–March 1961, Penguin, London.

CIG (1991) *Cross-Border Retailing in Europe*, The Corporate Intelligence Group, London.

Dawson, J (1993) *The Internationalisation of Retailing*, Department of Business Studies, University of Edinburgh, Working Paper Series No. 93/2.

Hollander, S (1970) *Multinational Retailing*, Michigan State University, East Lancing, Michigan.

Jefferys, J (1954) *Distribution of Consumer Goods*, Cambridge University Press, Cambridge.

Kacker, M (1985) *Transatlantic Trends in Retailing*, Quorum, Westport, Connecticut.

Kacker, M (1986) 'The metamorphosis of European retailing', *European Journal of Marketing*, 20(8), 15–22.

Kacker, M (1988) 'International flow of retailing know-how: bridging the technology gap in distribution', *Journal of Retailing*, 64(1), 41–67.

Levitt, T (1983) 'The globalization of markets', *Harvard Business Review*, 16(3), 92–102.

Loker, S, Good, L and Huddleston, P (1994) 'Entering Eastern European markets: lessons from Kmart', *Recent Advances in Retailing and Services Science Conference*, Banff, Alberta, Canada, 7–10 May.

McGoldrick, P and Fryer, E (1993) 'Organisational culture and the internationalisation of retailers', *7th International Conference on Research in the Distributive Trades*, Institute for Retail Studies, University of Stirling, 6–8th September.

McGoldrick, P and Holden, N (1993) 'Developments by Western retailers in East Europe and Russia', *Journal of Marketing Channels*, 2(3), 61–84.

MMC (1981) *Discounts to Retailers*, Monopolies and Mergers Commission, HMSO.

MMC (1985) *The Dee Corporation PLC and Booker McConnell PLC,* Monopolies and Mergers Commission, HMSO.

Morganosky, M (1993) 'International direct marketing: a perspective by US retailers', *7th International Conference on Research in the Distributive Trades,* Institute for Retail Studies, University of Stirling, 6–8th September.

OXIRM (1994) *The European Retail Digest,* Oxford Institute of Retail Management, Oxford, Issue 1, Winter.

Piercy, N and Alexander, N (1988) 'The status quo of the marketing organisation in UK retailing: a neglected phenomenon of the 1980s', *The Service Industries Journal,* 8(2), 155–175.

Reynolds, J (1994) 'Managing local markets across Europe: issues for retailers', *Recent Advances in Retailing and Services Science Conference,* Banff, Alberta, Canada, 7–10 May.

Robinson, T and Clarke-Hill, C (1994) 'Competitive advantage through strategic retailing alliances – a European perspective', *Recent Advances in Retailing and Services Science Conference,* Banff, Alberta, Canada, 7–10 May.

Salmon, W and Tordjman, A (1989) 'The internationalisation of retailing', *International Journal of Retailing,* 4(2), 3–16.

Treadgold, A (1988) 'Retailing without frontiers', *Retail and Distribution Management,* 16(6), 8–12.

Treadgold, A (1989) '1992: the retail responses to a changing Europe', *Marketing and Research Today,* 17(3), 161–166.

Treadgold, A (1990) 'The developing internationalisation of retailing' *International Journal of Retail and Distribution Management,* 18(2), 4–11.

Treadgold, A and Davies, R (1988) *The Internationalisation of Retailing,* Oxford Institute of Retail Management, Longman, London.

Treadgold, A and Reynolds, J (1989) *Retail Saturation: Examining the Evidence,* Oxford Institute of Retail Management, Longman, London.

Vink, N (1992) 'Historical perspective in marketing management, explicating experience', *Journal of Marketing Management,* 8, 219–237.

Williams, D (1992a) 'Motives for retailer internationalization: their impact, structure, and implications', *Journal of Marketing Management,* 8, 269–285

Williams, D (1992b) 'Internationalization: an empirical inquiry', *European Journal of Marketing,* 26(8/9), 269–285

Williams, D (1994) 'Motives for international retailer expansion: a comparative analysis', *Recent Advances in Retailing and Services Science Conference,* Banff, Alberta, Canada, 7–10 May.

CHAPTER 5

International sourcing: patterns and trends

Hong Liu and Peter J McGoldrick

INTRODUCTION

With the globalisation of business and markets, one dimension of the internationalisation of wholesale and retail operations has largely been overlooked: sourcing. Since the late 1980s, international sourcing by manufacturing firms has been a buzzword in the leading journals of purchasing and international business. Global or international sourcing by manufacturing firms has been seen as critical to the success of those firms in the 1990s (Min and Galle, 1991; Monczka and Trent, 1991a).

Hitherto, most empirical research on international sourcing has largely concentrated on US manufacturing firms or European and Japanese multinationals in the USA (Kotabe and Murray, 1990; Kotabe and Omura, 1989; Monczka and Trent, 1991a, 1991b; Min and Galle, 1991). Although it is evident that many international retailers have actively engaged in global sourcing operations, both conceptual and empirical work on international retail sourcing has been very limited. Studies of international wholesale sourcing are few and far between, although Larsen and Rosenbloom (1993) examined the role of wholesalers within the development of international channel structures.

This chapter is presented in three main sections. Following a definition of international sourcing, the factors that have stimulated and those that have inhibited its development are firstly discussed. Different forms of international sourcing are then examined, including the special issues associated with sourcing from developing countries and the nature of Japanese international sourcing. The final section considers the international sourcing process, noting that the choice between international and domestic sourcing may be more a matter of degree than a clear dichotomy.

Although based primarily upon a review of relevant literature, this chapter also draws upon in-depth discussions during 1993–94 within four UK retailing organisations. Because of the sensitivity of some of the issues, it has been agreed that the individual respondents and companies will not be named. Two of the organisations operate primarily in the clothing sector, two within the food sector. Within each of the two sectors, one organisation had developed international sourcing channels over many years, whereas the other is at the early development stage.

Definition of international sourcing

In this chapter, 'international sourcing' denotes 'international *wholesale and retail* sourcing'. The product spectrum of 'wholesale sourcing' is confined to manufactured consumer goods in order to exclude sourcing relating to manufacturing firms. Requirements and considerations can be quite different between sourcing supplies for manufacturers and for consumers. For manufacturing firms, international sourcing can have an impact on product quality, flexibility, time to market and product design as well as manufacturing costs (Carter and Narasimhan, 1990; Monczka and Trent, 1991b). The influence of delivery delays, for instance, on manufacturers may be even greater than on wholesalers or retailers.

Both wholesale and retail international sourcing involves the following activities:

- developing corporate objectives and buying policy;
- determining market wants;
- defining the needs for international sourcing;
- identifying, evaluating, and selecting overseas sources of supply;
- negotiating prices and terms of sale; and
- managing the contract and transferring the title of merchandise.

Bunn (1994) identified four key constructs associated with the buying functions of organisations, namely: (a) procedural control, (b) proactive focusing, (c) use of analysis techniques and (d) the search for information. While procedures and analysis are also important in the context of international sourcing, it requires an especially strong measure of constructs (b) and (d), i.e., proactive focusing and information search.

There is a difference between international sourcing and traditional importing. International sourcing implies that wholesalers and retailers tend to be more proactive in the acquisition of sources of supply and their own strategies dominate in the decision-making as to where, when, what, how much and from whom to buy. In the case of traditional importing, wholesalers and retailers often play a passive role in obtaining merchandise, with suppliers taking the initiative in providing goods.

5.1 THE GROWTH OF INTERNATIONAL SOURCING

International wholesale and retail sourcing is by no means a new phenomenon. As early as AD 1200, a significant amount of wholesale trade was conducted at an international level (import and export) in Europe (Luqmani *et al,* 1991). Nowadays, many international retailers espouse the philosophy that 'healthy profitable sources are critical for ensuring an uninterrupted supply of high quality products' (Kacker, 1988). With the globalisation of markets, global sourcing is increasingly becoming a precondition for an international firm's success in the 1990s (Monczka and Trent, 1991a; Fagan, 1991). It is notable that increasing numbers of retail firms from developed countries have been setting up buying offices in developing countries (United Nations, 1985). Figure 5.1 summarises the benefits and costs that have, respectively, driven and constrained the growth of international sourcing.

5.1.1 Driving forces

Cost reduction

The retailing industry in many Western countries has been undergoing two simultaneous processes: concentration and fierce competition. As a result, the opportunity for a retailer to raise retail prices in order to increase profits has been limited. Retailers are now pursuing the alternative profit-enhancing strategy of reducing the costs of their supplies. The sourcing efforts of many price-sensitive US firms have shifted their purchases of supplies from Japan and South Korea, where wage levels are rising, to the Peoples' Republic of China, Indonesia, Thailand and Malaysia (Kacker, 1986).

Competitive overseas products

Over the last two decades, developing countries have become increasingly competitive in the area of manufactured products. In 1980, developing countries accounted for 26.7 per cent of total US imports of manufactured goods, 25.1 per cent of Japanese manufactured imports, and 9.6 per cent of total European manufactured imports (United Nations, 1985). Many products with higher quality or a combination of low price and quality can be found in developing countries (Fagan, 1991; Monczka and Trent, 1991b).

For instance, Wine Schoppen, a UK wholesaling firm, headed the formation of a wine wholesale buying group for independent specialist wine shippers and wholesalers. It offers member firms exclusive labels from the major wine producing regions of the world. The managing director who set up the group claimed in 1992 that the group is quality conscious, not price-conscious.

Availability

Some companies source globally in order to enhance the reliability of their supply, to supplement their domestic sources or to meet increased demand. For many retailers, sourcing abroad is necessary due to the fact that certain products can only be found overseas.

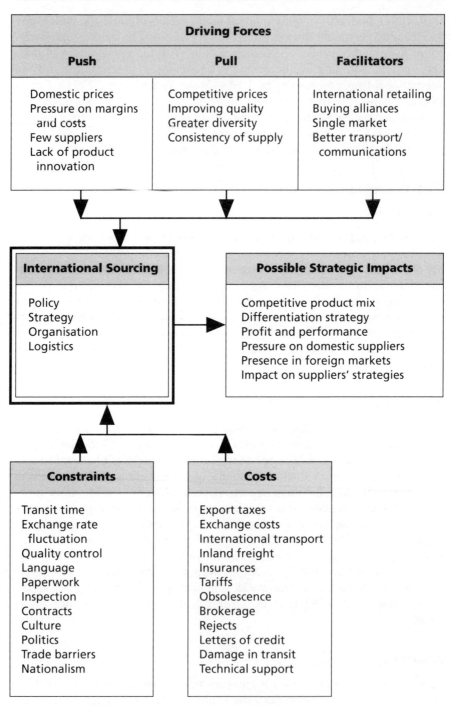

Fig. 5.1 International sourcing: costs and benefits

Impact of the Single European Market

The Single European Market represents an enormous challenge as well as opportunity both to distribution companies and to manufacturers. Many of the large distribution companies are already trading successfully across internal EU borders. In addition, a growing number of European wholesale and retail alliances have been established in order to achieve pan-European economies of scale (see Chapter 7).

Internationalisation of retailing

The internationalisation of retailing can have an impact on the sourcing patterns of international retailers. It appears that many international retailers operating in overseas markets are gradually developing local sources for both local and home markets. For instance, Sears purchases as much as it can from the countries where it is operating as a matter of corporate policy. At five of its seven overseas subsidiaries, over 90 per cent of their merchandise is purchased locally (Kaynak, 1988). This policy reflects the fact that, after a learning period, the company understands better its sources of supply as well as the culture in which it is operating. This enables the company to manage more effectively and exercise control over the variety and quality of supplies. Meanwhile, using local sources gains substantial cost savings since local merchandise is often less costly (for US and European firms operating in developing countries) and long-distance transportation, together with other transaction costs and import taxes, are avoided.

One example comes from the garment group Wing Tai Holdings which, after acquiring the UK garment wholesale and buying house Campari Holdings, sought to buy out three US apparel wholesale and buying companies. These acquisitions should provide Wing Tai with important distribution and sourcing links to the US and UK markets (Tan, 1990). In addition, the United Nations reported that the 'internationalization of the retail sector has not only led to the spreading out of buying offices, but the leading retailers are beginning to discover the third world as a consumer' (United Nations, 1985).

5.1.2 Inhibiting factors

Constraints on international sourcing

International sourcing involves a number of potential problems over and above those associated with local sourcing. These may include: (a) transportation delays; (b) foreign exchange rate fluctuations; (c) travel costs; (d) quality assurance uncertainties; (e) language; (f) paperwork; (g) inspection procedures; (h) contract terms; (i) culture/customs; (j) political stability; (k) trade barriers; (l) nationalism. The first five factors have been ranked as the most important impediments to effective international sourcing (Min and Galle, 1991).

International sourcing can also entail the following 'softer' obstacles: (a) an inadequate understanding of international business and purchasing practices; (b) human and organisational resistance to change; (c) domestic market nationalism; (d) an insufficient working knowledge of international sources, language and cultural differences (Monczka and Trent, 1991b).

A study by Scheffer (1992) has provided many insights into the internationalisation of production and sourcing within the clothing industries of Belgium, France, the Netherlands and the UK. Lead times and transit times were clearly a major issue, both for manufacturers and for retailers involved in international sourcing. Table 5.1 illustrates the lead times typically involved in dealing with various world regions. The times varied according to whether the garments were sourced on a contract basis, the supplier buying its own cloth, or on a 'cut, make and trim' basis (CMT) where the customer supplies the cloth.

Table 5.1 Lead times and transit times: clothing sourcing

Source area	Lead time (days)		Transit time (days)
	Range	Mean	
European Union (CMT)	10–25	15	2–6
S & E Europe (CMT)	15–50	25	2–10
S & E Europe (contract)	45–180	110	3–5
N Africa (contract)	30–165	110	8–20
Far East (contract): air	60–180	120	2–7
Far East (contract): sea	110–270	150	25–50

Adapted from Scheffer (1992).
Note: CMT = cut, make and trim.

Costs of international sourcing

Moreover, international sourcing incurs various additional costs compared with domestic sourcing, including: (a) export taxes; (b) cost of money; (c) international transportation costs; (d) inland freight cost; (e) insurance and tariffs; (f) risk of obsolescence; (g) brokerage costs; (h) cost of rejects; (i) letter of credit; (j) damage in transit; (k) technical support (Carter and Narasimhan, 1990).

A difficult decision on volume and frequency in international sourcing is the potential costs associated with inventory buffers. Too large a buffer may incur excessive costs, whilst too small a buffer may result in delivery difficulties, customer complaints or lost customers. Stocking the optimum inventory size depends on the accurate measurement of lead time, which differs greatly between domestic and overseas sources. Generally, overseas supplies, particularly those from developing countries, involve longer lead time and greater uncertainties (Fagan, 1991).

5.2 FORMS OF INTERNATIONAL SOURCING

5.2.1 International wholesale sourcing

Generally, a wholesaler's customers consist of a large number of small and medium-sized retailers. The wholesaler predicts what retailers will require, searches for and acquires the goods, and has them ready to be purchased by retailers. Hence, to pursue effective international sourcing, a wholesaler needs to meet two conditions: it must anticipate retailers' requirements, which are a function of market fluctuations, and possess good knowledge of international sources of supply.

In the case of more basic goods, it is relatively easy for a wholesaler to anticipate retailers' requirements and obtain the merchandise to make them available. However, in certain areas of manufactured goods, particularly fashion goods, a wholesaler is constrained by the physical distance which separates the wholesaler from consumer markets, and this makes it difficult to anticipate retailers' requirements (ultimately consumer wants). In addition, the internationalisation of wholesaling has been far slower to develop (Commission of the European Community, 1990), and this results in the wholesalers having limited knowledge of overseas supply markets.

Retailers, on the other hand, benefit from an international retail presence, which enables them to understand and approach sources of supply easily. Aided by their enhanced understanding of consumer markets, retailers' international placement enables them to make efficient decisions as to what, when, how many or how much to buy. By contrast, wholesalers face the disadvantages of being distant from both consumer markets and sources of supply. Therefore, it can be hypothesised that international wholesale sourcing will develop to a lesser degree than international retail sourcing.

To overcome the limitations of wholesalers in the pursuit of international sourcing, two strategies seem to have emerged. The first strategy has been the *formation of international wholesale alliances*. One example is the alliance formed between the Co-operative Wholesale Society (UK) and Group Nordisk. Alliances allow the wholesaler to achieve both a better understanding of overseas sources of supply and better buying conditions. The second strategy has been *alliances between wholesalers and retailers*. In the last few years, the number of European wholesale and retail alliances has increased; detailed discussion of these is contained in Chapter 7.

5.2.2 International sourcing by manufacturers

A study of factors leading to international sourcing by US manufacturing firms reveals that the most important factor inducing firms to undertake such a strategy is often the pursuit of quality purchases. The next most important factor is low price. Other reasons include the non-availability of items in the USA, more advanced technology abroad, willingness to solve problems, negotiability and association with a foreign subsidiary (Min and Galle, 1991).

The reasons for sourcing abroad can differ from company to company (Monczka and Trent, 1991b). Other motivations for international sourcing include the following: (a) increasing exposure to worldwide technology; (b) improving delivery; (c) introducing competition to the domestic supply market; (d) establishing a presence in an overseas market.

The empirical study of Min and Galle (1991) suggests that far more manufacturing firms engage in international sourcing than retailers and wholesalers. One reason for this is that high quality and less expensive manufacturing components and parts are often available from foreign sources. Another important factor is that, in general, wholesale and retail firms have been smaller than manufacturing firms.

Official statistics provide little help in trying to disaggregate international sourcing by retailers, wholesalers and manufacturers. The situation is further confounded by the complex network of domestic and international manufacturing arrangements, discussed further in section 5.3.3. General trade flows are, however, reported in some detail within the Business Monitor series MM20 for extra-EU trade, and series MQ20 for trade within the EU (CSO, 1994a, 1994b). A comprehensive discussion of import and export data relating to the UK clothing trade is provided by Jones (1994). A guide to official data sources in other EU countries is available within Eurostat (1993).

Table 5.2 summarises the balance of garment trade within five broad categories. This is a sector within which international sourcing, at all levels, is well developed to the extent that imports are over four times the level of exports. Only in the relatively small niche of clothing accessories are the trade flows almost balanced. There is currently a major problem in the analysis of long-term patterns within Europe. Since 1992, trade within the European Union has been monitored through returns on VAT forms rather than through customs data. Such flows are now described as 'arrivals' and 'despatches'; the data are difficult to reconcile with those up to 1992 on imports and exports within Europe.

Focusing upon imports from outside the EU, Table 5.3 indicates the main regions and countries from which clothing is sourced. Only countries from which imports in excess of £10m are listed, although sources are also being developed in many other regions. The importance of some of the Mediterranean sources is indicated, including Turkey, Cyprus, Israel and Morocco. It spite of the long lead times and transit times (Table 5.1) usually characteristic of sourcing from the Far East, these areas are clearly of great significance. It is interesting to reflect that garments sourced from or through Hong Kong exceed the value of (extra EU) exports from the UK.

Table 5.2 Balance of garment trade (extra EU: 1993)

Category (SITC codes)	Imports £000	Exports £000	Balance £000
Male outerwear, underwear and nightwear (841 + 843)	1,011,478	176,812	−834,666
Female outerwear, underwear and nightwear (842 + 844)	1,040,872	252,915	−787,957
Other textile garments (845)	1,061,242	217,874	−843,368
Clothing accessories (textile) (846)	134,315	123,838	−10,477
Non-textile apparel (848)	213,207	54,248	−158,959
Total (SITC div. 84)	3,461,114	825,687	−2,635,427

Source: Jones (1994), based upon UK Overseas Trade Statistics, MM20 (CSO, 1994a).

Table 5.3 Main sources of garment imports, 1993

Region/country	Imports £000	Region/country	Imports £000
EFTA	96,718	S Africa	29,575
Newly Industrialised Asia	1,459,099	Mauritius	72,311
Commonwealth	1,939,107	Japan	11,852
Sweden	14,876	Hong Kong	1,019,513
Switzerland	19,569	Malaysia	112,956
Austria	50,914	Singapore	84,305
Malta	15,065	S Korea	80,544
Turkey	164,959	Taiwan	72,697
Poland	15,659	Thailand	89,083
Czech Republic	10,303	Pakistan	104,866
Hungary	20,757	India	256,365
Rumania	38,292	Sri Lanka	86,700
USA	76,952	Bangladesh	98,952
Morocco	67,282	Macao	26,277
Egypt	17,102	China	253,221
Cyprus	48,475	Philippines	55,495
Israel	94,744	Indonesia	169,000

Derived from Jones (1994), based upon UK Overseas Trade Statistics, MM20 (CSO, 1994a).

5.2.3 Sourcing from developing countries

The classical and neoclassical body of international trade theories applies largely to the following two contexts: (a) trade in primary goods between two countries where absolute or comparative advantages exist, and (b) trade in manufactures between developed countries or between developing countries. Furthermore, the trade theories tend to explain patterns of international business from an exporter's point of view. These theories generally fail to explain the growth of trade in manufactures between developed and developing countries, particularly importing from developing to developed countries.

An important characteristic of the current international trade is that developed countries are importing an increasing number of manufactures from developing countries. The traditional pattern of international trade between two countries is more complementary, namely one country imports from another the goods which do not exist or are scarce at home. The recent pattern of international sourcing to a large extent involves importing competitive manufactured goods which are replacing or competing with existing domestic goods.

Therefore, theories explaining the new pattern of international trade (sourcing) need to introduce the dimension of product attributes. It is the combination between low factor costs and product attributes that determines the potential for trade in manufactures between developed and developing countries. Imports of manufactured goods ought to have: (i) the quality of being comparable to or better than domestic goods; (ii) cost advantages from an importer's point of view; and (iii) be compatible with the cultural traits of the home country.

A notable phenomenon in the development of the internationalisation of retailing and international sourcing is the growing use of own labels (private brands/labels) by multiple retailers. In recent years, own-brand sales growth has consistently outpaced total retail sales growth. In the USA, own brands have become major players in the grocery, health and beauty, and department store sectors (Euromonitor, 1992). In the UK, Sweden, France and Belgium, the penetration level of private brands is high, over 30% of groceries in the UK being retail branded.

Developing countries are now well able to produce manufactured goods to a high quality, yet the cost and time involved in building a manufacturer brand is very great (Jones, 1986). Manufacturing goods for sale as retailer brands offers the opportunity to be accepted by consumers in developed countries without expensive brand building. The retailer, for its part, is able to add a high margin to the low cost imports by setting a premium price. International sourcing can also add distinctive differences to the retailers' range of own brands (Shaw *et al*, 1992).

5.2.4 Japanese international sourcing

Since Japan's international distribution system is quite different to those in the USA or the EU countries, Japanese international sourcing practices merit special examination. In Japan, trading companies play a dominant role in procurement and distribution in both Japan and abroad, in addition to their other various important functions (Yoshino, 1971; Eli, 1990); hence, this section concentrates on the characteristics of Japanese trading companies' international sourcing.

Japanese trading companies or general trading companies are known as *sogo shosha*. There are 16 companies constituting *sogo shosha*, but generally only the nine largest of them are referred to as true *sogo shosha* (Eli, 1990). The nine largest *sogo shosha* handle about 20,000–25,000 products, and involve 8 per cent of world trade. They rank among the largest companies in the world in terms of turnover (United Nations, 1985). The activities of the *sogo shosha* encompass marketing, distribution, purchasing, financing, transportation project management, production of high technology and service (Yoshino, 1971; Barrett and Gehrke, 1974; United Nations, 1985).

Sogo shosha have established a worldwide network of offices and communication linkages. In 1982 the nine largest *sogo shosha* had 1,040 overseas bases with 6,207 Japanese and 17,311 indigenous employees. This has positioned *sogo shosha* well for the effective pursuit of international sourcing. Developing new suppliers and new markets for Japanese industry has been the key to the success of Japanese trading companies over the last 100 years. *Sogo shosha* have invested heavily in gathering, communicating and analysing information. Every individual *sogo shosha* has developed its own global communications network. The information systems of the *sogo shosha* enable them to pursue global sourcing strategies which assist them in outperforming their competitors.

In contrast, the development of international sourcing by US manufacturing firms has been an evolutionary process, involving four phases: (a) domestic purchasing; (b) overseas buying based on need, with limited international operating capabilities; (c) overseas buying with international sourcing strategies emerging; and (d) integrated global sourcing strategies. From the 1960s to 1970s, most US firms were operating in the first phase. In the early 1980s, US firms in some industries were pushed into the second phase by intensifying competition. These two phases are characterised by passively reacting to competitive forces in seeking overseas sourcing to improve performance. The third phase uses proactive international sourcing strategies with a view of the market from a global perspective. Newly established firms in fiercely competitive industries in the 1990s are operating at this stage. The fourth phase features integrated global sourcing efforts, involving worldwide information systems, cross-function teamwork, and the full support of top management (Monczka and Trent, 1991). According to this model, it seems that *sogo shosha* have for a long time been operating at this phase: considerably longer than US and EU firms.

5.3 THE INTERNATIONAL SOURCING PROCESS

The preceding discussion illustrates the diversity of approaches and contexts for international sourcing. A model of the sourcing process can offer therefore only a simple abstraction, as suggested in Figure 5.2. The main elements of this model are now explained.

5.3.1 Analysis of needs

Increasingly intensifying competition in the marketplace requires retailers to be even more customer orientated, determining a firm's overall assortment based on market requirements. Information about market requirements can be gathered from various sources, including the following: (a) market research; (b) EPOS data; (c) customer complaints and enquiries; (d) salespersons' insights and suggestions; (e) returned goods; (f) overseas branches and subsidiaries; and (g) trade magazines, newspapers and other publications. This information constitutes a major input to a firm's decision making concerning the overall assortment.

The overall assortment is also subject to a firm's objectives, policy and strategies. An apparent example is the firm's profitability and sales goals. Many retail firms have a policy concerning the breadth of assortment. Other relevant policies include those on purchases direct from manufacturers as opposed to those from wholesalers or jobbers, those on centralised buying as opposed to decentralised buying, and those on buying independently as opposed to joint buying with other retailers. Corporate buying policies and information about markets can also have an impact on the extent to which a firm's merchandise is sourced internationally. For instance, a major UK retailer has a policy of promoting British sources of supply and acquires 80 per cent of its merchandise from the UK (Silver, 1993).

5.3.2 Domestic sourcing

The benefits of domestic sourcing include the shorter lead and transit times, the ability to monitor closely the total production process and the lower costs in terms of management time and communications. In general, a retailer may accept higher prices in exchange for the lower risk and cost usually associated with domestic sourcing. The study of clothing sourcing by Scheffer (1992) suggested that retailers in general would pay a 15 per cent premium for goods provided by domestic suppliers. A study by Kurt Salmon/Texco (1991) confirmed that 41 per cent of retailers interviewed would pay that premium.

Such estimates of the premium potentially associated with domestic sourcing are however subject to wide variations. Clearly, sourcing costs from a distant and underdeveloped country may be far greater than those from a relatively adjacent country. There is also the issue of fixed and variable

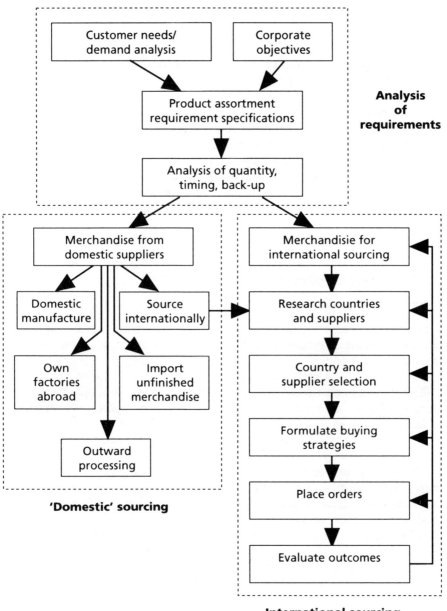

Fig. 5.2 Product sourcing process

costs. A retail organisation with an established buying office and/or retail operation in a distant country may consider only the short-term marginal costs of increased international sourcing. Under such circumstances, the premium that the retailer would be willing to pay for domestic sourcing may be somewhat less than 15 per cent.

In Figure 5.2, the label for this category of sourcing is enclosed within inverted commas. This reflects the fact that many domestic suppliers do, in any event, source partially or entirely internationally. In some cases, it is simply a case of delegating the task of (or distancing from) international sourcing. In other cases, the domestic supplier owns factories in countries with lower wage rates. Another approach is to import goods which are 'finished' in local factories. Almost the converse of this is outward processing trade (OPT), whereby the companies in developed countries export, for example, material or parts of garments for processing elsewhere, then re-import them to the home country.

5.3.3 International sourcing

Country and supplier selection

After the firm has made the decision on the merchandise which is appropriate for sourcing overseas, research needs to be undertaken on potential countries and suppliers.

The process of country selection involves scanning: (a) the economic environment, including the economic system, economic structure, resources, demographic information, infrastructure and economic performance; (b) the trade environment such as export control and bilateral trade relationships; (c) the political environment such as political stability; and (d) the legal system.

There are a number of channels whereby information about suppliers in a particular country can be secured, including professional contacts, trade journals, directories, trading companies, import brokers, trade fairs, foreign trade offices, trade associations and trade lists.

Many firms have adopted a policy of sourcing from multiple countries. For instance, Nike sources its shoes from South Korea, Taiwan, Thailand and Hong Kong. For different target markets, a firm may source the same product from different countries. An empirical study of international apparel sourcing has found that Italy dominates the designer label field, whilst Hong Kong is the leading choice for retailers' own labels (Harris and Heppell, 1991).

Selection of suppliers is one of the most important decisions a retailer makes in the process of international sourcing. The principle of purchasing used by both industrial and retail buyers is 'making the right goods available at the right price at the right time' (Webster, 1984). One study has suggested the following general considerations for selecting suppliers (in order of importance): selling history, mark-up, delivery, quality, fashionability, reputation, country of origin and service (Wagner *et al*, 1989). The criteria used by some US manufacturing firms in selecting foreign suppliers include the following: (i) supplier's foreign experience and management expertise; (ii) financial strength of the supplier; (iii) the ease of communication with the supplier; and (iv) factors that impact on inventories, such as the supplier's size and location (Carter and Narasimhan, 1990).

Retailers must also decide whether to source a product from a single supplier or from multiple suppliers. Considering the two options, the firm needs to balance the trade-off between operating costs and risks, particularly in the international context. Single sourcing has the benefit of cost reduction, but bears the risks of 'putting all the eggs in one basket'. Single sourcing has found favour amongst many manufacturing firms (Newman, 1989), and 75–90 per cent of a leading UK retailer's total range of products is single-sourced.

Purchasing strategies

Having chosen a supplier, the firm should develop a purchasing strategy concerning the volume, frequency, target price, time of delivery and trade channels.

A retailer has a number of alternative trade channels to organise the transaction, including the use of an international trading firm, overseas buying office, internal buyers and/or a buying group. Many retailers may prefer the use of overseas buying offices in that a direct contact with suppliers can reduce the possibility of misunderstanding or poor communication between the two parties. The choice of trade channels also depends on the expected volume and frequency of purchase.

There are mainly two types of buying offices which buyers use for sourcing tasks, namely affiliated buying offices (or representative offices) and independent offices. The majority of the largest retailing firms use their own (affiliated buying) offices to deal exclusively with purchasing. Independent buying offices act as a buying agent for several independent retailers and are often a co-operative which encompasses a number of retailers.

The major tasks of an affiliated buying office include the following: (a) identifying foreign suppliers for the firm; (b) soliciting RFQs (Requests for Quotations); (c) managing shipments; (d) negotiating supply contracts; (e) assuring clear communication between buyer and seller; (f) securing samples; (g) representing the firm to the supplier; and (h) dealing with payments.

Having defined the purchasing strategy, the firm is involved in negotiating prices and terms with a foreign supplier based on the chosen purchase strategy. In addition, a very important task is to manage the retailer–manufacturer relationship. Because of the importance of co-operation between retailer and manufacturer in the area of manufactured goods, a healthy and harmonious long-term business relationship is beneficial both to retailers and to manufacturers.

The corporate buying committee should evaluate the strategy and performance of international sourcing over time. This will help the firm identify problem areas, learn from mistakes and revise strategies accordingly, including the balance between domestic and international sourcing.

CONCLUSIONS

Sourcing is one of the most important functions in wholesaling and retailing firms. The accelerating globalisation of business and the marketplace opens up a new dimension for buying functions: international sourcing. Intensifying global competition is pushing more and more retailers to source abroad. Many retailing firms find a better combination between price and quality for manufactures in developing countries. International sourcing is increasingly becoming a competitive weapon for wholesalers and retailers. Hence, it can be expected that international wholesale and retail sourcing will continue to grow, mainly the latter.

A retailer's differentiation strategy is to a large extent realised through the deployment of the overall assortment. International sourcing contributes to the overall assortment, and thus can have a significant impact on the implementation of retail strategy. Wholesalers face more difficulties in the development of international sourcing in certain areas of manufactured goods compared with retailers. The decision between domestic and international sourcing requires the evaluation of many potential advantages, constraints, risks and costs.

In view of its current and, more especially, its likely future importance, the subject of international sourcing has received surprisingly little research attention. A major problem exists even in assessing the scope of the trend, given the level of aggregation within most national statistics. It is also an area of some sensitivity, many retailers and wholesalers being reluctant to 'admit' to the full extent of their international sourcing. It is, however, a major issue for researchers and practitioners alike, as the internationalisation of retailing and supply chains continues to gather pace.

REVIEW QUESTIONS

1. Assess the attractions of the international sourcing option for retailers operating in:
   (a) the clothing sector;
   (b) the grocery sector.

2. How would you evaluate the costs, both 'hard' and 'soft', of sourcing from the Mediterranean regions outside the EU?

3. What are the particular challenges of sourcing from developing countries?

4. Why has international sourcing by Japanese firms evolved to a high level of sophistication?

5. With reference to the clothing trade, explain the wide diversity in the origins of items purchased from domestic suppliers.

6. What are the main tasks involved in international sourcing? What forms of organisation may be utilised to perform these tasks?

REFERENCES

Barrett, M E and Gehrke, J A (1974) 'Significant differences between Japanese and American business', *MSU Business Topic*, 24 (Winter), 41–49.

Bunn, M D (1994) 'Key aspects of organizational buying: conceptualization and measurement', *Journal of the Academy of Marketing Science*, 22(2), 160–169.

Carter, J R and Narasimhan, R (1990) 'Purchasing in the international marketplace: implications for operations', *International Journal of Purchasing and Materials Management*, 26 (Summer), 2–11.

Commission of the European Community (1990) *The Internal Market: A Challenge for the Wholesale Trade*, Office for Official Publications of the European Communities, Luxembourg.

CSO (1994a) *Overseas Trade Statistics of the United Kingdom with Countries Outside the European Community*, (Series MM20), HMSO, London.

CSO (1994b) *Overseas Trade Statistics of the United Kingdom with Countries Within the European Community*, (Series MQ20), HMSO, London.

Davis, H L, Eppen, G D and Mattsson, L G (1974) 'Critical factors in worldwide purchasing', *Harvard Business Review*, 52 (November/December), 81–90.

Eli, M (1990) *Japan Inc.: Global Strategies of Japanese Trading Corporations*, McGraw-Hill, New York.

Euromonitor (1992) *The Own Brands Report*, Euromonitor, London.

Eurostat (1993) *European Statistics: Official Sources*, Eurostat, Luxembourg.

Fagan, M L (1991) 'A guide to global sourcing', *The Journal of Business Strategy*, 12 (March/April), 21–25.

Felgner, B H (1989) 'Retailers grab power, control marketplace', *Marketing News*, 23(2), 1–2.

Harris, R J and Heppell, J (1991) 'Apparel sourcing: a survey of retail buyers' attitudes in Canada, the USA, and Western Europe', *EIU Textile Outlook International*, 18 (November), 87–97.

Jones, J P (1986) *What's in a Name?: Advertising and the Concept of Brands*, Lexington Books, Toronto.

Jones, R M (1994) 'Market trends: statistical section', *Journal of Clothing Technology and Management*, Spring, 70–113.

Kacker, M P (1986) 'Coming to terms with global retailing', *International Marketing Review*, 3 (Spring), 7–20.

Kacker, M P (1988) 'The role of global retailers in world development', in Kaynak, E (ed.), *Transnational Retailing*, Walter de Gruyter, Berlin, 33–42.

Kotabe, M and Murray, J Y (1990) 'Linking product and process innovations and modes of international sourcing in global competition: a case of foreign multinational firms', *Journal of International Business Studies*, 21(3), 383–408.

Kotabe, M and Omura, G S (1989) 'Sourcing strategies of European and Japanese multinationals: a comparison', *Journal of International Business Studies,* 20 (Spring), 113–130.

Kurt Salmon/Texco (1991) *Encouraging the Competitiveness of the Soft Goods Industry through Cooperation in the Post 1992 European Community,* Report to the EC, Dusseldorf/Milan.

Larsen, T L and Rosenbloom, B (1993) 'A functional approach to international channel structure and the role of independent wholesalers', *Journal of Marketing Channels,* 2(4), 65–82.

Luqmani, M, Goehle, D, Quraeshi, Z A and Yavas, U (1991) 'Tracing the development of wholesaling practice and thought', *Journal of Marketing Channels,* 1(2), 75–99.

Min, H and Galle, W P (1991) 'International purchasing strategies of multinational US firms', *International Journal of Purchasing and Materials Management,* 27 (Summer), 9–18.

Monczka, R M and Trent, R J (1991a) 'Evolving sourcing strategies for the 1990s', *International Journal of Physical Distribution and Logistics Management,* 21(5), 4–12.

Monczka, R M and Trent, R J (1991b) 'Global sourcing: a development approach', *International Journal of Purchasing and Materials Management,* 27 (Spring) 3–8.

Newman, R G (1989) 'Single sourcing: short-term savings versus long-term problems', *Journal of Purchasing and Materials Management,* 25 (Summer) 20–25.

Shaw, S A, Dawson, J A and Blair, L M A (1992) 'The sourcing of retailer brand food products by UK retailers', *Journal of Marketing Management,* 8, 127–146.

Scheffer, M (1992) *Trading Places: Fashion, Retailers and the Changing Geography of Clothing Production,* PhD thesis, Department of Geography, University of Utrecht, The Netherlands.

Silver, C (1993) 'Manufacturing without factories: relationships with suppliers', *Profits from Progress: Conference Proceedings,* London, Department of Trade and Industry, 22–29.

Tan, J (1990) 'USA: Wing Tai to pay S$60m for 3 US apparel firms', *Business-Times,* 27 July, 26.

United Nations (1985) *Transnational Trading Corporations in Selected Asian and Pacific Countries,* ESCAP UNCTC Publication Series B, No. 6.

Wagner, J, Ettenson, R and Parrish, J (1989) 'Vendor selection among retail buyers: an analysis by merchandise division', *Journal of Retailing,* 65(1), 58–79.

Webster, F E, Jr (1984) *Industrial Marketing Strategy,* John Wiley & Sons, New York.

Yoshino, M Y (1971) *The Japanese Marketing System: Adaptations and Innovations,* MIT Press, Boston.

Yoshino, M Y and Lifson, T B (1986) *The Invisible Link: Japan's Sogo Shosha and the Organization of Trade,* MIT Press, Boston.

CHAPTER 6

The legislative environment as a measure of attractiveness for internationalisation

Gary Davies and Maureen Whitehead

INTRODUCTION

Retailers, much as any business, are constrained in what they can do by the law of the land. There are, however, a number of types of legislation which particularly affect a retailer's ability to exploit a marketplace. The most obvious is planning legislation and the formal guidelines that help those responsible for its implementation to interpret the law. Such law often restricts the size of a shop, limiting any economy of scope, or it places barriers to the building of new shops, thus limiting the speed at which a retailer can expand and raising the cost of doing so.

Less obvious legislation is that which aims to protect smaller retailers, not only certain planning legislation, but also legislation which restricts the negotiating power of the retailer with its suppliers. This chapter aims to provide a way of understanding whether legislation offers a real barrier to entry to a particular country/market by comparing the development of the retail sector in a country with that country's economic development. We argue that as an economy develops, shops reduce in number and increase in size unless there is legislation to constrain this process. Assessing the structure of the retail sector against others in a similar stage of economic development provides a way of measuring whether legislation is restrictive to retailers.

6.1 LEGISLATION AND RETAILING

Large-scale retailers considering entry into different national markets need to examine a number of factors that might affect their potential to make a profit. A multiple retailer would be concerned *inter alia* with its potential to develop similar or greater economies of scale or scope to those it might enjoy in its domestic market. This chapter is concerned with examining the significance of the legislative environment in deciding upon the attractiveness of individual national markets. Legislation in this context is taken to refer to that which is specifically aimed at affecting retailing: planning legislation, legislation affecting negotiation with suppliers and legislation affecting price competition.

Existing views differ on the significance of legislation to the structure and competitive nature of the retail sector. Much of the literature concerning the internationalisation of retailing treats legislation as one of a number of environmental variables which can impact upon the strategic direction of any business, the other variables being economic, social and cultural (Treadgold, 1990; Kacker, 1983). This perspective reflects work within individual countries on the structure of distribution channels as a whole. Sybrandy *et al* (1991), for example, in their review of much of the literature on channel structure, cite numerous examples where legal factors were seen as significant, but conclude that many environmental factors affect market structure without indicating whether any one is more important than any other or whether particular combinations of factors are more potent than others.

Empirical studies have been conducted within individual markets to assess the effect of specific legislation but have come to different conclusions. Leunis and François (1988) explained the slow growth of large stores in Belgium as being due to the Padlock Law first introduced in 1975. Treadgold and Sanghavi (1990) claim that the Loi Royer in France slowed the development of larger outlets in that country but Burt (1984) suggests that other factors (such as economic conditions and organisational trends) might have been more instrumental.

6.1.1 The role of legislation in channel development

Legislation has often been introduced to affect the power relationships within distribution channels generally, so as to ensure greater or fairer competition by confining 'the use of coercive and reward power', (Stern and El-Ansary, 1977). What 'fair competition' means is an issue, as much legislation relevant to retailing seems designed to support the independent sector against the power of the large multiple. Hollander and Omura (1989) recall that the Robinson-Patman Act in America was nicknamed 'the anti A and P law', as one main effect of the law was to constrain the negotiating power of the large multiple with its suppliers. A and P (Atlantic and Pacific), were one of the largest American retailers at the time. CNW (1991) identify the Baunutzungsverordnung passed in 1977 in Germany – planning legislation limiting the growth of larger stores – as being a 'direct response to pressure from independents' (CNW, 1990). An examination of the legislative frameworks in a number of European countries led the same source to conclude that 'the nature of the planning environment is often the principal determinant of a market's cost structure and therefore its margin structure'. They concluded that only in a relatively liberal planning environment were relatively high retail operating margins possible (CNW, 1991b).

Legislation to protect the small retailer or to limit the economies of scale of the large retailer or to limit the negotiating power of the large retailer acts as a constraint on market development. How much of a constraint remains an issue; is legislation the potentially dominant effect that County Natwest Woodmac (CNW) assert, or is it one of a number of individually less important issues as might be implied from some of the academic literature?

To understand whether legislation might be a determinant of the potential for large-scale retailing it is useful to ask the question *how* legislation might affect market structure. The main body of theory that should provide an answer is that of marketing channels.

6.2 CONCEPTS FROM THEORY

The body of theory that attempts to explore the nature and structure of distribution systems in general is that of marketing channels. Gattorna (1978) reviewed the extensive literature in the area and identified a number of 'schools of thought' therein. He identified the 'behavioural' school as the one holding the greatest potential, in that its exponents recognise that socio-political influences are an important factor in understanding how channels emerge and what their structures are. The 1970s saw a deal of research with this focus using concepts such as power, conflict and co-operation. However, Gattorna held that much research in the entire area of marketing channels was descriptive and lacking in a theoretical base.

Somewhat later, Gaski (1984) quoted an anonymous reviewer as doubting whether 'we really know anything about power and conflict in distribution'. Gaski's own paper attempted to identify some of the fundamental conceptual issues that remained to be resolved. Four years later still, Stern (1988) repeated much the same criticisms as Gattorna and Gaski in claiming that, apart from one monograph by Bucklin in 1966, 'almost all other studies in the channel area have been descriptive'. He argued that it was time to move on to using theory to predict processes and outcomes rather than simply to describe them.

Bucklin's work as cited by Stern lay within that of the microeconomic school but even by 1973 his models were presented without being tested on empirical data (Bucklin, 1973). There have been a number of later attempts to produce a universal theory or model of marketing channel behaviour. Some address particular aspects of channel behaviour such as leadership (Price, 1991), conflict (Perry, 1990/1) or dependence (Lewis and Lambert, 1991; Keith *et al*, 1990). Others rely upon behavioural concepts developed elsewhere in the social sciences such as expectancy theory (LaFleur *et al*, 1989). As yet there is no universally accepted model emerging from the channels literature that can be used to predict the outcome of any combination of circumstances pertaining within any particular marketing channel. Few models appear to have been tested empirically, and, remarkably, none of those mentioned give prominence to the legal environment, apparently taking it as given and not treating it as a potentially important, even dominant, variable.

6.2.1 Power and the effect of legislation

While theoretical development in the channels literature has been slow, the behavioural perspective has succeeded in giving us a number of well-established concepts, among which 'power' stands out as being important. Definitions of this particular concept vary somewhat in the literature, but Rosenbloom (1990: 140) suggested that all refer to the 'capacity of a particular channel member to control the behaviour of another channel member'. The ideas of French and Raven (1959) have been particularly influential over earlier research into power within marketing channels. They suggested that there were five bases for power between two parties: reward, coercive, legitimate, referent and expert. A totally different perspective on the bases that can provide one party with power over another comes from the more recent strategic literature and in particular from that of Porter (1980). He proposed three factors: the relative concentration of firms in the two sectors forming the two stages of a marketing channel, the switching costs of either party within a particular relationship to leave that relationship (exit costs), and the significance of the product being exchanged to whatever is the receiving party's end-product (dependency).

As one purpose of manufacturing and retailing businesses is to make a profit, in most if not all business relationships power will tend to be used to improve the share of the total profit to be made from the channel of the party with the greater power. Understanding the circumstances in which a manufacturer or retailer is more likely to be in a position of relative power, and understanding why, is going to be important both for the practitioner and the theorist. There has been research using the ideas of French and Raven into whether the source of power affects the type of relationship between channel members (see, for example, Etgar, 1976, 1978), but this is less important to the practitioner than what circumstance is likely to produce greater profit, something to which the concepts from business strategy are more likely to have direct relevance. There is evidence to support the significance of sector concentration from the PIMS and other databases (Buzzell and Gale, 1987: 70) in that the higher the absolute market share of a firm, the higher its profitability (market shares will be higher generally in markets that are more highly concentrated). In a retail context there is evidence that as a retail sector becomes more concentrated than the manufacturing sector supplying it, the profit in the retail sector rises relative to that in manufacturing (OFT, 1985: 31).

Power is not an issue between manufacturer and retailer unless a significant relationship exists (Emerson, 1962), but once the relationship exists then the level of power one player holds over another will vary with how dependent one player is on the other (El Ansary and Stern, 1972). Less attention has been paid to the issue of power over the other competitors at the same level in the distribution channel, in this instance the power a large retailer can exert over a smaller retailer because of the potential the larger competitor has to exert greater influence over the shopper. Unless legislation restricts the negotiating power of the large retailer and/or its ability to discount, the larger firm can use economies of scale in bulk buying. Economies of scope by offering a wider selection in a larger store can also lead to economies of scale as both the transaction and operating costs fall.

To summarise, power can be seen to be a desirable goal for a multiple retailer in a marketing channel, although how important power is will depend upon the circumstances within the particular market. There is no proven model that can be used to determine which market offers the retailer greater opportunity for power. Some generalisations can be made, in particular that the higher the level of retailer concentration in a market, the greater the potential for retailer power and for power that can be used to increase retailer profit, particularly at the expense of the supplier. Markets where multiple retailers can build larger stores are likely to be more profitable than others due to the potential for market power achieved through scale. Alternatively markets where it is unclear whether economies of scope and scale can be achieved present higher risks to the potential entrant. So although the channels literature itself places little emphasis on the significance of the legislative environment, if, as seems likely, legislation is the main force shaping the *power structure* in a retail market, then a significant contribution will be made to an understanding of retail markets and their attractiveness to new entrants from understanding the legislative environment as it affects the development of the retail market.

6.3 A SIMPLE MODEL OF LEGISLATIVE EFFECT

Legislation in a number of countries is aimed at restricting the power of large-scale retailers either by restricting the potential for economy of scope (limiting the size of stores) or the potential for economy of scale (limiting the size and number of stores and their negotiating power). By supporting the independent retail sector such legislation acts to restrict concentration in the retail sector. (Other legislation or government powers to limit merger activity may also be important in limiting concentration.) Restrictions on the negotiating power of retailers, specifically on their ability to obtain preferential discounts, will also be important in determining the profitability of the retail sector and may contribute indirectly to constrain retail concentration because the ability to obtain preferential discounts provides motivation for concentration.

As concentration in the retail sector grows, the negotiating power of the manufacturers supplying it falls. Retailer profits will rise unless some other factor intervenes, such as limitations on the retailer's ability to attract custom particularly through price promotion. Resale price maintenance persists in some countries and within some sectors even though such legislation became less important in many countries during the 1950s and 1960s (Edwards, 1966).

Figure 6.1 presents a simple model of the effect of legislation on retail power and profitability. Other factors may also affect retail concentration and retailer profitability, but markets which are described by Figure 6.1 may be inherently more attractive than those which are not.

The model postulates that the most significant effect of the relevant legislation is to constrain the power of large-scale retailers. In the absence of such legislation, or where the legislation has no effect, retailers will increase economy of scope by building larger outlets and will increase economy of

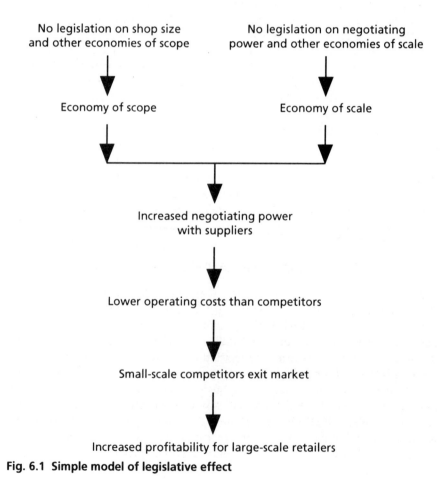

Fig. 6.1 **Simple model of legislative effect**

scale and thus negotiating power, and this will ultimately lead to increased profitability through the exercise of channel power both vertically and horizontally.

6.3.1 Methodological issues in testing the model

Thus far in the literature the significance of the legal environment has been argued in a deductive way, or merely assumed. Proving that legislation is a *determinant* of retailer concentration is more difficult. One immediate problem is the difficulty of 'measuring' legislation as a variable. In a perfect world legislation could be treated as a dichotomous variable, in that it either exists or it doesn't. In practice, legislation that is similar in concept differs in its effectiveness in application. For example, British manufacturers tended to choose not to enforce resale price maintenance after the law was modified in the 1960s (Edwards, 1966). RPM existed in law but was not enacted in practice. Recently the Loi Royer has been the subject of scrutiny in France due to the discriminatory way in which the legislation has allegedly been applied in favour of certain operators and against others.

Even if the legislative environment is a determining factor, other macro-factors may be equally important making a comparison between markets less valuable unless such factors can also be modelled. Of the other environmental factors, the economic environment can at least be quantified. As an economy develops, fixed retail outlets grow in numbers as disposable income increases and specialism in retailing becomes economic. In the absence of legislation there will be a time when the increase in shop numbers will be checked or reversed by the tendency to increase shop size to achieve scope and scale economies, unless there is legislation that prevents this. Economic development can be quantified and measured by assessing the per capita income of the national market. There are no obvious equivalent measures for the social and cultural environments.

Over the long-term a longitudinal study of the market either side of a change in legislation may reveal an apparent causal relationship between legislation and market structure. This approach has been used by Leunis and François (1988) and Davies and Harris (1990: 7). A relationship can be inferred between legislation and market structure but other variables may intervene to make such inferences unsafe.

Different retail sectors can be compared within the same country at the same time where legislation is applied to one sector but not to another. This is the case, for example, in Britain where resale price maintenance (RPM) still applies (at the time of writing) to pharmaceuticals, newspapers, magazines and books. Table 6.1 presents data on the concentration levels in food retailing (not subject to RPM) and in newspaper and periodical retailing and drug and medicine retailing. The concentration levels in the two sectors subject to RPM do appear to be lower than those in food but the comparison with all retailers is not so convincing.

Table 6.1 Concentration levels in sectors subject to RPM

Retail sector	% of sector sales from largest 5 retailers	% of sector sales from largest 10 retailers
Food	40.7	52.8
Newspapers and periodicals	18.3	22.5
Drugs, medicines, etc.	24.1	27.3
All types	19.3	30.1

Source: Business Monitor SDA 25, *Retailing,* Business Statistics Office, HMSO, 1988.

An alternative approach would be to compare different retail markets at the same point in time – in the context of this chapter that involves mainly different national markets. This approach presents its own problems of comparability of data and definitions. If these problems are of secondary importance then it may be possible to compare retail markets by comparing their structural development with the economic development of the country concerned. Markets that deviated from any norm would be markets where the legal environment had constrained the retail sector.

Figure 6.2 suggests how the number of fixed shops varies with economic development, the number of shops rising as the economy develops and falling as the average size of shops increases in an unrestricted market due to retailers achieving economies of scope.

Figure 6.3 suggests how the number of retail businesses varies with economic development: the number grows as the economy grows and then falls if legislation does not restrict economic development. As the relationships in Figures 6.2 and 6.3 are similar, one measure may be used as a surrogate for both.

In developed economies retail markets will have passed the peak

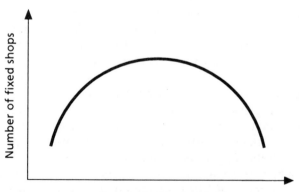

Economic development

Fig. 6.2 The effect of development on the number of shops

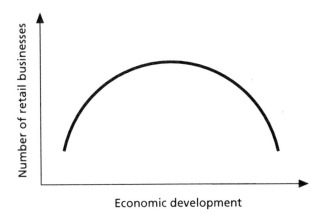

Fig. 6.3 **The effect of development on the number of retail businesses**

positions in Figures 6.2 and 6.3, in other words the number of shops will be decreasing relative to economic development. The more advanced the economy the greater this effect should be, unless legislation provides an effective constraint.

6.3.2 Empirical evidence for the model

Figure 6.4 presents data on the number of retail outlets in a country compared to that country's economic development as measured by GNP. The data are made comparable by expressing both variables per head of population and by converting GNP in national currencies to US dollars. The countries included are all those developed nations for whom data was available from the same Euromonitor source (Table 6.2). The correlation in the data is significant at the 95 per cent level (two tail test, 22 degrees of freedom, $R = 0.479$). The value of R^2 at 0.23 implies that a quarter of the variation in the data is explained by the postulated relationship. Just as important in assessing the significance of the relationship is an examination of those countries which are furthest from the correlation line. At one extreme is Italy where the planning regime is generally held to be highly restrictive, at the other is the USA where the planning regime is held to be relatively liberal. Austria appears to have a relatively liberal legislative environment, closely followed by the UK, Canada, Sweden and Germany. Spain, Japan and Ireland appear to have relatively restrictive environments.

The planning regime in Germany appears to be quite restrictive from what is written about it but our analysis shows it to be relatively liberal. Going back to the detail of the German legislation, we found that restrictions on the size of new shops applied only outside of town or city boundaries. Large shops could be, and were, being built in town centres or within the boundaries of quite small settlements but which were close to a large conurbation.

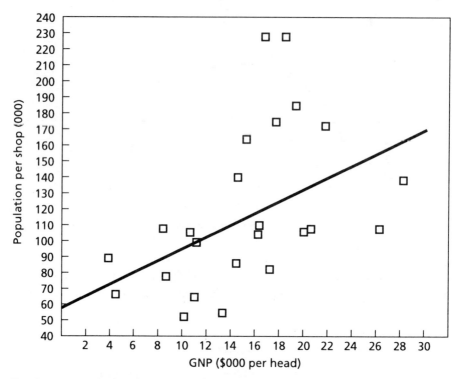

Fig. 6.4 Economic development and shops per head

The planning regime in Britain is also sometimes seen as restrictive. Britain has few large out-of-town shopping centres similar to those in America. That said, British retailers have been adept at influencing local authorities to allow them to build superstores out of town. The development of retail parks rather than shopping centres, where retailing is used to infill open space in towns and cities, is common practice in Britain. In 1994 the planning regime appeared to change. Government guidelines, reissued in 1993 for retail development – the so-called PPG6 – had expressed concern over the environmental damage caused by out-of-town development due to increased car usage and the possible damage to the town centre if most retailing moved into the suburbs. The equivalent guidelines issued in 1994 for transport, PPG13, placed even greater emphasis on the town centre as the location for retailing. Clearly the government's position had changed and the *de facto* change in legislation will doubtless have its effect on the structure of the British retail market in years to come unless the planning regime changes yet again.

The position of Spain in Figure 6.4 is interesting. Spain's legislative environment is regarded as relatively free, yet our model implies the opposite. However, the data for Spain is from 1988, not long after the end of what had been a restrictive phase in retail planning legislation under General

Table 6.2 Retail concentration and economic development

Date	Country	Outlets (000)	Population (000)	Population per outlet	GNP/head ($000)
1985	Japan	1,880.4	121,049	64	10.95
1986	Australia	160.2	15,602	100	10.72
1990	New Zealand	42.0	3,307	79	8.57
1990	Israel	45.8	4,038	106	10.43
1988	Canada	134.5	25,309	185	19.38
1986	USA	1,441.2	226,546	228	18.56
1987	Belgium	113.7	9,849	87	14.57
1985	Denmark	48.7	5,124	105	20.08
1989	France	518.7	54,335	105	16.32
1988	W Germany	348.5	60,651	174	18.86
1985	Greece	148.9	9,740	65	4.72
1988	Ireland	31.7	3,443	109	8.31
1988	Italy	1,043.9	56,557	54	13.37
1988	Luxembourg	3.3	365	111	16.44
1990	Netherlands	160.5	13,060	81	17.28
1989	Portugal	109.6	9,833	90	3.97
1988	Spain	728.7	37,746	52	10.06
1989	UK	334.6	55,089	165	15.34
1988	Austria	33.2	7,555	228	16.84
1986	Finland	36.6	4,785	131	14.67
1987	Iceland	1.9	205	108	26.34
1987	Norway	38.6	4,091	106	20.46
1988	Sweden	48.0	8,320	173	21.95
1989	Switzerland	45.0	6,366	141	28.07

Source: Euromonitor.

Franco. During the 1980s, under a more liberal regime, many retailers looked to Spain as a foreign market. The attractiveness of the country stems from both its rapid economic development since joining the EU *and* the relaxation of its planning regime.

The explanation for the large number of shops in Japan could well be connected with the legislation allowing wholesalers considerable market power and restricting the ability of large retailers to deal directly with manufacturers. In such circumstances retailers are less able to exercise any market power.

6.3.3 Implications of the model

Given the problems of comparability in data, the correlation level in Figure

6.4 is surprisingly high. The relationship between population per retail outlet and economic development as an indirect measure of legislative effect is
given further face validity from the position of those countries whose planning regimes are deemed to be either relatively restrictive or relatively liberal. It appears highly likely that planning legislation can and does constrain
the ability of retailers to achieve the economies of scope and scale inherent
in operating larger outlets. The relationship provides strong evidence to support the view that legislation is a highly significant variable in retail development rather than something of secondary significance.

The implications for retailers are that markets which fall above the correlation line in Figure 6.4 are likely to be easier to develop within and those
below the correlation line should only be entered if the retailer believes that
the legislative regime is about to change. Within such markets it is possible
that large-scale retailers would benefit by applying pressure towards more
liberal planning legislation.

Significant differences appear to exist in terms of the evolution of the
retail sector between countries which are members of the EU or who were
negotiating to join at the time of writing. For example, Britain has only a
third of the number of shops per head of population compared to Italy.
Large-scale retailers will find it easier to enter and to compete within the
British rather than the Italian market. Is this reasonable in a single market?
While legislative barriers that reduce competition in the trading of products
are being reduced within the EU, no similar moves appear to be planned to
facilitate greater competition between retailers. A retailer considering internationalisation is likely to avoid entering a market where the legislative
environment is restrictive. This in turn acts to protect established retail businesses within the country with such restrictive legislation.

CONCLUSIONS

The correlation between shop numbers and economic development suggests
that shop numbers provides a useful measure of retail market development.
No attempt has been made in this chapter to assess the profitability of the
retail sectors under different legislative regimes. As British retailers appear
to be more profitable than their American counterparts and Italian retailers
do not appear to be totally disadvantaged by their planning regime, then
clearly the development of the sector is only one part of the profit equation.
That said, the disadvantages of entering a market with a restrictive legislative environment do seem to be as significant as CNW (1990) assert. What
is also clear is that there is an issue for the EU to address on whether there
should be such differences in legislative environment between member
states.

Retailers need to consider the effects of legislation on their type of business operation within the foreign country they seek to target. They also

need to identify whether there are any likely changes in legislation which will affect the structure of the retail sector. For example, if the legislative regime in Italy changes, then there will be significant opportunities for large multiple retail businesses to establish themselves. In Britain, changes in the planning guidelines in 1993 and 1994, rather than any formal legislation, may prove to be a barrier to any retailer seeking to develop a new chain of larger stores away from the town centre.

REVIEW QUESTIONS

1. List the types of legislation you would expect to affect a retailer's profitability. Explain how each could do so.

2. What is meant by 'economy of scale' and 'economy of scope'? Give examples of both.

3. Graph the number of shops in three different countries per 1,000 of population over a number of years. Explain any trends you observe.

4. Does the fact that planning legislation varies throughout the EU act as a barrier to fair competition between retailers of different countries? If so, how?

5. What are the arguments for and against the development of out-of-town retailing?

6. How would you find out what was the relevant legislation in any one country?

REFERENCES

Bucklin, L P (1973) 'A theory of channel control', *Journal of Marketing*, 37 (January), 39.
Burt, S (1984) 'Has the Loi Royer had any effect?', *Retail and Distribution Management*, (January/February), 16.
Buzzell, R D and Gale, B T (1987) *The PIMS Principle*, Free Press, New York.
CNW (1990) *Focus on German Food Retailing*, Country Natwest Woodmac, London.
CNW (1991) *Focus on European Food Retailing*, Country Natwest Woodmac, London.
CNW (1991b) *Focus on Food Retailing in Southern Europe*, Country Natwest Woodmac, London.
Davies, G and Harris, K (1990) *The Independent Retailer*, Macmillan, London.
Edwards, C D (1966) *Trade Regulations Overseas*, New York, Oceana.
El-Ansary, A and Stern, L W (1972) 'Power measurement in the distribution channel', *Journal of Marketing Research*, 9 (February), 47.
Emerson, R M (1962) 'Power dependence relations', *American Sociological Review*, 27 (February), 31.
Etgar, M (1976) 'Channel domination and countervailing power in distribution channels', *Journal of Marketing Research*, (August), 254.
Etgar, M (1978) 'Selection of an effective channel control mix', *Journal of Marketing*, (July), 53.

French, J R P and Raven, B (1959) 'The bases of social power', in Cartwright, D (ed.) *Studies in Social Power,* University of Michigan, 612.

Gaski, J F (1984) 'The theory of power and conflict in channels of distribution', *Journal of Marketing,* 48 (Summer), 9.

Gattorna, J (1978) 'Channels of distribution conceptualisations: a state of the art review', *European Journal of Marketing,* 12(7), 471.

Hollander, S C and Omura, G S (1989) 'Chain store developments and the political, strategic and social interdependencies', *Journal of Retailing,* 65(3), 299.

Kacker, M (1983) *Transatlantic investment in retailing,* Research Bulletin No. 138, Conference Board, New York.

Keith, J E, Jackson, D W and Crosby, L A (1990) 'Effects of alternative types of influence strategies under different dependence structures', *Journal of Marketing,* 54 (July), 30.

LaFleur, E K, Arnold, D R and Smith, G D (1989) 'Expectancy theory: a framework for analysing relationships between dependent yet autonomous channel members', in Pellegrini, L and Reddy, S K (eds.), *Retail and Marketing Channels,* Routledge, London, 138.

Leunis, J. and Francois, P (1988) 'The impact of Belgian public policy upon retailing', in Kaynak, E (ed.), *Transnational Retailing,* de Gruyter, New York.

Lewis, M C and Lambert, D M (1991) 'A model of channel member performance, dependence and satisfaction', *Journal of Retailing,* 67(2), 205.

OFT (1985) *Office of Fair Trading, Competition and Retailing,* OFT, London.

Perry, M A T (1990/91) 'Channel member conflict and performance: a proposed model and research agenda', *International Review of Retail Distribution and Consumer Research,* 1(2), 233.

Price, R (1991) 'Channel leadership behaviour: a framework for improving channel leadership effectiveness', *Journal of Marketing Channels,* 1 (Spring), 87.

Rosenbloom, B (1990), *Marketing Channels,* 4th edn, Dryden, Orlando, Florida.

Stern, L W and El-Ansary, A (1977) *Marketing Channels,* Prentice-Hall, New Jersey, 318.

Stern, L W (1988) 'Reflections on channels research', *Journal of Retailing,* 64(1), 1.

Sybrandy, A, Pirog, S F D and Tuninga, R S J (1991) 'The output of distributive systems: a conceptual framework', *Journal of Macromarketing,* Fall, 19.

Treadgold, A (1990) 'The developing internationalisation of retailing', *International Journal of Retail and Distribution Management,* 18(2), 4–11.

Treadgold, A and Sanghavi, N (1990) *Developments in European Retailing,* Dover House, Yeovil, Somerset.

PART THREE

Strategies for internationalisation

CHAPTER 7

International alliances in European retailing

Terry Robinson and Colin M Clarke-Hill

INTRODUCTION

Strategic alliances of one sort or another have been a common feature in manufacturing industry for many years (Harrigan, 1985, 1986, 1988; Hergert and Morris, 1987; Kogut, 1988; Nielsen, 1988). Cravens, Shipp and Cravens (1993) use the analogy of the 'lone wolf' organisation which competes independently with other firms in a market as being an anachronism in the increasingly global markets of the 1990s. Co-operative relationships, which may or may not be strategic alliances between independent businesses, are major components in the business and marketing policies of industries operating in the aerospace, information technology, electronics, pharmaceuticals and automotive sectors. Kanter (1989), among others, has suggested that co-operative relationships are of escalating importance to firms seeking to improve their competitive advantage. Co-operative relationships may take a variety of forms and may occur at different points in an organisation's value chain. Typically such relationships might be termed vertical alliances or horizontal alliances. The focus of this chapter is to concentrate on alliances between retailers that are both horizontal, i.e. retailer to retailer, and also international, in that they cross the boundaries of nation states.

Retail alliances are not a new phenomenon in Europe, having existed for many years as predominantly national buying clubs, particularly in France. However, with the exception of alliances within the Co-operative movement and some specialist retail sectors, international retail alliances emerged, particularly in the grocery sector, in the mid to late 1980s. An important feature of this new wave of alliances is the existence of a central secretariat, usually at a neutral location, to facilitate co-ordination between members. This has meant that a large and increasing share of the European grocery market is now in the hands of international alliances. In the United Kingdom, two of the top four grocery retailers by market share are currently members of international alliances. The most recent addition, J Sainsbury, announced an alliance, entitled SEDD, in April 1994 with

Esselunga of Italy, Docks de France and Delhaize of Belgium. Tesco have so far avoided direct alliance membership and Asda, after spending a short period as a member of the Deuro Buying alliance, subsequently withdrew.

This chapter reviews the extent of horizontal retail alliances within Europe, with specific focus on food retailing. The chapter defines alliances in this context, identifies the retailers involved in the two most significant alliance types and describes the common features in the workings of these alliances. It extends the scope of alliance definition and discusses the advantages derived from alliance membership.

7.1 MONITORING ALLIANCE ACTIVITY

7.1.1 Definitions

The term 'strategic alliance' is fairly new in the literature and is applied to organisations which are co-operating and forming partnerships and coalitions based on mutual needs. Whilst there has been extensive discussion in the literature on how alliances work through the analysis of numerous case histories, there has been little work in developing a general definition of what constitutes a strategic alliance within the context of retailing. However, the existence of horizontal co-operation between retailers is not new and has existed, for example within the Co-operative movement, for many decades, along with the early development of voluntary chains. What is new is the acceleration of such horizontal co-operation through institutionalisation and internationalisation. In this chapter, we do not intend to resolve the dilemma of definition as, in the past, attempts at definition have proved to be limited to particular forms of alliance (Dawson and Shaw, 1992; Robinson and Clarke-Hill, 1993). We believe that a working and deliberately broad definition as follows would suffice:

> An alliance is a coalition of two or more organisations intended to achieve mutually beneficial goals.

Such a broad definition is useful, in that retailer alliances can be both strategic as well as operational in nature with multiple goals. This, we believe, is as far as we wish to go towards an all-embracing definition.

These alliances often involve companies that *may* be seen as competitors. Vertical alliances, usually buyer/supplier alliances, are specifically excluded from this chapter except in so far as horizontal alliances can often create their own vertical alliances within a web of relationships between retailer and retailer, retailer and supplier as well as alliances between supplier and supplier. Furthermore, alliances within European retailing can be seen as either compact and tight alliances, with highly developed interactions between alliance partners, or as a much looser concept of collaborative activity between retailers.

7.1.2 International alliances in Europe

The international alliance has become an ubiquitous part of the European retail picture in the early 1990s. This pervasive nature is illustrated in Table 7.1 overleaf which shows the alliances in place at the beginning of 1995, their members and respective turnovers.

Table 7.1 clearly demonstrates the extent to which alliances are a dominant part of European food retailing, representing over 300 bn ecu in total turnover, and involving some 130,000 retail outlets over all of the nations of the European Union. However, this only represents a 'snapshot' at the beginning of 1995 of a dynamic retail environment. Companies move into and out of alliances each year. For example, Asda spent only a short period in the Deuro Buying alliance and Edeka of Germany left the CEM (Coopération Européan de Marketing) alliance in July 1994 to join AMS in January 1995. This resulted in the dissolution of the CEM alliance. Superquinn of Ireland and Jerinimo Martins of Portugal have recently joined the AMS. Some alliances even join other alliances, for example, NAF joining Deuro in 1994, and the European Retail Alliance of Ahold, Argyll and Casino (being a majority holder in the AMS) and Nisa (a domestic UK alliance) within the EMD, thus creating the phenomenon of 'alliances within alliances'. Nor do alliances preclude retailers entering into bilateral agreements with each other, for example, Sainsbury and Docks de France had such an agreement before the formation of SEDD. Alliances even spawn their own sub-alliances, for example, the VRA (Viking Retail Alliance) between Kesko of Finland, Hakon of Norway and ICA of Sweden, all of which are partners in the AMS.

Examination of Table 7.1 also reveals some quite fundamental differences in the nature of the type of retail outlets that comprise the alliances. For example, the NAF alliance is comprised of many small outlets, particularly in the former eastern bloc. Even within alliances themselves there are some strange looking partners such as the co-ops of NAF (28 bn ecu from 12,000 shops) to the hypermarket dominated Carrefour with 18.5 bn ecu from 647 stores.

7.2 ALLIANCE TYPES AND FUNCTIONS

Two types of formal retail alliance have become apparent so far in this analysis: (a) those that include a cross shareholding between members which can be described as 'equity participating alliances', and (b) those which have no such sharing of equity but have a central secretariat to administer the work of the alliances and are thus described as 'alliances with central secretariats'. The cross shareholding alliance is found in only one case, the European Retail Alliance (ERA) between Ahold, Argyll and Casino. This alliance is depicted in Figure 7.1.

Table 7.1 European retail alliances (as at January 1995)

Alliance name (formation)	Alliance centre	Members	Domicile	Turnover (bn ecu) (1993)	No. of outlets (1993)
Associated Marketing Services (AMS) (1989)	Switzerland	Ahold	Netherlands	12.46	2,132
		Allkauf	Germany	3.3[1]	292
		Argyll	UK	7.19	841
		Casino	France	9.48	3,311
		Hakon	Norway	1.84[1]	416[1]
		ICA	Sweden	5.55	2,840[1]
		Kesko	Finland	3.83	2,007[1]
		Mercadonna	Spain	1.14	160
		Rinascente	Italy	3.13	740
		Superquinn	Ireland	0.13[2]	21
		Jer. Martins	Portugal	0.59	169
		Edeka[3]	Germany	15.30	11,618
		Total		48.65	24,547
Deuro Buying (1990)	Switzerland	Carrefour	France	18.57	647
		Makro	Netherlands	4.44	171
		Metro	Switzerland	29.6	1,434
		NAF[4]	Netherlands	28.8[1]	12,088[1]
		Total		81.41	14,340
European Marketing Distribution (EMD) (1989)	Switzerland	Markant	Germany	33.78	24,276
		Markant	Netherlands	1.49	2,218[1]
		ZEV	Austria	2.98	2,407[1]
		Euromadi	Spain	5.43	6,801[1]
		Selex	Italy	2.13	1,100[1]
		Uniarme	Portugal	0.69	68[1]
		Nisa	UK	12.80	3,040[1]
		Musgrave	Ireland	1.14	387[1]
		Supervib	Denmark	2.45	666[1]
		Total		62.89	40,340
Eurogroup (1988)	Germany	GIB	Belgium	7.70	1,768
		Vendex	Netherlands	4.78	705
		Rewe Zentr.	Germany	23.25	8,479
		Co-op Schw.	Switzerland	5.61	1,729
		Total		41.34	12,681
Buying Internat Group Spar (BIGS) (1990)	Netherlands	Spar	Austria	2.15	n/a
		Unidis	Belgium	0.41[1]	n/a
		Bernag Ovag	Switzerland	0.10[1]	n/a
		Dagrofa	Denmark	0.86[1]	n/a
		Spar	UK	1.64[1]	n/a
		Hellaspar	Greece	0.17[1]	n/a
		Despar	Italy	2.23[1]	n/a
		BWG/Spar	Ireland	2.38[1]	n/a
		Unil	Norway	0.09[1]	n/a

▶

Table 7.1 (continued)

Alliance name (formation)	Alliance centre	Members	Domicile	Turnover (bn ecu) (1993)	No. of outlets (1993)
		Unigro	Netherlands	2.04[1]	n/a
		Dagab	Sweden	1.63[1]	n/a
		Tukospar	Finland	1.78[1]	n/a
		Total		15.48	
Inter Coop/ NAF Internat (1971)	Denmark	CCU	Bulgaria	1.83	13,000
		FDB	Denmark	3.54	1,276
		BVK	Germany	3.41	1,120
		SOK	Finland	3.02	1,138
		Tradeka	Finland	0.80	726
		FNCC	France	n/a	n/a
		CWS	UK	8.66	4,600
		AFEOSZ	Hungary	0.93	12,739
		Coop Union	Iceland	0.42	177
		Coop Italia	Italy	4.91	1,245
		JCCU	Japan	20.98	2,450
		NKL	Norway	2.23	1,291
		KF	Sweden	5.65	1,812
		Coop Union	Slovakia	0.49	6,636
		Total		56.87	48,210
SEDD (1994)	Not known	Sainsbury	UK	13.21	419
		Esselunga	Italy	1.49[1]	75[1]
		Delhaize	Belgium	8.06[1]	1,377[1]
		Docks de France	France	4.84[1]	1,451[1]
		Total		27.60	3,322
Total of all alliances				305.26[5]	131,975[6]

Notes:
1. 1992.
2. Estimate.
3. Edeka joined AMS in January 1995. Edeka owns 1,650 shops itself and supplies 9,950 independent retailers (Handelsblatt, 1994).
4. NAF is an alliance itself.
5. NAF is excluded from Deuro to prevent double counting.
6. Excludes BIGS.

Source: Adapted from IGD (1994).

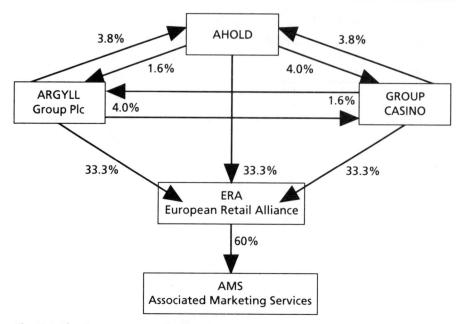

Fig. 7.1 The European Retail Alliance

Previous work (Robinson and Clarke-Hill, 1993) examined the differences between the ERA and its operational subsidiary the AMS and concluded that the ERA was more concerned with the strategic interrelationships between its members and was in particular aimed at developing potential synergies between them. A caveat must be made concerning the nature of the cross shareholding between the partners in that it is really more token in nature than a true attempt at an equity stake in each other. Indeed, the ERA could be seen as being championed by one man, namely Albert Hejn, the chairman of Ahold. An important feature of the ERA is that it is confined to only the three founding members who see no further additions in the foreseeable future. The ERA owns 60 per cent of the AMS, which is a looser form of alliance where there is evidence of members entering and leaving over time. The ERA's long-term benefits were described by Sir Alistair Grant, chairman of Argyll, as follows: 'Perhaps above all, the retail alliance has helped our team become serious about Europe. I believe that our successors will be grateful for this.' Kanter (1994) suggests that: 'Externally, the ERA opens borders. Inside member companies, it opens minds.'

The second alliance type, namely the alliance with central secretariat, extends further than the equity participating alliance in terms of the number of alliances and the retailers that comprise their membership. Such an alliance can be defined as:

An international alliance of a number of retail groups that form together and create a central secretariat for the purpose of co-ordinating operational activities — buying, branding, expertise exchange and product marketing. (Robinson and Clarke-Hill, 1994)

The distinguishing feature is the existence of a formal centre, often in a neutral location, to act as a focal point for the group. To date, the range of activities performed by the centres is limited, and excludes order processing and central payments, but over time these roles are likely to take on a more strategic focus with the development of pan-European retailer brands.

There are a number of common (and uncommon) features in the working of these retail alliances (Robinson and Clarke-Hill, 1995), as detailed below.

7.2.1 Supplier selection

A key constituent of any retail alliance is the benefit that members derive from operating as a coherent group rather than as individuals. This implies a functional shift of supplier selection away from the individual member towards the group centre.

There is no evidence yet of the alliance centre being solely responsible for supplier selection decisions. In some instances, supplier selection is jointly undertaken between the individual retailer and the alliance centre. In other instances, supplier selection remains firmly in the domain of the individual retailer. In two cases, there were variations within the alliance itself.

In most instances, a change of supplier is based on criteria of price and performance. However, in the case of the AMS, strategic motives were present in the change of suppliers as members attempted to move towards a pan-European supply network.

7.2.2 Buying price policy

The international nature of much of the supply side suggests that the lowest supply price to any individual member of the alliance will act as a 'benchmark' price for the alliance as a whole. Where central purchasing is in existence, price advantage flows to all members, suggesting that the alliance is attempting to countervail the power of the supplier.

Often the presence of common pricing, discounts, sharing of 'deals' and other price matters exists amongst members. It is important to note that price relationships involve two-way flows between the alliance centre to the member company, as well as the flow from one member company to the centre and then onwards to other members. This creates a network of price intelligence and bargaining positions.

7.2.3 Operational order processing

As retail alliances develop, the nature of the alliance will evolve from a loose federation of members seeking price advantages, into an institution-alised form that would suggest a 'tighter' relationship. To some extent, this evolution is taking place – but slowly. With the exception of InterCoop (NAF), it is the company rather than the alliance centre that raises the order, processes routine reorders and pays the supplier. InterCoop (NAF) operates in a different way and is worthy of separate mention. In certain cir-cumstances, orders are raised by both the company and the centre and rou-tine reorders are channelled through, consolidated and paid for by the group. This could be explained by the import activity on the non-food side of NAF, where there are significant differences in buying methods when compared with grocery purchasing. The other interesting exceptions to the rule are that some form of centralised payment system is likely to be devel-oped by the EMD, and the Inter Group (BIGS) alliance is currently partially operating centralised payment. In both cases, these are groups that tend to consist of a large number of small size stores.

7.2.4 Co-ordination within the alliances

All the retail alliances have a central organisation of some kind that deals with alliance matters and contact with member companies. The member companies usually, but not always, have an executive who is responsible for company/alliance co-ordination. The organisational seniority of co-ordinators from member companies to the alliance centre varies consider-ably and is dependent on national differences. Two Co-op retailers reported no designated executive charged with alliance co-ordination. In those two companies, the relationship with the centre was essentially at the lower product buyer level. In addition to co-ordinator to centre liaison, co-ordinators of member firms also meet together. The frequency of these meetings varies by alliance and even within an alliance itself. Product buyers' contacts tends to be more frequent and are dependent on types of product being purchased. Clearly, some form of transfer of learning is taking place.

7.2.5 Matters discussed at alliance meetings

The following topics are 'always' discussed at co-ordinator meetings: prices, range policy, supplier relationships, discount structures. On the other hand, promotions and merchandising are only discussed on a 'sometimes' basis, the exception being the AMS alliance meetings where promotions are dis-cussed regularly and the terminology of the 'fighting brand' is used to describe marketing strategy. Other discussion topics include budgets and policy, buying methods and organisation, private label strategy, new market information, transportation and logistics, as well as other operational details.

These activities suggest that this type of alliance operates more as a 'buy-ing club' than an alliance with a truly strategic focus. The benefits of alliance membership, as perceived by some of their members, are broadly operational in nature, namely: better prices, control of quality, marketing information, new product ideas, training and education, better European deals, own-label development, better European communications. However, as competences are transferred and organisational learning is institutionalised, these alliances may evolve from a mainly operational to a strategic focus. Thus the alliances will become of strategic importance to individual retailers: 'Business alliances are living systems, evolving progressively in their possibilities' (Kanter, 1994).

7.3 ALLIANCES: A WIDER PERSPECTIVE

Significant parts of the retail literature have examined the international nature of retailing, for example Hollander (1970), Jefferys (1973), Salmon and Tordjman (1989), Segal-Horn and Davison (1992), Dawson and Burt (1989), Treadgold (1988, 1989, 1990), Kacker (1988), Burt (1989, 1991) and Pellegrini (1991). This body of literature has mainly studied cross-border movements and internationalisation motives rather than the mechanisms involved in international retailer activity. The two alliance types described above provide only a limited explanation of the phenomenon of retailer internationalisation. In addition to these two alliance types, a number of other 'alliance' types can be identified.

7.3.1 Loose affiliations

These are defined as organisations whose primary functions are to act as focal points for their members. Essentially, these are trade bodies engaged in research and dissemination of market data as well as political lobbying. Examples include the Retail Consortium and the Institute of Grocery Distribution in the UK. In mainland Europe, most nation states have similar trade bodies, e.g. Conseil National du Commerce in France and Hauptgemeinschaft des Deutschen Einzelhandels in Germany. In addition, there is a Europe-wide trade body entitled CECD (Confédération Européenne du Commerce de Détail) (Eurostat, 1993). Also within this category can be included 'task forces' set up by retailers with specific objectives to achieve. Examples include: the examination of in-store security at both local and national levels, the analysis of trends in music hardware and software which would impact on range policy, and retailer-to-retailer arrangements to share the distribution costs in the supply of goods to stores in remote locations.

7.3.2 The national buying club

These are defined as buying organisations that exist for the benefit of their members predominantly within one nation state, whose main purpose is the procurement of merchandise and maximisation of purchasing power. Often members of buying clubs compete with each other in the same market. Typically, this form of alliance has been in existence in France for many years and examples include Paridoc and FNCC. In some instances, a buying club may have a very limited transnational dimension, e.g. Diffra (France) which has included the Belgian Delhaize group.

Within the UK, the Nisa Today group falls into this category, along with Tiger, which is a buying group of independent electrical retailers. A recent paper on UK domestic buying groups (Shaw *et al*, 1994) develops this point very clearly.

7.3.3 Co-marketing agreements

Co-marketing alliances are a form of working partnerships that are defined by Anderson and Narus (1990) as: '... the mutual recognition and under-standing that the success of each firm depends in part on the other firm ...' Bucklin and Sengupta (1993) suggest that such alliances are:

> contractual relationships undertaken by firms whose respective products are com-plements in the marketplace, and are intended to amplify and/or build user aware-ness of benefits derived from these complementarities. They involve co-ordination among the partners in one or more aspects of marketing.

The Bucklin and Sengupta definition must be slightly adapted from the high technology sector, on which the research was based, into the retailing con-text. This entails a broader definition of the word 'product' to encompass retailing skills and competences, retail formats, brand values and space assets. Thus, this definition is wider in scope, encompassing a range of co-marketing activities whereby one retailer joins with one or more partners for the specific purpose of engaging in some form of marketing activity. A co-marketing agreement may later develop into a joint venture.

This activity is illustrated by the business format franchising of Benneton, Tie Rack and Sock Shop. Marks & Spencer's co-marketing activities, in the form of the operation of shops within shops and licensing agreements with partners in Spain and Hungary, also fall into this category. Other examples include Storehouse's franchising agreements for its Mothercare brand in the Middle East, Burton Group's in-store concessions in the Spanish department store Galarias Preciados, Sears' shop-in-shop operation under its Olympus format also in Galarias Preciados, and Alexon's concessions in a number of mainland European department stores.

7.3.4 Joint ventures

Harrigan's (1988) definition of joint ventures as being 'business agreements where two or more owners create a separate entity' can be said to apply equally well to retailer joint ventures as to those in other industrial sectors.

They involve one or more partners joining together to create a new identity with a specific purpose.

Examples at a national level of such joint ventures include Boots and WH Smith's UK joint venture in creating the Do It All chain. At a transnational level, this format can be illustrated by J Sainsbury (UK) and GB (Belgium) forming the UK DIY chain Homebase, Littlewoods and Gostinyi Dvor (Russia) opening a department store in St Petersburg, Kingfisher and Staples (US) to form the Office Superstore, Sears and Groupe André (France) to develop André Deutchland and Sears Hoogenbosch (Netherlands).

7.3.5 Partial acquisition and equity participation

Such an alliance is defined as one retailer acquiring a minority equity stake in another retailer, for the purpose of either achieving strategic leverage in terms of technology transfer in either or both directions, or as a precursor to a full acquisition. In all cases, this form of alliance can be seen as strategic.

Examples of such alliances include the French mail order company La Redoute's minority stake in the UK's Empire Stores, Carrefour's holding in Costco of the USA, Littlewoods' 20 per cent stake in Price Costco Europe, Sainsbury's 1994 purchase of a minority stake in Giant Stores of the USA, and Rewe's 29.4 per cent holding in Budgens.

7.3.6 Controlling interest or full merger with retained identity of subsidiary

This type of alliance involves the acquisition of the majority equity of another retailer where control passes to the acquirer; this may also involve a total acquisition or a majority controlling interest. In this case, the identity of the acquired company is retained, otherwise it could not be said to be an alliance. Often this form is used as a means of market entry to sidestep barriers to entry. Examples of this type include Tesco's control of Catteau (France), Kingfisher's acquisition of Darty (France), Marks & Spencer's purchases of Brooks Brothers (USA), Kings Supermarkets (USA) and D'Alliards (Canada), Sainsbury's purchase of Shaws (USA) and Iceland's acquisition of Au Gel (France).

7.3.7 Summary

The six alliance forms described above can be combined with the two alliance types discussed earlier in the chapter to form a hierarchy of alliance types. It is useful to view this hierarchy in terms of the degree of organisational infrastructure linkage between members in a 'loose to tight' continuum of organisational relationships. Figure 7.2 overleaf, conceptualises this in diagrammatic form.

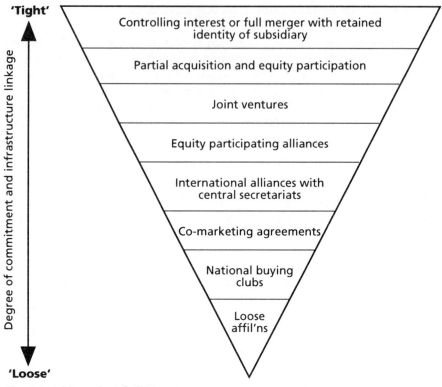

Fig. 7.2 A hierarchy of alliance types

7.4 MULTIPLE ALLIANCE STRATEGIES

Use of the various methods outlined in the hierarchy above should not be seen as mutually exclusive. Retailers may, and often do, pursue multiple alliance strategies and strategic goals. Such a case is Marks & Spencer, with their co-marketing activities in Europe and the Far East, as well as their history of acquisitions in North America. In some instances, notably among smaller retail groups, a 'nested' hierarchy of alliances may occur, operating at both the national and the international levels. An example of this is the UK domestic buying club of Nisa, which in turn is a member of the larger European alliance EMD.

Many retailers follow a simple multi-alliance strategy. However, in the case of J Sainsbury, the company is involved in a web of alliance relationships. It has entered into a joint venture with GB Inno of Belgium in order to enter the UK DIY market; a partial acquisition leading to full control with retained identity of Shaws in the USA in order to enter the US grocery market; a formal alliance with a central secretariat, namely SEDD; co-marketing agreements in its Homebase operation with Laura Ashley; and the 1994 acquisitions of minority holdings in Giant of the USA and Docks de France.

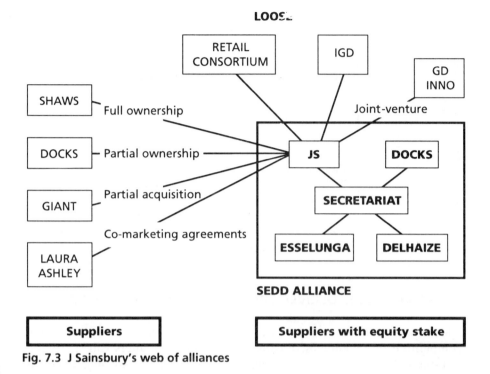

Fig. 7.3 J Sainsbury's web of alliances

Along with these alliances, the company is also involved in trade associations. Thus, one retailer is pursuing six separate alliance strategies simultaneously. This horizontal web of relationships is further complicated by the inevitable vertical web of relationships within the supply chain, including some partially and wholly owned suppliers. Horizontal alliances often result in suppliers and systems being transferred among alliance members to their mutual advantage.

The complexity of this is shown in Figure 7.3. The vertical web of relationships is specifically excluded, as the diagram would lose its clarity.

The concept of a hierarchy of alliances can be linked with the national versus international dimension of such alliances. This concept is illustrated in Figure 7.4 (overleaf).

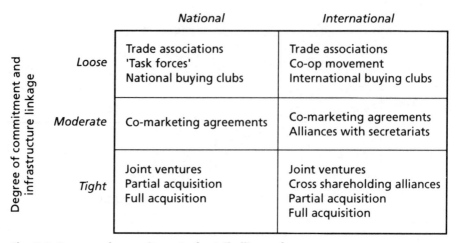

Fig. 7.4 Scope and commitment of retail alliance forms

7.5 ADVANTAGES DERIVED FROM ALLIANCE MEMBERSHIP

Alliances are formed in order to overcome certain inherent, or perceived, competitive disadvantages. By forming alliances, retailers can share and transfer skills and capabilities among their partners. The advantages accruing from membership are both strategic and operational in nature. Typically, they would include: economies of buying, brand image transfer, trading format transfer, market entry, enhanced competitive position and financial power. Different alliance forms may achieve different benefits to members.

Table 7.2 on page 146 tabulates likely benefits within predominant alliance types. It does not specifically label those advantages as either operational or strategic in nature. The reason for this is that often members of an alliance have differing motivations for membership.

CONCLUSIONS

In concluding this chapter, more questions are perhaps raised than answers are offered. In order to understand fully retail alliances, *all* of the horizontal linkages that bind retailers together must be studied rather than merely studying a limited range of alliance types.

In summary five sets of issues can be highlighted for further investigation and discussion.

1. Alliances are ubiquitous in Europe and are growing by the day. They represent a considerable and increasing number of retailers and collective market share. This raises the question – will retailer autonomy eventually be eroded?

Table 7.2 Key benefits and alliance types

Key benefits	Predominant alliance types
1. Common voice in the trade/political arena	• Loose affiliations (trade associations)
2. Situation-specific and short-term advantages	• Loose affiliations (task forces)
3. Buying economies/buying power	• National buying clubs • International alliances with central secretariats
4. Brand and image transfer	• International alliances with central secretariats • Co-marketing agreements • Equity participating alliances • Partial acquisitions • Full acquisition
5. Trading format skills	• International alliances with central secretariats • Equity participating alliances • Joint ventures
6. Procurement in specific product areas	• National buying clubs • International alliances with central secretariats
7. Promotional skills	• International alliances with central secretariats • Equity participating alliances • Co-marketing agreements
8. Systems and technology skills	• International alliances with central secretariats • Equity participating alliances
9. High speed international growth and geographic market extension	• Joint ventures • Partial acquisition • Full acquisition
10. Market entry into new product segments and trading formats	• Co-marketing agreements • Joint ventures
11. Financial investment	• Joint venture • Partial acquisition • Full acquisition
12. Protection from market entry	• International alliances with central secretariats • Equity participating alliances • Partial acquisition • Full acquisition
13. Protection from takeover	• International alliances with central secretariats • Equity participating alliances • Partial acquisition • Full acquisition
14. Enhanced competitive position for subordinate players	• National buying clubs • International alliances with central secretariats • Equity participating alliances

2. Is Europe becoming a single entity in the context of greater consumer convergence, with the likelihood of Euro-manufacturer brands competing with Euro-retailer brands?
3. Is alliance formation merely a question of retailers retaliating to the increasing power of the manufacturer? Are horizontal relationships between retailers being created to countervail the power of horizontal relationships between manufacturers, particularly in the food industry?
4. Does the formation of retailing alliances change the way in which competitive advantage in retailing is achieved? Issues of competition, co-operation and collusion need serious analysis. Is the nature of competition going to change from 'retailer versus retailer' to one of 'alliance versus alliance' within a domestic market?
5. Will the European alliance concept extend to other parts of the globe? There is some evidence that this may be happening. For example, the US retailer Wal-Mart and Ito-Yokado have recently entered an agreement under which Wal-Mart will supply its own brand products to the Japanese retailer. Aoyama Trading, a leading Japanese menswear retailer, is to tie up with J C Penney, the US department store chain, to sell J C Penney's casual wear in Japan. Yaohan, a Japanese retail and distribution chain based in Hong Kong, will market Wal-Mart products in Asia. Wal-Mart in Mexico is opening a chain of warehouse clubs and discount stores in a joint venture with the Mexican retailer Cifra. The Wal-Mart link with Ito-Yokado is reciprocated by the Japanese retailer providing Wal-Mart with point-of-sale systems to improve Wal-Mart's efficiency in shelf management. In addition, the two companies are to jointly develop low cost products and plan to co-operate in expanding sales networks in Asia and Europe (*Financial Times*, 1994).

If this is the case, what impact do alliances have on the traditional way in which we view competitive advantage in retailing?

REVIEW QUESTIONS

1. To what extent does the 'global village' have 'global shops'?
2. Review the motives that retailers have for entering into horizontal alliances with other retailers. How do such retailers gain competitive advantage from alliance membership?
3. Discuss the way in which retail alliances of various types alter the traditional relationships between individual retailers and their suppliers.
4. Identify potential areas of conflict among members of retail alliances. Discuss how such conflict might be resolved.
5. 'Externally, the ERA opens borders. Inside member companies, it opens minds' (Kanter, 1994). Critically appraise this statement within the context of retail alliances in general.

6. Explain the ways in which alliances may co-operate in the future development of pan-European retail brands.

REFERENCES

Anderson, J C and Narus, J A (1990) 'A model of distributor firm and manufacturer firm working partnerships', *Journal of Marketing*, 54 (January), 42–58.

Bucklin, L P and Sengupta, S (1993) 'Organising successful co-marketing alliances', *Journal of Marketing*, 57 (April), 32–46.

Burt S L (1989) 'Trends and management issues in European retailing', *International Journal of Retailing*, 4(4), 1–97.

Burt S L (1991) 'Trends in the internationalisation of grocery retailing: the European experience', *International Review of Retail, Distribution and Consumer Research*, 1(4), 487–515.

Cravens, D W, Shipp, S H and Cravens, K S (1993) 'Analysis of co-operative interorganisational relationships, strategic alliance formation, and strategic alliance effectiveness', *Journal of Strategic Marketing*, 1, 55–70.

Dawson J A and Burt S L, (1989) *The Internationalisation of British Retailing*, Institute of Retail Studies, University of Stirling.

Dawson, J A and Shaw, S A (1992) *Interfirm alliances in the retail sector: evolutionary, strategic, and tactical issues in their creation and management, University of Edinburgh Working Paper Series*, No. 92/7.

Eurostat (1993) *Retailing in the European Single Market*, Commission of the European Communities Statistical Office, Brussels, p 212.

Financial Times (1994) 'Wal-Mart to supply Japanese chain', 24 March, p 30.

Groupe Casino (1990) *Annual Report*.

Handelsblatt (1994) Die Marktführerschaft in den neuen Bundesländern würde weiter ausgebaut, 24 March, p 27.

Harrigan, K R (1985) *Strategies for Joint Ventures*, Lexington Books, Lexington Massachusetts.

Harrigan, K R (1986) *Managing for Joint Venture Success*, Lexington Books, Lexington, Massachusetts.

Harrigan, K R (1988) 'Joint Ventures and Competitive Strategy', *Strategic Management Journal*, 9, 141–158.

Hergert, M and Morris, D, (1987) *Trends in International Collaborative Agreements*, in Contractor, F and Lorange, P (eds), *Co-operative Strategies in International Business*, Lexington Books, Lexington, Massachussets, pp 99–110.

Hollander S C (1970) *Multinational Retailing*, MSU, East Lancing.

Kacker M (1988) 'International flow of retailing know-how: bridging the technology gap in distribution', *Journal of Retailing*, 64(1), 4–67.

Kanter, R M (1989) 'Becoming PALS: pooling, allying and linking across companies', *Academy of Management Executive*, 3, 183–193.

Kanter, R M (1994) 'Collaborative advantage', *Harvard Business Review*, July/August, 96–108.

Kogut, B (1988) 'Joint ventures: theoretical and empirical perspectives', *Strategic Management Journal*, 9, 319–332.

Nielsen, R P (1988) 'Co-operative strategy', *Strategic Management Journal*, 9, 475–492.

Pellegrini L (1991) 'The Internationalisation of Retailing and 1992 Europe', *CESCOM*, Note de Ricerca 23, Università Bocconi, Milan.

Retail Directory, (1993), 47th edn, Newman Books, London.

Robinson T M and Clarke-Hill, C M (1990) 'Directional growth by European retailers', *International Journal of Retail and Distribution Management*, 18(5), 3–14.

Robinson, T M and Clarke-Hill, C M (1993a) 'International alliances in European retailing', *ESRC Seminar on International Retailing*, UMIST, Manchester, March 1993.

Robinson, T M and Clarke-Hill, C M (1993b) 'European retail alliances: the ERA experience', in Baker, M (ed.), *Perspectives in Marketing Management,* Vol.3, J Wiley, Chichester, UK, pp 47–63.

Robinson, T M and Clarke-Hill, C M (1994) 'Competitive advantage through strategic retail alliances: a European perspective', presented at *Recent Advances in Retailing and Service Science Conference,* University of Alberta, Canada, May 1994.

Robinson, T M, and Clarke-Hill, C M (1995) 'International alliances in European retailing', *International Review of Retail, Distribution and Consumer Research,* January.

Salmon W J and Tordjman A (1989) 'The internationalisation of retailing', *International Journal of Retailing,* 4(2), 3–16.

Segal-Horn S and Davison H (1992) 'Global markets, the global consumer and international retailing', *Journal of Global Marketing,* 5(3), 31–62.

Shaw, S A, Dawson, J A and Harris, N (1994) 'The characteristics and functions of retail buying groups in the United Kingdom: results from a survey', *International Review of Retail, Distribution and Consumer Research,* 4(1), 83–105.

Treadgold A (1988) 'Retailing without frontiers', *Retail and Distribution Management,* 16(6), 8–12.

Treadgold A (1989) '1992: the retail response to a changing Europe', *Marketing Research Today,* 17(3), 161–166.

Treadgold A (1990) 'The developing internationalisation of retailing', *International Journal of Retail and Distribution Management,* 18(2), 4–11.

CHAPTER 8

Retail franchising in Britain and Italy

Angelo Manaresi and Mark Uncles

INTRODUCTION

A franchise is a legal agreement where one party, the franchisor, allows another, the franchisee, the right to sell a product or conduct a business that has been developed by the franchisor. Hoffman and Preble (1991) identify three different bases for a franchise: product, business or business conversion. Typically, a retail franchise is an example of a business franchise and a product franchise rolled into one. Thus the Body Shop operates with very much the same design of shop and with the same operating systems throughout the world. Also many of the same Body Shop products are sold throughout the world. Customers of the retail franchise may not be aware that they are shopping at a private business, that of the franchisee. To them a franchised chain appears very much as any multiple retailer.

In general, franchising has become a major force in many Western nations. Some estimates show that one-third of all retail sales in the USA come from franchises, but these claims are based on a broad definition that includes gasoline service stations and automobile dealers which together account for 70 per cent of total sales (Stern and El-Ansary, 1988). Even using a narrower definition, we can say that by 1988 there were 2,200 franchisors in the United States, operating through 370,000 franchised outlets and accounting for $190 bn in sales (Mendelsohn, 1992: Table 1.1).

A similar situation has arisen in much of Europe, stimulated by the European Commission which sees franchising as a way to encourage and develop entrepreneurship. Regulation 4087/88 (30 November 1988) allows members of a franchise to act in ways which would otherwise violate normal EC competition rules (Mendelsohn, 1992: Appendix B) – particularly with regard to exclusive territorial rights, location clauses, the sale of exclusive goods and the protection of franchisor know-how.

Any retailer who is intending to expand internationally, or who is already operating in different countries, is likely to have a keen interest in franchising – if only because the costs and risks of developing and managing overseas operations can be huge, and franchising represents a way to contain these problems. The main attractions are similar to those which apply in domestic markets, notably the use of the financial resources of franchisees to bring about geographical expansion. In an international context this also means gaining access to local banks and other lenders, assembling local business knowledge, and being close to local customers (Stern and El-Ansary, 1988; Welch, 1987). However, there are some dangers – the brand is not necessarily known overseas, the franchisor's know-how does not necessarily transfer, and the economic system will differ (in terms of culture, language, lifestyle, habits, business attitudes and legislation). The onus, therefore, is on the franchisor to prove himself (with a pilot scheme, say) before entering a new market on a large scale.

Despite these barriers, the appeal of franchising is illustrated by the fact that in the 1980s it became a major mode of entry into overseas markets by British retailers, accounting for 24 per cent of all foreign retail investments, up from a mere 3 per cent in the 1960s (Burt, 1995). On a wider scale, franchising has become one of the most popular entry modes for Western firms moving into the newly opened Eastern European markets.

When the franchise option is being considered as the vehicle for internationalisation rather than for growth in a domestic market, a number of issues arise. For example, compatibility of culture is often used as a criterion for identifying attractive markets to export a product or a business format. If the franchise has to be modified substantially to make it acceptable to a different culture, then the benefits of franchising as a means of international growth are reduced by the added complexity to the core business.

The more obvious changes to a retail franchise that might be required are changes to the trading format due to differences in legislation between countries or to differences in consumer tastes. Less obvious, but by no means less important, are possible differences in management style and method. Is it possible to use the same internal management of franchises in different geographical markets?

The purpose of this chapter is to explore the question of internal management by comparing retail franchises operating in Britain and Italy. Somewhat surprisingly, we find that many aspects of management are similar in the franchises operating in the two countries, despite differences in language and culture. This is not to say that everything is identical, but rather that enough commonalities exist to show that imposing a common management style may not be an issue in the geographical expansion of a franchise.

8.1 FRANCHISING IN ITALY AND BRITAIN

We will be concentrating on *Italy* and *Britain*, two countries where franchising is now well established. One factor that makes this comparison particularly relevant is that among British retailers franchising is the most popular entry mechanism when investing in South European markets such as Italy (Burt, 1995). In these cases the perception of risk is quite high (there are important cultural and linguistic differences, commercial practices differ, regulations have yet to be harmonised despite the European Union – all these considerations affect the manager's perception of risk).

Although this study is confined to two countries, we suggest that a multi-country study would be even more revealing for managers, and this is something which we would strongly encourage for the future. It is our view that international research demands carefully conducted replications, and a two-country study of the type reported here is only the first step in this direction (Kale and McIntyre, 1991; Uncles *et al*, 1994).

Most Italian franchises are in the retail sector, with well-known brand names such as Stefanel, Buffetti, Coin, Gruppo Bata, Gruppo VeGe, and the retail operations of the telecom service, SIP. In 1988 there were 200 Italian franchisors (over 80 per cent of them retailers), with sales of $3.4 bn (excluding the auto industry). Many British franchises are in the retail sector too, notably catering/food, fashion and fast printing, with leading names such as Tie Rack, Clarks Shoes, Kall-Kwik and Prontaprint. Overall, the 380 franchisors in Britain generated some $7.6 bn in sales in 1990 (excluding the auto sector), and some 60 per cent of these were retail operations. (For a more exhaustive survey of the whole industry in Britain see Forward and Fulop, 1993.)

We see, therefore, that there are enough equivalent franchises for us to administer similar questionnaires and draw meaningful comparisons. The only problem with this focused approach is that we ignore service franchising – our ability to represent the breadth of British franchising is traded-off against our desire for matched comparisons.

8.1.1 Management issues

The nature of managing a franchise operation differs markedly from that of managing a subsidiary or a retail unit in a multiple operation. The franchisee and franchisor normally sign formal contracts. The franchisee contracts to operate the franchise in a prescribed way and remunerates the franchisor with a capital sum, a royalty or by agreeing to purchase product for resale. In return the franchisor provides training, brand support, consultancy and exclusivity of territory.

Despite the existence of a legal agreement (or perhaps as a consequence of this) conflict often occurs between the two parties. In theory, conflict can be resolved by the franchisor exerting power over the franchisee, demanding compliance or agreement under threat of ending the franchise agreement. But, unless both are losing money or see an obvious advantage in going their separate ways, they are bound together by their mutual dependency. Both need the other to ensure the success of their business, although the franchisee's dependency will generally be higher than that of the franchisor.

Relationships between members of any marketing channel can be complex and there has been a great deal of academic research into a number of aspects of channel relationships. In this chapter we report the results of a study of relationships between franchisees and franchisors using a number of the concepts found by such research to be important in the management of marketing channels.

8.2 THE STUDY OF FRANCHISOR–FRANCHISEE RELATIONSHIPS

For our in-depth research study, data were collected from both franchisors and franchisees to obtain a rounded picture of the relationships between the two parties. For practical reasons we undertook a sample survey by randomly selecting franchises and then identifying key informants.

8.2.1 The sample

Listed in the official directories of each local franchising association were roughly 200 retail franchises (Associazione Italiana del Franchising, 1990; British Franchising Association, 1990). Our final sample of 30 franchises in each country represented 15 per cent of all these retail franchises. In each case a personal interview was held with the franchisor and with at least one franchisee, and a larger number of franchisees were randomly selected from company lists for a mail survey. This resulted in 120 personal interviews (30 franchisors from Britain, and another 30 from Italy; 30 franchisees from Britain, and another 30 from Italy). These were supplemented by 293 replies from a mail survey using the same questionnaire (147 franchisees returned questionnaires in Britain, and another 146 in Italy).

8.2.2 The survey

The person responsible for managing channel relationships (usually called the franchise manager) was our key franchisor informant; these individuals were readily identified during an initial telephone call. The person who ran the franchise unit (usually the one who signed the franchise contract) was our key franchisee informant, and these were randomly selected from lists provided by franchisors. This approach suffers from survivor bias in that we focus on existing franchises, and do not consider those who have failed, nor those who are eagerly waiting to sign a contract. This common bias can be tackled using long-run cohort studies, but these have problems of their own. What we are able to provide here is a snapshot – a picture that includes those about to fail and those who have only just joined a franchise, as well as true survivors.

For the personal interviews a structured questionnaire was administered to respondents; this enabled us to obtain complete answers and monitor the context of the interview. On the downside, this meant that the sample was smaller than it might otherwise have been – 120 personal interviews. However, a further 293 mail questionnaires were completed by other franchisees in the same franchises.

All groups of respondents were asked virtually identical questions, with only minor changes of wording to allow for the slightly different roles of the two different sets of managers. A number of descriptive questions were asked to help us characterise the franchises (size of company, years of experience, etc.). These were followed by a list of perceptual questions, enabling us to gauge respondents' views of power, dependence and so forth.

A particular problem was the translation of the questionnaire into the respondents' mother-tongue; to deal with this questionnaires were prepared in English, translated into Italian by the first author, and translated back into English by a native speaker. The two English versions were compared and the differences analysed and normalised. This procedure of double translation was designed to ensure consistency and comparability of the answers (Sechrest, Faye and Zaidi, 1972). A thorough pilot study was also undertaken (see Manaresi, 1993, for details; also Manaresi and Marcati, 1991).

8.3 A MODEL OF RELATIONSHIPS IN A FRANCHISE

To help guide our research we constructed a model of how a number of factors or variables might interact within a franchise organisation (Figure 8.1). We examined each factor by asking similar questions of franchisees and franchisors concerning their relationships. Each variable was appraised by asking a number of similar questions, placed at different points in the questionnaire. For example, the variable 'power' (the potential of one party to get the other to do

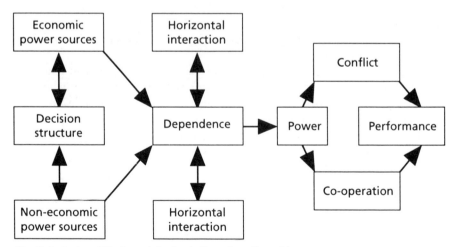

Fig. 8.1 A simplified model of relations in a franchise

something they might not otherwise have done) is measured using 16 different questions or statements that respondents were asked to agree with or not (by marking a Likert scale). Here are two examples:

> Because of its position, the franchisor has the right to influence our behaviour. If we do not do as the franchisor suggests, our life will be made difficult.

If a franchisee agreed with both of these statements it would indicate that their franchisor was perceived to exercise power over him. There was something that would ensure the franchisee complied with the franchisor's wishes.

Respondents were asked about their perception of the ability of the franchisor to control hours of operation, product displays, local advertising, stock levels, etc. Each question took the form of a seven point scale ranging from strongly agree to strongly disagree.

A 'score' for power could then be calculated by averaging the responses for all the power questions for all respondents of each type. In the tables of results given later in this chapter, the variable POWER is used to label these particular results. The higher the scores, the greater the perceived level of power. This can differ from the actual control exercised by the franchisor (Dahl, 1957; Hunt and Nevin, 1974) but it is generally held that the potential to influence or direct is more relevant than the exercise of actual power.

The source of power is also held to be an important issue (French and Raven, 1959; Pfeffer and Salancik, 1978; Gaski, 1984). In common with many previous studies we differentiated between sources which were 'hard' or economic such as financial rewards, penalties (coercion) and legal (legitimate) obligations, and those which were 'soft' or non-economic such as an acknowledgement that one party was more expert than the other. (The two sample questions mentioned earlier represent different sources of power.) In earlier studies the use of hard sources for power has been linked to an increased likelihood of conflict. The five sources used were those of French and Raven (1959) and labelled as REWARD, COERC (coercion) and LEGIT (legitimate), the hard sources of power, and EXPERT and REFER (reference), the soft sources. Three questions were asked for each of the first four variables and four for REFER.

Conflict occurs when the objectives of two parties differ. The common objective for both franchisee and franchisor is to develop the franchisee's business. How this is best achieved and who should be responsible for what are sources of conflict, although we would expect the level or frequency of conflict to be low in a continuing relationship (Lusch, 1976; Etgar, 1978a; Brown and Day, 1981). Fifteen questions were asked for the variable CONFREQ (conflict frequency).

The antithesis of conflict is co-operation, the view that 'we're all in this together'. Some co-operation is essential in a franchise (Schul and Babakus, 1988) but the intensity or level of co-operation will vary. The intensity of co-operation, its strength and relevance, were measured using six questions for the variable CO-OP.

How dependent the franchisee and franchisor are on each other will determine the willingness of either party to continue with the relationship. The difficulty of exiting from such a relationship is another measure of dependency (Emerson, 1962; Aldrich, 1976). Four questions were used to assess the variable DEPN (dependency).

The way decisions are reached in a marketing channel can be very formalised or it can be participatory. A formulated approach is typified by the use of written guidelines and instructions. A participatory approach would involve the franchisee in matters such as setting standards or allocating promotional budgets. The measure FORMAL (formality of decision making) was assessed using three questions and the measure PARTIC (participation in decision making) assessed using three questions.

The level of interaction between members of the same franchise could determine views on operational matters. Franchisees could be considered to represent a network and analysed as such (Cook and Emerson, 1978) although typically such relationships will be informal. The variable HORZ-INF (horizontal interaction) used fifteen questions to assess this issue.

Finally, the outcome from the franchise relationship will affect perceptions of the relationship. We chose to assess perceived performance by measuring satisfaction with the outcome versus expectations and an assessment of performance trends. PERF1 (expectations) and PERF2 (trends) were the names used to represent these variables.

8.4 RESULTS AND FINDINGS

8.4.1 The characteristics of the sample

Ideally we would like the samples of Italian and British franchises to match in every possible way so that any differences in management relationships are likely to be due to country-specific factors rather than differences in the type of business in each sample. Table 8.1 identifies the size of franchises sampled. Most had more than 50 outlets and the samples are very similar on this measure. Table 8.2 shows that the majority of franchisees had been

Table 8.1 The size of franchises

Number of outlets in franchises	% of franchisees		
	Italy	Britain	Total
$5 \leq n < 50$	39	40	40
$n > 50$	61	60	60
Total	100	100	100

Note:
1. No franchises in the sample have less than five franchised outlets.

members for more than two years. This figure may have been affected by the economic recession when the data were being collected (October 1991 to February 1992) as fewer new franchisees would have been started during this period. There is little difference in experience within the two sub-samples but there is some difference in the backgrounds of the managers. Both sub-samples contained large numbers who were not experienced managers or entrepreneurs. This is particularly true of the British sample. As envisaged by the EU, franchising has helped to create a new cadre of entrepreneurs at least in Britain.

In Italy the picture is somewhat different – well over a third of the sample had previously been independent retailers working in the same sector (often in fashion). Partly this situation arose because it is hard to obtain a licence from the local government to operate as a retailer in Italy, so franchisees tend to be drawn from those who already have a licence (i.e. the independent retailers). The appeal of franchising for an Italian manager, who might be in business already, is to obtain products and a store image that can help increase sales, whereas for the British manager it is also to foster the entrepreneurial spirit in a way that might otherwise be too hard or risky.

The benefit of obtaining exclusive products is reflected in the 64 per cent of franchisees who buy at least three-quarters of their product range from the franchisor or controlled suppliers – something that is common to Italy and Britain (Table 8.2(c)). With exclusive distribution the franchisor can create a form of dependence and control over the store image, and yet still find willing partners if the product assortment is itself appealing to franchisees and final customers.

Thus, in many respects the Italian and British samples are comparable. In addition to the characteristics described above, by design both samples were drawn from equally dispersed populations (from the North and South of both countries), and in equal measure from large and small towns (roughly 50 per cent from towns above 100,000 people and 50 per cent from smaller towns).

The only noteworthy differences are in the number of franchisees in some specific retail sectors (Table 8.3). While we have confined our analysis to retail franchising, and while similar numbers are drawn from the clothing and furniture sectors, there is a distinct bias towards stationery and bag retailers in Italy, and food and shoe retailers in Britain. These differences appear to reflect true differences in the structure of retail franchising in the two countries.

It is also the case that the degree to which the franchisor is willing or able to control the assortment of the franchisees varies across retail sectors and that there are some differences between the two national samples (Table 8.3). This is particularly so in the stationery, food and furniture sectors (where products can be prepared or assembled on site, depending on the business culture); by contrast, fashion assortment in the clothing and shoe sectors tends to be heavily controlled by franchisors in both nations.

Table 8.2 Some characteristics of the franchisees

Characteristics	% of franchisees		
	Italy	Britain	Total
(a) Duration of the franchise relationship:			
Less than 6 months	5	4	5
6 months to 1 year	11	10	11
1 to 2 years	17	11	14
2 to 5 years	34	44	39
More than 5 years	34	29	31
Missing values	0	2	1
Total	100	100	100
(b) Previous activity of the franchisees:			
Retailer in the same sector	37	16	27
Employed in another sector	17	32	24
Employed in the same sector	13	20	16
Owner/manager in another sector	13	16	14
Retailer in another sector	9	10	9
Franchisee in another franchise	5	4	5
Missing values	7	2	5
Total	100	100	100
(c) Percentage of assortment supplied or controlled by the franchisor:			
0%	1	18	9
1–25%	6	7	7
26–50%	11	7	9
51–75%	10	7	9
76–99%	36	26	31
100%	34	32	33
Missing values	2	2	2
Total	100	100	100

Notes:
1. Figures relate to franchisee responses from mail surveys and personal interviews.
2. Totals may not exactly add to 100 because of rounding.

Table 8.3 Retail sectors in which the franchisees operate

Retail sector	% of franchisees in specific retail sectors			Number of franchisees	% of assortment supplied or controlled by the franchisor		
	Italy	Britain	Total	Total	Italy	Britain	Total
Clothing	21	20	20	71	88	100	94
Stationery	30	10	20	71	68	19	55
Shoes	7	23	15	54	85	91	89
Food and restaurants	2	26	14	50	(33)	54	52
Furniture	14	12	13	46	79	30	55
Bags and accessories	12	1	6	22	99	(30)	96
Sports equipment	4	5	5	16	(100)	(77)	87
Telephones and computers	2	2	2	7	(26)	(20)	(24)
Beauty products	3	1	2	7	(94)	(85)	(91)
Lingerie	3	0	1	5	(88)	NA	(88)
Toys	2	0	1	4	(92)	NA	(92)
Total	100	100	100	353	80	66	73

Notes:
1. Figures relate to franchisee responses from mail surveys and personal interviews.
2. Each sub-section is arranged in accordance with the 'Total' column rank orders.
3. Totals may not exactly add to 100 because of rounding.
4. Classes where the number of responding franchisees is smaller than 10 are shown in round brackets – these figures should be treated with caution.

8.4.2 Relational variables in franchises

Here we compare the mean scores of the Likert scales with respect to the relational variables listed in section 8.3. Recollect that we are reporting the perceptions of the different respondents, not observed facts. The detailed figures are shown in Table 8.4.

The following conclusions are drawn from comparisons within each column:

1. Non-economic power sources (expert and referent power) are used heavily in most franchises (average scores on the 7-point Likert scales are above 5 for EXPERT and REFER, and, although we do not show them in the table, standard deviations are as low as 1.5). These scores exceed almost all others, indicating the perceived strength of non-economic power sources on the behaviour of franchisees.
2. By contrast franchise systems are largely managed without the heavy-handed use of coercive power sources (COERC), and reward power (REWARD) is also fairly neutral in its effect. The only economic power source to feature prominently in franchisees' perceptions is that associ-

Table 8.4 Average responses across the sampled franchises

Relational variable	Franchisees: Mail survey and personal interviews		Mail survey		Personal interviews		Franchisors: Personal interviews	
	Italian (176)	British (177)	Italian (146)	British (147)	Italian (30)	British (30)	Italian (30)	British (30)
Power sources:								
Non-economic								
EXPERT	5.7	5.1	5.7	5.2	6.0	4.7	6.5	5.7
REFER	5.4	5.3	5.4	5.3	5.4	5.0	5.5	5.6
Economic								
COERC	—	—	—	—	3.2	3.1	3.6	2.5
REWARD	—	—	—	—	3.5	3.1	3.5	4.3
LEGIT	—	—	—	—	3.6	4.8	4.9	5.5
FORMAL	5.0	5.0	5.0	5.1	4.7	4.5	5.2	5.9
PARTIC	4.8	4.8	4.9	4.9	4.0	3.9	5.1	5.7
DEPN	3.7	3.7	3.7	3.8	4.0	2.9	4.5	4.9
HORZINF	1.0	1.0	1.0	1.0	1.2	1.4	—	—
POWER	—	—	—	—	3.0	3.3	4.6	4.5
CONFREQ	3.1	2.9	3.2	2.8	2.6	3.4	3.0	3.1
COOP	—	—	—	—	1.8	1.7	2.6	3.6
PERF1	4.2	3.6	4.2	3.5	4.5	4.0	4.4	3.9
PERF2	4.5	4.1	4.4	4.0	4.8	4.5	4.4	4.5

Notes:
1. Sample sizes are in brackets.
2. Unmeasured variables are shown as '—'.
3. All variables except HORZINF are measured with 7-point scales: a response of 7 means 'high' or 'very much', 4 is a neutral mid-point, and a response of 1 means 'low' or 'not at all'. HORZINF is measured with a 5-point scale: 4 means frequent exchange of information; 0 indicates no exchange.

ated with legitimation (LEGIT). This implies that the contractual arrangement applied in most franchises, even if not very tight, is a constant point of reference for all parties.

3. Overall perceptions of power (POWER) are such that franchisees and franchisors believe they have an equal say over decision-making, i.e. each party is confident about its own say over commercial policies at the retail level. In part this arises from the counterbalancing of power sources, but it may also reflect the desire of all concerned to think they have power (whether or not they actually do).

4. Given the use of non-economic power sources over economic ones, and the perception that power is evenly balanced, it is not surprising to find low levels of conflict (average scores on the 7-point Likert scales for

CONFREQ are about 3). Conflict is infrequent because an established franchise depends on all parties 'getting along together' or, at worse, 'muddling through'. If there were major conflicts we would expect the franchise agreement to be terminated (something that we were unable to explore in this study).

5. This view of established franchises is reinforced by the perception among franchisees that their decision-making is very formalised and participatory; i.e. that it is clear what has to be achieved, who has authority, and how involved in decision making the different parties are (FORMAL and PARTIC). Use of these variables helps to minimise conflict and allay the concerns of franchisees in the established, mainly large, franchises in our sample. This implies a reasonably effective managerial relationship with everyone working as a team and financial performance in line with expectations, but it does not mean that in practice there is equality.

6. Another manifestation of the effective working relationship that exists between franchisees and franchisors is the absence of horizontal information exchange, especially at a formal level (HORZINF). Franchisees do not see the need to exchange information with their peers. It is possible that informal contacts are maintained, by telephone or from chance encounters, but these do not appear to be very frequent, important or memorable.

If we now look in particular at the responses of franchisors and franchisees to the personal interviews, we see that the perceptions are all fairly similar:

7. Both parties claim that conflict is infrequent, that their decision-making processes are very formalised but participatory, and that this ensures financial performance is in step with expectations (see (4) and (5) above).

8. Their view of power sources is similar in that both groups say non-economic power sources (expert and referent power) are used heavily in contrast to the light-handed use of coercive power sources (see (1) to (3) above). However, franchisors systematically report higher scores on the Likert scales, perhaps because they overestimate their own power sources and in so doing stress that they are in charge.

For two of the relational variables we draw somewhat different conclusions:

9. Franchisors think that franchisees are very dependent on them, although this is not how others perceive the relationship (DEPN). This may be an expression of hope on the part of franchisors, or it may be a genuine perception based on direct experience. (Within a large franchise we would expect the level of direct control to vary, so in thinking about dependence franchisors might focus on the cases where they have fuller control than usual.)

10. Franchisors claim that the level of cooperation is much higher than franchisees' perceptions would suggest (COOP). Again, this may be an expression of hope or the result of distorted perceptions in that franchisors might recall the best examples from their organisation. However, we should not read too much into this – it might be that most managers are reasonably clear about their tasks and they can proceed without entering into intense discussions.

The closeness of the Italian and British responses indicates that the relationships are perceived in similar ways in both countries (i.e. compare across columns):

11. Virtually all the conclusions listed under points (1) to (8) apply whether we are looking at the internal management of franchises in Italy or Britain. Moreover, given the consistency of these results we can be confident about them.
12. There are a couple of discrepancies. For instance, responses from the personal interviews suggest that Italian franchisees feel they are much more dependent in their dealings with franchisors than their British counterparts (DEPN). Another discrepancy is that Italian franchisors view their relationships as somewhat less cooperative, although they still score more than franchisees in either country (COOP). These isolated cases beg a number of questions, but in neither instance are these results supported by other data in Table 8.4. Certainly there is nothing here as systematic as the perceptual differences discussed in points (8) to (10).
13. Similarly, there are isolated differences between mail survey and personal interview averages, but no systematic effects are apparent.

Finally we should note that the perceptions listed here are widely held – on the whole they apply for most of the categories described earlier. For instance, the perceptions of managers in large franchises are broadly similar to those in small franchises (we do not show the tables).

8.5 OVERVIEW AND EXTENSIONS

Retail franchising is now commonplace in most Western nations, and among international franchises the front-of-house format is usually standardised (e.g. Hertz, Body Shop, Stefanel). The most notable finding from this study is *the extent to which franchise management is also standardised* between Italy and Britain, despite all the obvious linguistic and cultural differences, and sector-specific differences (such as the need for a commercial licence to trade in Italy, or the more sympathetic attitudes of British banks).

Using findings from the questionnaire we are also in a position to address questions such as who decides on minimum order sizes, product display and size of retail territories, to what extent there is disagreement over these decisions, and what sources of power there are. We have found that some important aspects of internal management are performed along similar lines in these two culturally diverse countries, and this is likely to have a bearing on the key strategic question of whether to use franchising for market entry and overseas expansion.

8.5.1 Further development

The findings reported in this chapter are based on simple descriptive comparisons of the data from Italy and Britain; these comparisons show how channel members perceive their interactions and behaviour. However, they do not constitute a fully-fledged model of the interrelationships in franchises.

An extension would be to capture the relationships using a multivariate statistical procedure, such as structural equation modelling (as used by Brown, Lusch and Muehling, 1983, and Schul and Babakus, 1988, in their influential research studies). In Manaresi (1993) and Manaresi and Uncles (1994) this approach is used to isolate the direct and indirect effects of variables on each other and to explore the generality of these relationships across countries. These formal methods add credibility to our results, and add to the body of well-established research in this field (particularly with respect to power sources theory, resource dependence theory, and exchange network theory).

The research reported in this chapter was confined to *retail franchising* in just *two* countries. In principle, however, many of the issues raised here apply to any situation where the exercise of power is asymmetric and yet where there is need for co-operation and conflict management – for example, the relations between independent retailers and their suppliers, or the relations between contractors and contractees. We would expect to see further studies in which retail franchising is compared with other forms of retailing (such as the relationship between headquarters and individual outlets in a supermarket chain) and other types of franchising (for example, plumbers and builders) (see Etgar, 1978b, on this point). The managerial value would be to help firms when they are deciding which retail formats to adopt – not only should they consider the cost structure of their options, but also check whether they possess the sources of power that are required to work in a specific type of channel.

Likewise, replication studies are needed to determine the generality of our findings in other countries (there is already an implicit generalisation in that much of the literature we quote is based on US experience, while our own work describes some of the European experience). There are many calls for empirical studies along these lines (for example, Kale and McIntyre, 1991), but little has been published and our contribution is only a start. Replication studies would be of direct assistance to managers operating or expanding overseas who are faced with large development costs, and for whom the similarities and differences in internal management might make or break their business plans.

CONCLUSIONS

There is no evidence from our research to discourage those retailers who would use franchising as their vehicle for internationalisation. In fact the absence of substantial differences in managerial relationships should encourage those who might have rejected the idea of using franchising to expand into markets where the culture is markedly different from that where the franchise concept originated. The temptation must always be to expand into markets where language, race and culture are similar. While our work cannot prove that such logic is flawed (as we can offer data from only two countries) it does provide a counter to the conventional wisdom that barriers to market entry due to cultural differences are always high. Our results may also tempt retailers who have not adopted franchising in their existing markets to consider it as a vehicle for further expansion.

REVIEW QUESTIONS

1. For a specific case, describe how a franchisor exercises power over a franchisee. What are the main sources of power in this case?

2. Typically, what conflicts arise between franchisees and franchisors? Discuss how such conflicts are or might be resolved.

3. For retail franchising, consider two specific examples of conflict. Discuss how these conflicts might be handled, drawing a comparison between British and Italian approaches.

4. If you were a potential retail franchisee in Italy, and you were approached by a British franchisor, what would convince you to sign the franchising contract? Explain your decision.

5. What stresses are placed on a vertically integrated system, which does not involve actual ownership, when an attempt is made to introduce the system to a new overseas market?

6. If you were considering entry into a specific Eastern European market, what lessons about the internal management of franchises in Western markets would you take into account? Justify your remarks.

REFERENCES

Aldrich, H (1976) 'Resource dependence and interorganizational relations', *Administration and Society*, 7, 419–454.

Associazione Italiana Del Franchising (1990) *Annuario del Franchising*, Milan.

British Franchising Association (1990) *Directory of Franchising*, London.

Brown, J R and Day, R L (1981) 'Measures of manifest conflict in distribution channels', *Journal of Marketing Research*, 18 (August), 267–274.

Brown, J R, Lusch, R F and Muehling, D D (1983) 'Conflict and power dependence relations in retailer–supplier channels', *Journal of Retailing*, 59(4), 53–80.

Burt, S (1995) 'Temporal trends in retailer internationalisation' in McGoldrick, P J and Davies, G (eds.), *International Retailing: Trends and Strategies*, Pitman Publishing, London.

Cook, K S and Emerson, R M (1978) 'Power, equity, and commitment in exchange networks', *American Sociological Review*, 43 (October), 721–739.

Dahl, R A (1957) 'The concept of power', *Behavioral Science*, 2 (July), 201–218.

Emerson, R M (1962) 'Power-dependence relations', *American Sociological Review*, 27 (February), 31–41.

Etgar, M (1978a) 'Intrachannel conflict and use of power', *Journal of Marketing Research*, 15 (May), 273–274.

Etgar, M (1978b) 'Differences in the use of manufacturer power in conventional and contractual channels', *Journal of Retailing*, 54(4), 49–62.

Forward, J and Fulop, C (1993) *Issues in Franchising*, City University Business School, London.

French, J R P Jr and Raven, B (1959) 'The bases of social power', in Cartwright, D (ed.), *Studies in Social Power*, University of Michigan, Ann Arbor.

Gaski, J F (1984) 'The theory of power and conflict in channels of distribution', *Journal of Marketing*, 48 (Summer), 9–39.

Hoffman, R C and Preble, J F (1991) 'Franchising: selecting a strategy for rapid growth', *Long Range Planning*, 24(4), 74–82.

Hunt, S D and Nevin, J R (1974) 'Power in a channel of distribution: sources and consequences', *Journal of Marketing Research*, 11 (May), 186–193.

Kale, S H and McIntyre, R P (1991) 'Distribution channel relationships in diverse cultures', *International Marketing Review*, 8(3), 31–45.

Krackhardt, D and Hanson, J R (1993) 'Informal networks: the company behind the chart', *Harvard Business Review*, July–August, 104–111.

Lusch, R F (1976) 'Channel conflict: its impact on retailer operating performance', *Journal of Retailing*, 52(2) (Summer), 2–12.

Manaresi, A (1993) 'Franchise channel relationships: a cross-country comparison', unpublished PhD thesis, London Business School, London.

Manaresi, A and Marcati, A (1991) 'Integration mechanisms in franchise systems: a pilot study on Italian franchises', *Sixth World Conference On Research in the Distributive Trades*, The Hague, The Netherlands, 4–5 July.

Manaresi, A and Uncles, M D (1994) '*Relationships among franchisees and franchisors: a two-country study*', Working Paper, University of Bradford Management Centre, Bradford.

Mendelsohn, M (ed.) (1992) *Franchising in Europe*, Cassell, London.

Pfeffer, J and Salancik, G (1978) *The External Control of Organizations: A Resource Dependence Perspective*, Harper & Row, New York.

Ruekert, R W and Churchill, G (1984) 'Reliability and validity of alternative measures of channel member satisfaction', *Journal of Marketing Research*, 21 (May), 226–233.

Schul, P L and Babakus, E (1988) 'An examination of the interfirm power-conflict relationship: the intervening role of the channel decision structure', *Journal of Retailing*, 64(4), 381–404.

Sechrest, L, Faye, T L and Zaidi, S M H (1972) 'Problems of translation in cross-cultural research', *Journal of Cross-Cultural Psychology*, 3(1), 41–56.

Stern, L W and El-Ansary, A (1988) *Marketing Channels,* (3rd edn), Prentice-Hall, Englewood Cliffs, New Jersey.

Uncles, M D, Hammond, K A, Ehrenberg, A S C and Davis, R E (1994) 'A replication study of two brand-loyalty measures', *European Journal of Operational Research,* 76(2), 375–384.

Welch, L S (1987) 'Diffusion of franchise system use in international operations', *International Marketing Review* (Autumn), 7–19.

CHAPTER 9

International market appraisal and positioning

Peter J McGoldrick and Debbie Blair

INTRODUCTION

Retailers have a battery of techniques and information sources to assist their location and positioning decisions within home markets. These include checklists, analogues, regression models and geographic information systems. In spite of the greater risks involved in developing stores internationally, such decisions are frequently made with rather less opportunities for mathematical modelling. In new markets, analogues or regressions constructed elsewhere are of limited value. Furthermore, the range of variables to be considered on entering new markets is far more diverse.

The first objective of this chapter is to suggest a broad framework, a checklist of some of the issues to be considered in entering new markets. Inevitably, the components of such a checklist and the relative importance of each component vary greatly according to the planned entry strategy and the particular strengths/limitations of the company.

Marks & Spencer started its process of internationalisation some 25 years ago, representing now a valuable case study of market evaluation, entry techniques and positioning. The company has developed a variety of formats and positions in many parts of the world. The international moves by the company since 1972 are summarised briefly before new data from a study of its image in France and the UK are examined.

Marks & Spencer's competitive positioning is compared with that of C & A and a local competitor in two different national markets. Images are also compared with those recorded in an earlier study of Marks & Spencer in Hong Kong. A model is suggested of some of the determinants of international image and positioning, drawing attention to the additional importance of awareness and learning in such international contexts.

9.1 FRAMEWORK FOR INTERNATIONAL MARKET APPRAISAL

Before focusing upon the specific issues of market positioning, it is appropriate to take a broad view of the task of evaluating international market

Table 9.1 International market appraisal checklist

Spending power

Total GDP

Disposable incomes:
- spending patterns
- spending improvements
- seasonal fluctuations
- taxes on incomes
- taxes on spending
- savings ratios

Population size:
- age profile
- cultural/ethnic groupings
- expatriates and tourists
- lifestyles
- religion

Residential structure:
- urban vs rural
- housing density
- ownership levels

Adjacent markets:
- cornerstone status
- market proximities
- market similarities
- market accessibilities

Barriers and risks

Entry barriers:
- tariffs
- quotas
- development restrictions
- competition laws
- barriers to foreign entry
- religious/cultural barriers

Political risks:
- change of government
- nationalisation or controls
- war or riot
- international embargoes

Civil risks:
- effectiveness of policing
- rate of theft
- rate of murder/violence
- level of organised crime

Economic risks:
- inflation
- exchange rate fluctuations
- employment structure and stability
- taxes on business

Other risks:
- geological
- climatic

Costs and communications

Factor costs:
- land availability and costs
- costs of acquisition targets
- taxes on business
- energy costs
- labour availability and costs
- training costs
- development costs

Logistics and costs:
- road networks
- rail transport
- air freight
- sea freight
- available carriers
- distances between markets
- transport safety
- transport reliability

Competition

Existing retailers: competition
- same or similar formats
- indirect competition
- specialist retailers
- other marketing channels
- price competitiveness
- extent of differentiation

Existing retailers: co-operation
- synergies from partnerships
- international alliances
- franchising activities
- cumulative attraction
- acceptance of format

Saturation levels:
- structure of outlets by sector
- concentration levels
- primary/secondary markets   ▶

Table 9.1 (continued)

Costs and communications	*Competition*
Communications and costs: • telephone/fax lines • automatic international dialling • available international lines • costs of calls	Gap analysis: • positioning of competitors • viability/size of gaps • reasons for gaps • age of existing stores
Marketing communications: • TV/radio advertising • direct mail agencies • outdoor advertising • print/magazine advertising • cable TV penetration	Competitive potential: • site availability • financial strength of home retailers • attractions to international retailers • opportunities to reposition

opportunities. Following from the early work of Nelson (1958), elaborate checklists have been developed to assist retailers in their domestic location decision (McGoldrick, 1990). While not providing the answers, such checklists have helped to provoke the questions that should be asked in evaluating a location. They have helped numerous retailers to avoid expensive and potentially disastrous pitfalls in their expansion programmes. They have also helped to identify information gaps which, within many domestic markets, have been filled by the various data providers (Mitchell and McGoldrick, 1994).

It would appear worthwhile therefore to develop a checklist to assist in the evaluation of international markets. Table 9.1 offers an initial attempt at such a list, the refinement of which is the objective of a study of internationalised retailers in the UK, Holland, Germany and Italy. This study, currently in progress from the International Centre for Retail Studies in Manchester, is also seeking to establish the information sources relevant to each major element of the checklist. It is accepted that this checklist overlaps with lists utilised to appraise specific locations, yet it does not supersede these. Table 9.1 is designed to help appraise national opportunities; specific locations must then be evaluated.

Table 9.2 has been derived from one of the relatively few studies that has set out to provide decision tools for retailers wishing to expand internationally (Coopers & Lybrand, 1993). Based upon 5-point scales, from 'very unfavourable' (1) to 'very favourable' (5), the analysis offers scores on seven elements of market attractiveness for some 20 countries/zones. This provides an indication of how retailers could set about scoring market attractiveness, although further detail would inevitably be required. The four main areas of the checklist in Table 9.1, however, will first be discussed briefly.

Table 9.2 Rating market attractiveness

	1997 GDP	Urban adult pop.	Risk	Infra-structure	Spending improvements	Competition	Entry barriers
USA	5	5	5	5	3	1	4
Japan	4	3	5	5	3	2	1
Germany	4	3	5	3	4	1	1
France	3	2	5	5	3	1	1
Italy	3	2	5	3	3	3	1
Great Britain	3	2	5	5	3	1	1
Republic of Korea	2	2	4	2	4	5	1
Spain	2	2	5	4	3	2	1
Canada	2	2	5	4	2	1	3
Netherlands	2	1	5	5	3	1	2
Australia	1	2	5	3	3	1	1
Mexico	2	3	4	2	4	4	3
India	1	5	2	1	4	5	1
China	2	5	1	1	4	5	1
Turkey	1	2	3	3	4	4	1
Hong Kong	1	1	3	3	4	4	1
Chile	1	1	3	2	4	4	2
Argentina	1	2	1	3	3	4	1
Brazil	2	3	1	1	3	4	1
Russia	1	3	1	1	2	5	1

Key: 5 = Very favourable, 4 = Somewhat favourable, 3 = Neutral, 2 = Somewhat unfavourable, 1 = Very unfavourable.
Derived from Coopers & Lybrand (1993).

9.1.1 Spending power

The market size, or rather the accessible spending power, is a primary consideration in market evaluation. A number of official sources can provide estimates of a country's Gross Domestic Product (e.g. OECD, 1994) and of trends in the movement of consumer spending. Seasonal fluctuations are clearly of importance, not least because many international retailers establish their early 'bridgeheads' in areas of high tourism. The factors that intervene between incomes and disposable incomes are numerous; still more factors intervene between disposable incomes and spending in stores. Information on the savings ratio and taxation regimes will provide further insights, as will information on housing, transport and energy expenditures.

Population sizes are readily accessible data, as are details of age profiles. Median ages differ greatly between 35–40 in the cases of Germany and Sweden, around 25 in Korea and Taiwan, yet under 20 in Turkey and

Mexico (Coopers & Lybrand, 1993). Such profiles clearly provide insights both into market opportunities and into future market growth. Less consistently available is information into cultural/ethnic groupings or lifestyles, although the latter are the subject of extensive study within the more highly developed markets.

While measures of total spending power are important, the accessible spending power depends upon residential dispersion. A high proportion of urban population is generally more accessible to the retailer, especially if the urban population also holds a disproportionate amount of the spending power. Table 9.2 shows that India, while rating low on GDP, rates favourably on the level of urban adult population. Levels of home ownership, and the balance between apartments and houses, also influence spending propensities in various home-related product categories.

The size and spending power of adjacent markets may also be a factor in evaluating markets in regions new to a specific retailer, the term 'cornerstone' market has been used to describe markets that may provide a foundation for a wider, regional strategy. Thus Brazil, in spite of its levels of risk and modest GDP, may be regarded as a cornerstone for entry to South America. Not that such tactical springboards need to be large in themselves. The special characteristics of Hong Kong have attracted a great deal of tactical investment (Goldstein and Rowley, 1990), including the transfer of the Yaohan Department Store Corporation's corporate headquarters from Japan to Hong Kong (*Tokyo Business Today*, 1989).

9.1.2 Barriers and risks

Barriers to entry and obstacles to development within various countries are the foci of chapters 12 and 6 respectively. Further elaboration is therefore unnecessary at this point, other than to confirm their importance within any international market appraisal checklist. The specific issues of cultural differences and barriers represent an especially complex area of analysis, being of relevance to many aspects of retail positioning and internal management. Martenson (1988) examined cross-cultural differences within the context of multinational retailing.

Levels of risk are given a single rating in Table 9.2, yet are certainly multi-dimensional. It may be true that some aspects of political risk tend to go hand-in-hand with economic risks, but the individual components of risk do merit close scrutiny and analysis. Relatively stable countries, such as the UK, and USA, may get the most favourable ratings in a generalised risk analysis, yet some retailers react most adversely to a political swing to the left, seeing dangers of greater intervention. At the other end of the spectrum, the enormous upheavals in Russia represent a risk of altogether different proportions, yet a risk that some Western retailers have been prepared to take (Holden, 1994).

Within Table 9.1, a category headed 'civil risks' has been introduced to summarise various important attributes of a country's internal security. Theft is sadly an aspect of most countries, developed or developing, but its level varies greatly. The cost and viability of defending merchandise and stores varies accordingly. Organised crime has also spread well beyond its traditional heartlands, representing a major threat to property and to retail personnel in some areas.

Other risks include the potentially disastrous occurrences of major earthquakes, floods or typhoons; in regions susceptible to such risks, insurance against them may be exorbitant or unavailable.

9.1.3 Costs and communications

Analyses of cost factors will clearly differ according to the strategy that is being employed. If entry by acquisition or partnership is envisaged, the cost analysis will focus upon the valuation of the target company. In that many acquisitions or joint ventures are followed by a period of organic growth, the availability and cost of land are still likely to be of relevance. Labour availability and cost is an issue with all entry strategies. In some countries the labour may be abundantly available and inexpensive, but not experienced in the skills of retailing. Under such circumstances, the time and costs involved in training may be considerable. For example, trainers from the McDonald's operation in Canada were 'imported' to develop the staff skills required in the Moscow restaurants (McGoldrick and Holden, 1993).

The physical movement of goods, both to the market and within the market, is a major factor in the assessment of viability and cost. In some situations, retailers acquire an existing logistics network; in others, the international retail developments are closely linked to international product sourcing arrangements (see Chapter 5). The ratings for 'infrastructure' in Table 9.2 reflect a combination of transport and communications issues. The neutral rating for Germany is explained by the differences that remain between the former East and West Germanies.

While an abundance of telephone, fax and computer links is now taken for granted in highly developed countries, this assumption cannot be made in less developed areas. In 1991 it was estimated that France and the UK had approximately 50 telephone lines per 100 inhabitants, in contrast with 10 per 100 in Brazil or Mexico. From many countries, automatic international dialling is not available and extensive delays are experienced in trying to access an international line. In contrast, international retailers operating in Hong Kong or areas of the European Union are able to establish teleconference facilities to enhance the flow of information, reduce physical distance and minimise management travel time.

The marketing infrastructure is of greatest importance to retailers using direct entry or developing through franchising. Facilities taken for granted at home cannot be assumed. For example, Ikea employed the police to distribute leaflets in Budapest, being unable at the time to employ an agency for the purpose. Another problem encountered in post-communist societies is a distrust of media advertising, many people rejecting this as a continuation of propaganda (McGoldrick and Holden, 1993).

9.1.4 Competition

In any market evaluation, domestic or international, the existing retailers represent both threats and opportunities. This is especially true within the international context, given the scope for partnerships and international alliances (see Chapter 7). Even in the absence of such formal arrangements, existing retailers may help, rather than entirely hinder, market entry. For example, a retailer which has pioneered a particular format or established acceptance of a merchandise category may reduce the cost and risk of entry by others.

Threats posed by competitors should not, however, be underestimated, nor be assumed static. For example, Aldi encountered harsh opposition from UK retailers in terms of price retaliation and other measures seeking to block its development (McGoldrick and Ali, 1994). Even the world-class retailer Toys 'R' Us encountered serious retaliation on entering the French market, where hypermarkets had both the space and the cost structures to compete with an extensive, if seasonal, product range (Tordjman, 1994). The growth of other marketing channels, most notably teleshopping, may have been relatively slow but its competitive potential should not be underestimated by retailers attempting long-term evaluations (Reynolds, 1994).

Assessments of competition must not only consider the numbers of retailers, shop units, etc., they must also consider their positioning. Only in this way can gaps in the market be evaluated and attempts made to explain the gaps. As many retailers have discovered to their cost, gaps do not always represent opportunities if the market does not perceive the need for the format. For example, Carrefour did not achieve success in exporting the hypermarket concept to the USA, even though a gap appeared to exist (Burt, 1994).

The importance of international market positioning, in terms of both gap analysis and strategic repositioning, will now be examined in more detail. Firstly, the international expansion of Marks & Spencer will be summarised, illustrating an increasing skill in evaluating and adapting to new markets.

9.2 MARKS & SPENCER: A LEARNING EXPERIENCE

Marks & Spencer represents a useful case study of retail internationalisation, having utilised most of the entry strategies described within the introduction to this book. The company runs 72 stores outside the UK, plus 76 franchise outlets. Under different logos, the company also owns 133 Brooks Brothers stores in the USA and Japan, 19 Kings Super Markets (USA) and 106

D'Allairds stores (Canada). Table 9.3 summarises the contributions to turnover and profitability of the various regions in 1994.

Table 9.3 Marks & Spencer worldwide

	UK and Eire	Continental Europe	Rest of world
Number of stores	285	23	304
Turnover (£m)	5,598.1	246.9	609
Turnover % [1]	85.6	3.7	9.3
Operating profit (£m)	809.9	27.1	36.4
Operating profit %	92.7	3.1	4.2

1. A further £87.2m (1.3%) comprises direct exports.

Source: Marks & Spencer (1994).

9.2.1 North American acquisitions

The first steps towards international retail operations were taken in the early 1970s, with the acquisition of a 50 per cent shareholding in three Canadian chains (Whitehead, 1992):

- *People's:* budget priced general merchandise stores;
- *D'Allairds:* selling clothes primarily to women over 40;
- *Walkers Clothing Stores:* redeveloped as smaller versions of Marks & Spencer UK stores.

The company acquired controlling interest three years after the initial share acquisition. The initial investment in Canada was prompted by several 'push factors', including the oil crisis and even the threat of nationalisation by some labour politicians. The 'pull' and 'facilitating' factors of Canada included the use of the English language in most of the country, perceived cultural similarities (possibly overestimated), economic prosperity and stability, plus a tactical springboard into the lucrative United States market.

In retrospect, the Canadian venture was probably far too ambitious as a first step into international operations. The positioning of the acquired stores also presented difficulties in establishing the quality image that is central to the Marks & Spencer proposition. Since 1990, the company has reduced its Canadian operation from 275 stores to 146, and has considerably upgraded the image of the retained stores.

It was 1988 before the anticipated move into the USA market occurred, in the form of the acquisitions of Brooks Brothers and Kings Super Markets. The former was purchased from the Canadian Campeau organisation at the cost of $750m, which included 47 stores in the US and 21 in Japan. These numbers grew to 83 and 50 respectively by 1994. Described as a 'small strategic acquisition' (Whitehead, 1992), Kings had 16 food stores in New Jersey, the number having now grown to 19.

9.2.2 European developments

In contrast to the major acquisitions that have characterised most of the North American developments, Marks & Spencer's growth in Europe has been somewhat more incremental. The first store to open in 1975 was in the celebrated and high-cost retailing environment of the Boulevard Haussmann. The store is situated directly opposite to two of the most prestigious department stores of Paris, namely Printemps and Galeries Lafayette. The location has also benefited from a direct entry to the express underground service (RER) and underground links with the other department stores.

The variety store concept, au Marks & Spencer, was not familiar to the French market. Variety stores of a sort had been developed as low price subsidiaries of the major department stores, such as Monoprix of the Galeries Lafayette Group (Tordjman, 1993). With low productivity and inconsistent images, they gained only a 2.1 per cent share of retail trade, compared with 6.2 per cent in the UK. In contrast, the Marks & Spencer store on Boulevard Haussmann enjoys higher sales per square metre than any department store in France. This store has been joined by five others in Paris, with 16 in France as a whole.

The Brussels store was also opened in 1975, since joined by two more in Belgium and two in Holland. In common with the French operation, these are wholly owned by Marks & Spencer, which has gained extensive knowledge of these adjacent markets. A different approach was taken to the Spanish market, where the company entered a joint venture with Cortefiel. Marks & Spencer owned initially two-thirds of the business, the proportion having now increased to 80 per cent. This partnership has helped the company to enter and learn rapidly about this distinctive market.

9.2.3 Franchising worldwide

With exception of the North American and Hong Kong stores, most entries to more remote markets have been achieved via the franchise route (Whitehead, 1991). Table 9.4 summarises the locations of the 76 Marks & Spencer franchised outlets. Although many of these stores are small by UK standards, they serve as an important learning experience and also establish the company name within new markets.

The enormous difference between, for example, Greek and UK retailing may be illustrated by the typical scale of the former. Ninety per cent of Greek shops employ three people or less; against this background, Marks & Spencer stores of 4–5,000 sq.ft represent a significant increase in size. The Greek operation is run in partnership with the Marinopoulos family; a

Table 9.4 Marks & Spencer franchises

Area	Shops	Area	Shops
Austria	2	Indonesia	5
Bahamas	5	Israel	8
Bermuda	1	Malaysia	2
Canary Islands	3	Malta	3
Channel Islands	7	Norway	1
Cyprus	9	Philippines	7
Gibraltar	1	Portugal	4
Greece	7	Singapore	7
Hungary	2	Thailand	2

Source: Marks & Spencer (1994).

deputy manager from the UK is based permanently in Greece. Arrangements of this type offer a blend of expertise and local knowledge that is highly appropriate to markets so physically and culturally distant from the home market.

Some insights into the international positioning of Marks & Spencer were provided by Buckley (1994). In the Portuguese and Spanish markets, for example, the company rapidly gained supremacy in the sale of bras. Not that the company offered more choice in these markets; the competitive advantage stemmed from the fact that local retailers were decades behind in their assortments and merchandising techniques for intimate garments. In the company's latest Paris opening in the Rue de Rivoli, some of the best selling products are ready-meals, especially Indian meals, not widely available in France. These and many other examples illustrate the enormous diversity that still exists, even between adjacent markets. The inevitability that the stores' positioning will differ between markets, even if the stores could be made identical, is also illustrated.

9.3 INTERNATIONAL MARKET POSITIONING

A major challenge for international retailers is to identify and adopt the most appropriate positioning within other national markets. This requires careful appraisal of existing competition, possible gaps and customer needs within the target market. It is not difficult to find examples of retail formats, excellently positioned within their home markets, which have been unsuccessful outside those markets. Most require at least some adaptation to local expectations, shopping habits, customs and competition.

It is surprising that so little research attention has been given to the image and positioning of retailers operating outside their home markets. Davies and Brooks (1989) examined the relative positioning of British and German department stores within their domestic markets. McGoldrick and Ali (1994) compared the images of German and British grocery firms within the latter market. McGoldrick and Ho (1992) measured images of Marks & Spencer *vis-à-vis* Japanese department stores in Hong Kong.

Within this section, data from a recent study of Marks & Spencer and C & A images in Chester and Strasbourg are presented. In each case, the images of the British and Dutch retailers are compared with a local competitor. In the case of Chester, this is the Browns department stores; in Strasbourg, Printemps was chosen as the equivalent, well established, department store competitor. The study was regarded as exploratory, with British and French samples of around 120 each.

The methodology was essentially a replication of that described by McGoldrick and Ho (1992), allowing some comparisons to be drawn with the earlier study in Hong Kong. Interviews were conducted in French and English. On the basis of this exploratory study, directions for future research into international positioning are suggested.

9.3.1 Positioning in three markets

In line with the earlier study, some 14 image attributes were rated, using a scale of 1 to 10. As this seemed to cause respondents some confusion when applied to price ratings, a more simple, 1 to 5 scale was used for this particular attribute. Table 9.5 summarises the mean ratings for twelve of the attributes, broken down between the two samples and the three stores in each location.

A large number of t-tests are also summarised in this table, which indicate whether differences between means are statistically significant. A 'p' value of 0.001 indicates significance at the 99.9 per cent confidence level. Significance levels of less than 90 per cent (0.10) are declared as n.s. (not significant). Two directions of testing were undertaken. Within each of the two national samples, each store was compared with each of the other two. These results are summarised in the final three columns of Table 9.5. The ratings given to Marks & Spencer and C & A were then compared between the French and the British samples. Clearly, there was no point in comparing the ratings given to the 'other' competitors across the two markets.

In order to provide a graphic representation of some of these comparisons, Figures 9.1 and 9.2 show the relative positioning of the stores on major dimensions. Added to these figures are the ratings given to Marks & Spencer *vis-à-vis* two competitors in the Hong Kong market, both Japanese department stores. The details of the Hong Kong study are provided in McGoldrick and Ho (1992). No formal, statistical comparisons are attempted between the Hong Kong study and the recent study in France and England. The lapse of time would render such tests invalid. The positioning is plotted on these charts for illustrative purposes.

Price and quality are clearly dimensions of critical importance. In

Table 9.5 Comparisons of image ratings

Image component		Image ratings (means)			t-tests (p=)		
		M & S	C & A	Other[1]	M & S vs C & A	M & S vs Other	C & A vs Other
Merchandise quality	FR	8.0	5.9	7.8	(0.000)	(0.092)	(0.000)
	UK	8.5	5.6	7.8	(0.000)	(0.000)	(0.000)
t-test (p=)		(0.013)	(n.s.)				
Merchandise range	FR	6.5	6.4	7.5	(n.s.)	(0.000)	(0.000)
	UK	7.5	6.1	7.7	(0.000)	(n.s.)	(0.000)
t-test (p=)		(0.000)	(n.s.)				
Merchandise fashion	FR	6.6	6.4	7.2	(n.s.)	(0.007)	(0.001)
	UK	6.6	6.2	6.8	(0.019)	(n.s.)	(0.001)
t-test (p=)		(n.s.)	(n.s.)				
Level of services	FR	7.2	6.4	7.2	(0.001)	(n.s.)	(0.001)
	UK	7.9	6.3	7.5	(0.000)	(0.007)	(0.000)
t-test (p=)		(0.005)	(n.s.)				
Personnel	FR	7.0	6.3	6.3	(0.003)	(0.003)	(n.s.)
	UK	7.9	6.5	7.2	(0.000)	(0.000)	(0.000)
t-test (p=)		(0.000)	(n.s.)				
Store layout	FR	7.2	5.9	6.9	(0.000)	(0.038)	(0.000)
	UK	7.4	6.0	6.2	(0.000)	(0.000)	(n.s.)
t-test (p=)		(n.s.)	(n.s.)				
Atmosphere	FR	6.7	5.9	6.4	(0.007)	(n.s.)	(0.042)
	UK	7.1	5.8	6.7	(0.000)	(0.009)	(0.000)
t-test (p=)		(0.092)	(n.s.)				
Quality of display	FR	7.6	5.9	7.4	(0.000)	(n.s.)	(0.000)
	UK	7.6	5.6	7.1	(0.000)	(0.010)	(0.000)
t-test (p=)		(n.s.)	(n.s.)				
General reputation	FR	8.2	6.6	8.0	(0.000)	(n.s.)	(0.000)
	UK	8.9	6.5	8.2	(0.000)	(0.000)	(0.000)
t-test (p=)		(0.001)	(n.s.)				
After sales service	FR	7.8	7.3	7.6	(n.s.)	(n.s.)	(n.s.)
	UK	8.6	6.8	7.6	(0.000)	(0.000)	(0.000)
t-test (p=)		(0.037)	(n.s.)				
Image in general	FR	7.7	4.4	6.3	(0.000)	(0.000)	(0.000)
	UK	6.4	4.6	6.7	(0.000)	(n.s.)	(0.000)
t-test (p=)		(0.000)	(n.s.)				
Prices[2]	FR	3.9	2.1	4.1	(0.000)	(0.043)	(0.000)
	UK	3.9	2.4	3.9	(0.000)	(n.s.)	(0.000)
t-test (p=)		(n.s.)	(0.022)				

1. The other competitor rated is Browns in Chester, Printemps in Strasbourg.
2. Rated on scale from 1 (low price) to 5 (high price). All other components rated on a scale from 1 (very poor) to 10 (very good).

Fig. 9.1 Price/quality positioning
Source: Hong Kong data derived from McGoldrick and Ho (1992).

promoting its concept within the French market, Marks & Spencer modestly proclaims its exceptional quality and keenly maintained pricing. Figure 9.1 illustrates how these translate into consumer perceptions within the various markets. It is interesting to note that perceptions of Marks & Spencer prices are almost identical across all three markets, in spite of reports that their prices tend to be significantly higher outside the United Kingdom (Buckley, 1994). Such reports, however, ignore all the many complexities of comparing prices internationally, not least the issues of brand/product positioning, prevailing price norms, differential retail costs and logistical costs (McGoldrick *et al*, 1995).

Rather different positions are revealed on the quality dimension. In both Chester and Strasbourg, Marks & Spencer enjoys a quality perception at least on a par with that of the leading local department store. While comparisons with the Hong Kong study must be treated with caution, it is noticeable that Marks & Spencer is again on a par with the leading local

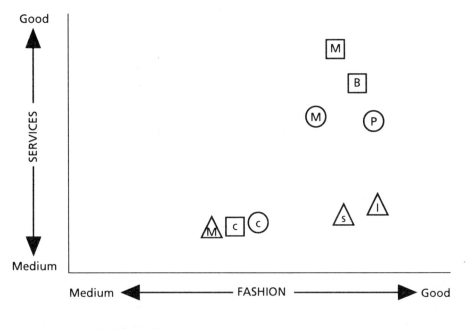

Key: See Figure 9.1

Fig. 9.2 Services/fashion positioning

department store competitor, Mitsukoshi. Quality ratings overall, however, were considerably lower in the Hong Kong study. Does this reflect a cultural reticence to give high quality ratings, or does it simply reflect the enormous diversity of high quality shopping opportunities in Hong Kong? It is likely that both factors contribute to this difference. By comparison, the gap between the Marks & Spencer quality ratings in Chester and Strasbourg is small. Part of this gap could be explained by the longer learning process associated with some elements of image, a theme developed further in section 9.3.3.

Fashion perceptions, both of Marks & Spencer and C & A, are not significantly different between the two markets. Again, however, the Hong Kong ratings are somewhat out of line. On this dimension, the temporal lag between the surveys may be especially important, as the company has made its range more cosmopolitan in recent years, not least because of the influence of more international trading.

The services ratings differ significantly between Chester and Strasbourg in the case of Marks & Spencer, but not for C & A. In that C & A has an established image in France, this again could be indicative of a learning process. It could also reflect the market context. As noted in 9.2.2, the strength of the department store concept *vis-à-vis* the variety store concept is greater in France than in Britain. It could well be that consumers' internal reference standards, when evaluating service levels, are somewhat higher in France.

This would certainly seem to be the case in Hong Kong, although it is noticeable that Marks & Spencer is on a par with its Japanese competitors on this dimension.

Although it is not possible to discuss in detail all the comparisons summarised in Table 9.5, it is of interest to note the overall juxtapositions of the Marks & Spencer and C & A stores. In virtually every case, Marks & Spencer gets the more favourable rating. Prices are the exception, although Marks & Spencer would not wish to be perceived as cheaper than average. The Strasbourg respondents considered the companies to be equivalent on range, but that is mostly a function of store size. On fashion, both companies are faced with the difficult balance between design flair and broad market appeal. The companies are also close, in the perceptions of the French consumers, on after-sales service. It would be of interest to repeat this survey in three years' time, to see if the gap opens up to the level perceived by the British consumers.

9.3.2 Perceptions of national origin

Some companies that trade internationally seek to emphasise their national origins, whereas others seem content to become identified with the adopted country. Certainly, Woolworths in the UK tended to be regarded as British by most consumers, even while still under US ownership (Mitton, 1987). In contrast, some retailers seek to promote their foreign origins to establish an important facet of their identity (Kapferer, 1986). An obvious example is the Scandinavian element of Ikea's identity.

C & A is an example of an organisation which seems content to become a local institution, rather than promote heavily its Dutch origins. Not surprisingly, customers in both our samples were generally not aware of the company's national origin (see Table 9.6). For a country with more than its share of Euro-sceptics, not to mention xenophobics, it is possibly surprising that the British sample did significantly better in this respect. The close proximity of Strasbourg to Germany may have contributed to the belief that C & A is an organisation of German origin.

In fact, C & A was founded by the Brenninkmeyer brothers Clemens and August (C & A) in Holland in 1841. The confusion with German origin is all the more understandable as the family were traders in the border town of Mettingen. In 1910 a store was opened in Berlin, then in 1922 a store was opened in London.

While remaining a private enterprise, C & A is run as a largely autonomous organisation in each of ten countries in Europe. C & A (Germany) is now amongst Europe's 50 largest retail organisations, having greatly outgrown C & A (Netherlands). Possibly because of the troubled history of Europe during much of its internationalisation, C & A has not chosen to promote its origins. In fact, many of its own shopworkers appear uncertain as to its national origin!

Table 9.6 Perceived country of origin

Country	M & S		C & A	
	France %	UK %	France %	UK %
France	0.0	1.8	15.1	5.6
Germany	0.0	0.9	42.5	14.0
Holland	0.0	0.0	8.2	23.4
UK	93.8	93.0	11.0	38.3
USA	6.2	3.5	19.2	17.8
Other	0.0	0.9	4.1	0.9
chi^2 (p=)	(n.s.)[1]		(0.000)	

1. For the purpose of this test, the perceived origins were dichotomised to UK vs Others.

In the Hong Kong study, some 87 per cent of respondents correctly allo-cated the national origins of Marks & Spencer. As the St Michael brand was long established in Hong Kong, it may have been expected that the percent-age would be even higher. Possibly because of sensitivities surrounding 1997, the company had not promoted its 'Britishness' quite as vigorously as in some near European markets.

In Spain, for example, the company invested in major displays within the British pavilion at EXPO 92, which closely followed the opening of a store in Seville. In France, the 'Britishness' is being promoted with great vigour. For example, prior to the opening of the store in the Rue Rivoli in 1994, the Paris Metro carried numerous advertisements proclaiming the location, opening date and a clear British stereotype. In one advertisement, Sherlock Holmes and Watson are depicted studying a map of Paris, with Holmes say-ing: 'Do you not have any other clues, Watson?' ... 'Yes Rue Rivoli.' Another such picture depicted two Buckingham Palace guards, also studying their Paris plan. To cater for the full range of British stereotypes, a third depicted two kilted gentlemen, also studying their Paris plan, the catchline being: 'McLeod, for your tweed trousers, do you go up to Glasgow?' 'No, you go down to Chatelet'. This established, by multiple repetition, the loca-tion of the nearest Metro station at Chatelet. It therefore comes as no sur-prise that the French consumers are equally aware of the British origin of Marks & Spencer.

9.3.3 International image development

The evidence presented from studies in the UK, France and Hong Kong offers only snapshots of Marks & Spencer's positioning at particular points in time. Of considerable value would be data that added two further dimen-sions:

- a *quantity* dimension, recognising that awareness of the store name is likely to be weak in the early stages of development;
- a *time* dimension, in that images will usually shift over time from an initial position, normally close to a neutral image.

The importance of brand awareness is widely recognised within the marketing literature (e.g. Aaker, 1991) and is incorporated within even the most basic of consumer behaviour models. Image research, however, has tended to focus upon the many different dimensions of image quality, tending to ignore the issue of image quantity. This no doubt reflects the fact that most image research has been conducted in domestic markets, in which awareness of the competing stores is assumed to be high. Furthermore, shoppers would typically be excluded from a survey if they were not aware of one of the stores under consideration.

In the international context, high levels of awareness clearly cannot be assumed. This can be illustrated through a short anecdote, drawn from a recent experience of one of the authors. On returning to Manchester from a conference in the south of Spain in 1992, a slow connection at Madrid allowed sufficient time to get to the city centre for a meal and a little retail tourism. A Marks & Spencer store having recently opened in Madrid, this became a natural way of using some of this time; as this was not a planned visit, the address had not been noted. Now, if you ask a taxi driver at Heathrow, or at Charles de Gaulle for that matter, to take you to Marks & Spencer, the reply is likely to be: 'which one?' In Madrid, however, some 19 taxi drivers were quizzed before one claimed to know of its location! This experience certainly emphasised the importance of establishing name and location recognition before and during the early weeks of trading.

Figure 9.3, although partly hypothetical, attempts to introduce the quantity and time dimensions to some of the cases discussed in this chapter. We have no 'hard data' on the movement of Marks & Spencer's Canadian image, yet anecdotal evidence suggests that it started from a generally unfavourable position. As the strength of the image grew with the development of the Marks & Spencer name, it still did not achieve the favourable qualities typical elsewhere. Only the recent refurbishment and repositioning have probably shifted the image in a more favourable direction.

The image track followed in Hong Kong is likely to differ somewhat, as the product brand name 'St Michael' had been sold for some 40 years through Dodwell's department stores (McGoldrick and Ho, 1992). Furthermore, the large expatriate community in Hong Kong ensured that, when the first store was opened in 1988, there was already a fairly high level of awareness. The intensive and glamorous competitive context of Hong Kong, however, presents a major challenge to the development of the quality dimensions of the image.

Our data suggest that Marks & Spencer has achieved a strong and favourable image in France, yet this has been achieved from a fairly slow

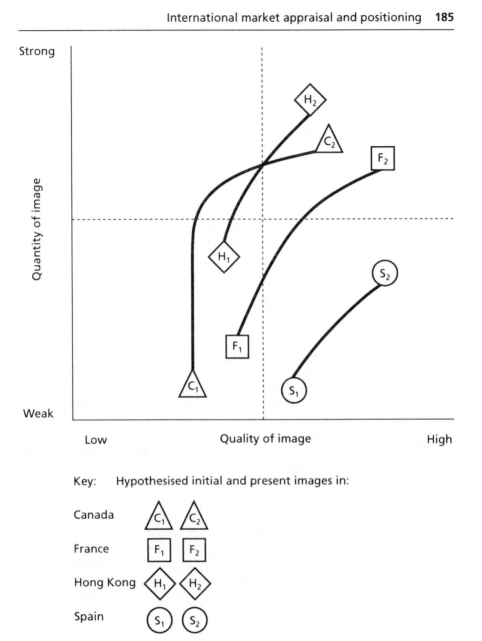

Key: Hypothesised initial and present images in:

Canada

France

Hong Kong

Spain

Fig. 9.3 Marks & Spencer: hypothesised path of image development

start. Given the close links between London and Paris, there would, how-ever, have been some degree of name awareness, even in 1975. The store in the Boulevard Haussman was, initially, rather smaller than its formidable department store competitors, which are situated on the 'right' side of the street. One can conjecture that predispositions were on the negative side of neutral, given the positioning of variety stores in France. The 'general image' rating of the Marks & Spencer store in Strasbourg (Table 9.5) would suggest that a favourable reputation has been developed over 20 years of trading in France.

The image trajectory depicted for Spain is based upon anecdotal evidence, plus discussions with retail researchers in that country. The Marks & Spencer name was well known to the British tourists and expatriates but not to the Spanish consumers in general. Predispositions towards British retailing and merchandise quality were, however, generally more favourable than those encountered in some other markets. Even the name of the country's leading department store, El Corte Ingles, no doubt contributed to the brand values of 'Britishness' in retailing. As reported earlier (Buckley, 1994), acceptance of the products and merchandising techniques has been very strong and favourable within the Spanish market.

9.3.4 Aetiology of international image

The determinants of image in new competitive contexts clearly differ from those within most domestic contexts. To stay with the example of Marks & Spencer, images of the company in Britain are started in childhood, in part handed down from generation to generation. As noted by Brown and Burt (1992), for many consumers Marks & Spencer actually retails 'trust' and 'safety'. Unlike the more immediate attribute characteristics of the category killer (Chapter 11), these beliefs take time to develop. While Marks & Spencer has been adopted enthusiastically as an innovation in Spain, it may take a generation to become an institution. In Paris, it has almost reached that stage in its image development.

Inevitably, the method of market entry will influence both the quantity and the quality of image. The early acquisitions in Canada probably slowed the development of the Marks & Spencer name, as well as suggesting a positioning not entirely congruent with the aims of the company. In the case of the Brooks Bros acquisition in the USA and Japan, the name was considered too strong to change. Entry methods can also be used to build image, prior to full-scale development. The use of licensing, franchising or concessions may be partly a learning experience, partly the development of brand equity in new markets.

Figure 9.4 depicts the situation where the retail name is being developed in an unfamiliar market. Customers will be heavily influenced in their early impressions by a number of expectations and predispositions. These are rooted in existing shopping habits and competition, but are also influenced by spending power, culture, climate, lifestyles, etc. Attitudes towards a retail newcomer will also be driven by various national stereotypes. For example, McGoldrick and Ho (1992) found Hong Kong shoppers to be strongly disposed towards Japanese retailers; it would appear that Spanish consumers are well disposed towards British retailing in general.

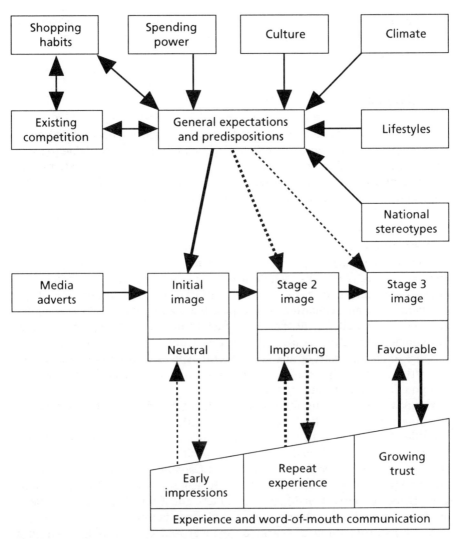

Fig. 9.4 Determinants of international image

Direct experience plays but a modest part in the formulation of initial impressions. Media advertising can contribute greatly at this stage to the development of name/location awareness and to the communication of core values. As experience grows, word-of-mouth communications become more prolific and the images of more immediate attributes are developed. While consumers may be aware of few prices (Wilson *et al*, 1995) they quickly develop an image of prices, and of fashion, range, etc. As noted earlier, the longer-term values take rather more time to develop, such as beliefs in relia-bility, quality and after-sales service. This degree of trust requires not only repeat use but also the tangible evidence that products last, that buying mistakes are indeed refunded, etc. In future research, it would be valuable to disaggregate the development over time of the different components of a store image.

CONCLUSIONS

It is paradoxical that retailers typically face the high-risk decisions to enter international markets with less reliable information than is available to assist domestic location decisions. A framework is proposed, which extends the concept of the location checklist to the international retailing arena. Population and spending power are crucial to location decisions at any level. In the international context, however, data on population growth, structure, incomes, etc., are typically apprised at the macro level. Further micro-scale analysis must inevitably follow, as specific sites are shortlisted.

International market appraisal also requires the analysis of entry barriers and entry risks. The risks include a range of political, civil, economic and other contingencies. In each case, the appraisal requires an estimate of the likelihood and an evaluation of the possible consequences. Cost estimates must be developed for all the major factors involved in the international development, including land, taxes, energy, labour, transport and communications. As in any market analysis, several aspects of the existing competitive structure must be examined, with projections made of likely reactions and potential new entrants to the market.

Marks & Spencer is an organisation with nearly 25 years of experience in retailing internationally. The acquisitions, development and franchising activities have served to illustrate the linkages between entry strategies, market appraisal needs and international positioning. Early acquisitions did not achieve the desired market position in Canada. Using a more incremental strategy, greater success was ultimately achieved in some European markets. Direct export of St Michael products and franchising has also been used, in part to develop brand equity within new markets.

A comparative study of Marks & Spencer and C & A images within a French and an English market revealed a fairly consistent juxtaposition between the stores on most key attributes. The Marks & Spencer quality rating had not quite achieved the level accorded by the British sample but the 'overall image' rating by the French sample was very strong. Although Marks & Spencer's prices in continental Europe are reported to be about 25 per cent higher than in the UK (Buckley, 1994), the price ratings by the British and French samples were identical. C & A prices were considered to be lower by the French consumers than by the British.

The level of services offered by Marks & Spencer was rated significantly better by the British sample; this could illustrate the slower learning process in the development of some image facets. Perceptions of national origin were generally accurate within both markets for Marks & Spencer, but inaccurate in the case of C & A. Marks & Spencer has chosen to project strongly its 'Britishness' within the French market.

Although of interest to retail managers and researchers, such analyses present essentially a static view of image. The movement of image, especially within unfamiliar markets, is likely to be very considerable. Two further dimensions need to be included, namely the strength or quantity of image (awareness), and the trajectory of image over time. A model is hypothesised, which suggests some of the determinants of retail images as they develop within new markets. New approaches to image research are clearly required to measure retail positioning at this crucial stage of commercial development.

REVIEW QUESTIONS

1. Study the ratings of market attributes in Table 9.2. How would you rank the relative importance of these in a market entry decision of your choice? Specify the nature of your entry decision and justify your ranking of the market variables.

2. Select a less developed country for an international market appraisal. What elements of risk are most salient to your appraisal and what information would you seek to help assess these risks?

3. As a consultant within a given national market, you have been commissioned to advise a foreign retailer wishing to enter that market. What competitor reactions should the foreign retailer anticipate in the short-term, and what new competition should be anticipated in the longer-term?

4. The major acquisitions by Marks & Spencer in Canada contrasted sharply with their incremental developments within continental Europe. Why do you consider that the latter have achieved greater success?

5. Why are images in different international markets often different, even if identical formats are used?

6. Select two national identities, including your own. Assume that a retailer from each country is intending to enter the other one. What are the main national stereotypes that will assist, or hinder, the development of image in each case?

7. What steps can a retailer take to increase initial awareness of its brand prior to developing stores within a new market?

8. What factors contribute to image in the early stage of development within a new market? How do these factors change as the image evolves over time?

REFERENCES

Aaker, D A (1991) *Managing brand equity*, Free Press, New York.

Brown, S and Burt, S (1992) 'Conclusion – retail internationalisation: past imperfect, future imperative', *European Journal of Marketing*, 26(8/9), 80–84.

Buckley, N (1994) 'Food for thought', *Financial Times*, 10 November.

Burt, S (1994) 'Carrefour group – the first 25 years', in McGoldrick, P J (ed,) *Cases in Retail Management*, Pitman, London, 154–164.

Coopers & Lyband (1993) 'Retailing in the 21st century: a global perspective', Chain Store Age Executive (Special Issue), 69(12), 4–81.

Davies, G and Brookes, J (1989) *Positioning Strategy in Retailing*, Paul Chapman, London.

Goldstein, C and Rowley, A (1990) 'Shogun wedding', *Far Eastern Economic Review*, 28 June, 70–71.

Holden, N (1994) 'Littlewoods in St Petersburg: a major development in UK–Russian retail co-operation', in McGoldrick, P J (ed.), *Cases in Retail Management*, Pitman, London, 194–201.

Kapferer, J N (1986) 'Beyond positioning: retailer's identity', *Retail Strategies for Profit and Growth*, ESOMAR, Amsterdam, 167–175.

McGoldrick, P J (1990) *Retail Marketing*, McGraw-Hill, Maidenhead.

McGoldrick, P J and S.A. Ali (1994) 'Discount store patronage and the multi-attribute attitude model', *Proceedings of the Annual MEG Conference*, Ulster, 657–666.

McGoldrick, P J, Bosworth, D, Betts, E and Duffy, M (1995) *International Retail Price Differences*, Office of Fair Trading, London.

McGoldrick, P J and Ho, S L (1992) 'International positioning: Japanese department stores in Hong Kong', *European Journal of Marketing*, 26(8/9), 61–73.

McGoldrick, P J and Holden, N J (1993) 'Developments by Western retailers in East Europe and Russia', *Journal of Marketing Channels*, 2(3), 61–84.

Marks & Spencer (1994) *Company Facts*, Marks & Spencer, London.

Mitchell, V W and McGoldrick, P J (1994) 'The role of geodemographics in segmenting and targeting consumer markets', *European Journal of Marketing*, 28(5), 54–72.

Mitton, A (1987) 'Foreign retail companies operating in the UK: strategy and performance', *Retail & Distribution Management*, 15(1), 29–31.

OECD (1994) *Quarterly National Accounts*, 2(2), OECD, Paris.

Reynolds, J (1994) 'Is there a market for teleshopping? The home shopping experience', in McGoldrick P J (ed), *Cases in Retail Management*, Pitman, London, 16–25.

Tokyo Business Today (1989) 'New globalization and a touch of dogma', December, 60–62.

Tordjman, A (1993) *Evolution of Retailing Formats in the EEC*, Groupe HEC, Paris.

Tordjman, A (1994) 'Toys 'R' Us', in McGoldrick P J (ed), *Cases in Retail Management*, Pitman, London, 165–184.

Whitehead, M (1991) 'International franchising – Marks & Spencer: a case study', *International Journal of Retail and Distribution Management*, 19(2), 10–12.

Whitehead, M (1992) *Marks & Spencer: Britain's leading retailer – quality and value worldwide*, CORTCO Case Study Conference, London.

Wilson, A, Betts, E J and McGoldrick, P J (1995) 'Consumer price cognition in contrasting shopping contexts', *Proceedings of the European Academy of Marketing Conference*, Paris.

CHAPTER 10

The internationalisation of limited line discount grocery operations

David Bennison and Hanne Gardner

INTRODUCTION

The rapid growth of internationalisation in the retail sector in the last decade has raised many questions about form, process and consequences. Once a subject of arcane interest, it has now become a major issue for retailers, and one whose significance can only continue to grow. The rise of the narrow focus, global retailer, expanding largely through franchising (for example, Benetton, Body Shop, McDonald's) preceded, and perhaps partly conditioned, the current growth in the international activity of the larger, more mainstream retailers. A wide range of factors on both the demand and supply sides of retailing have influenced the development of internationalisation, including, for example, the tightening of domestic market conditions, the declining cost and increasing capabilities of information technology, and the relaxation and removal of trade barriers in various parts of the world. The myriad interplay of many variables across different sectors, formats and countries produces pictures of activity that are both complex and dynamic, and which in turn pose a challenge to the development of a deeper understanding of the phenomenon.

One way of exploring the issue is to use case studies of particular sectors, companies and/or countries as the basis of an inductive approach to conceptual and theoretical formulation (Gill and Johnson, 1991). The value of this kind of work has been emphasised, for example, by Williams (1992), who characterised research on the motives for internationalisation as 'fragmented'. This chapter's contribution to the discussion is therefore to examine in some detail a particular retail sector – limited line grocery discount retailing – which has experienced substantial international activity in the last ten years. Through reference to the wider literature, it is then possible to highlight those parts of the process that are well understood and, equally important, to identify those where further research could be profitably directed. A limited line discount shop stocks predominantly commodity packaged goods (about 600 lines). A small number of fresh, chilled and frozen products are normally available.

Food retailing as a whole presents many examples of companies which have yet to involve themselves in trading outside their domestic markets, together with a smaller number which have become involved internationally, albeit usually on a modest scale relative to their domestic operations. However, while the overall position regarding mainstream superstore/ hypermarket operators is, as yet, generally fairly restrained, the sub-sector of limited line discounting stands out as one where some of the fastest and most vigorous internationalisation activity of any type of retailing is taking place, and, moreover, the companies involved are (unusually) adopting strategies of organic growth.

Discounting is hardly a new feature of the retail scene, although historically it has tended to be strongly associated with recession, and used by companies as a marketing tactic at appropriate times. What is much newer has been the emergence of discounting as a central, overriding philosophy of business from which its principal adherents do not deviate, and from which all operational and marketing activities spring. While three types of discount food retailer can be identified (Berry and Holmes, 1993), the limited line discounters stand out not only because they are very distinctive and focused in their style, but also because of their 'unprecedented disposition ... to transfer their formats across borders' (CIG, 1993), with the German firm of Aldi leading the way. The other two are extended range discounters (for example, Kwik Save, Lo-Cost), and discount superstores (for example, Pioneer, Food Giant, Dales).

This chapter focuses on the internationalisation of limited line discounters from the specific perspective of Denmark, and the experience of the Danish retailer Netto, which has quickly become Denmark's leading retail 'export'. The rationale for this particular choice is, first, that Denmark provides an example of a country which combines a sophisticated and progressive consumer market with a historically restrictive environment for the development of larger retail companies in general, and the establishment of foreign-based companies in particular. The introduction of the limited line discounters has fundamentally changed the structure of grocery retailing within only ten years. Secondly, the Danish company Dansk Supermarked has targeted the UK with its Netto format, and it is currently pursuing a programme of rapid store development and expansion within an economic environment where retail saturation has become a much discussed issue.

10.1 THE CONTEXT: RETAILING IN DENMARK

The population of Denmark (5.1 million) is amongst the most prosperous of the EU, and has for long enjoyed a high standard of living. Economic growth and stability have been underpinned by a Nordic tradition of social democracy, where state involvement in welfare and intervention in commerce have been deeply engrained, and where consumerist issues play an important role in the market (*ombudsman* is not only a Danish word, but also a Danish institution adopted by many other countries). Denmark has a strong rural tradition, and co-operatives have featured in local communities and have been strong for over a century, securing and maintaining a major role in retail provision. Operating in tandem with small independent traders, they were for many years protected from the encroachment of either indigenous or foreign multiples. As in many other countries, however, the 1980s saw the emergence of new economic and social pressures, which have inevitably impacted on the retail sector. To some extent the developments in Danish retailing are not dissimilar to the changes which gathered momentum in the UK thirty years ago; in other respects, they may offer some pointers to what can be expected here. Together, they provide a perspective on the nature and causes of retail change, and, in particular, on retail internationalisation.

10.1.1 Size and structure

Danish retailing has, on the whole, moved and developed relatively slowly. A recession in the late 1970s was replaced during the early part of the 1980s by a period of steady economic growth which was reflected in rising sales volumes of 2 per cent to 3 per cent per year up until 1987. There was then a second and sudden recession, deeper than the previous one, as the government introduced various fiscal measures to curb a rapidly escalating borrowing requirement and a balance of payments deficit. In 1987 and 1988 retail sales volumes declined by 3 to 4 per cent. Since 1990 modest economic growth has returned, but retail sales volumes have remained flat (Danmarks Statistik, 1994).

Food and drink sales account for about 60 per cent of total retail sales, and are dominated by the co-op and two multiples. Retail food provision is complemented by a large number of independent specialist shops (confectioners, bakers, greengrocers etc.). Outside of the broad food sector, Danish retailing has been dominated by small businesses, with multiples only significant in furniture, electricals and some clothing sub-sectors (CIG, 1990).

The level of international activity by Danish retailers is relatively low. Of the 311 European retail organisations with operations abroad recorded by CIG (1991), only nine (2.9 per cent) were Danish, the three largest being, in order of number of stores, Dansk Supermarked, Jensen Taepper (Carpetland), and Bang & Olufsen. Of the 34 foreign retailers recorded by CIG as operating in Denmark, the three largest were buying groups (Expert, Intersport and Edeka), and only eight retail store operators had more than ten units, the largest being Aldi (with 112 at that time in 1991).

10.1.2 Recent changes in the food sector

As might be expected in a country dominated by co-operatives, changes in food retailing in Denmark have tended to take place fairly gradually, with considerable constraints placed on the development of either large companies or large store units (see section 10.2.2). A watershed in Danish food retailing seems, however, to have been reached in 1987, with the onset of recession. The limited line discount sector, which had been introduced during an earlier recession, suddenly began to grow rapidly after a ten-year gestation period, at the expense of the more traditional supermarkets and grocers. By the end of 1992, the discount sector was taking 15.4 per cent of sales, and was forecast to grow to 17.6 per cent in 1996, and 18.5 per cent in 1999 (Hartvig-Larsen and Bahr, 1992). At the same time, it is being predicted that the number of hypermarkets may also be on the verge of a sudden rise in numbers, albeit from a low base: from 7 to 14 by 1995 in Jutland, for example (Hartvig-Larsen and Bahr, 1992).

The changes in food retailing result primarily from the activities of the three largest companies: FDB, Dansk Supermarked and Aldi, with, respectively, a 36.8 per cent, 15.6 per cent and 4.2 per cent share of sales in 1992 (Hartvig-Larsen and Bahr, 1992). The main features and developments of each are as follows.

FDB

FDB is the main Danish wholesale and producer co-operative (the equivalent of the UK's CWS). It moved into retailing in 1972 after constitutional constraints had been lifted in 1968. Its retail portfolio is dominated by food and it trades from a number of fascias (see Table 10.1). SuperBrugsen is the main supermarket chain and Fakta the co-op's discount chain.

A sluggish financial performance with trading losses in the early 1990s led to a major restructuring of the portfolio. The closure of about 40 unprofitable FDB supermarkets was followed by a noticeable shift to price-conscious formats, apparent most clearly in the fate of the Irma chain. Originally acquired in 1982, and seen in some respects as the Danish equivalent of J Sainsbury, Irma made record profits in 1985, only to find them turn to record losses by 1991. In 1993 FDB began to restructure the division. In January 65 stores were put up for sale, 30 were being converted to the new SuperBrugsen format (focusing on value-for-money and fresh food), and another 25 converted to Fakta discount stores. It is intended to continue to operate the remaining stores under their existing name, and possibly under a management buy-out. Indeed, there is the possibility that the success of the remaining stores may lead to some expansion (*Politiken Weekly*, 1993).

Table 10.1 Co-op food retailing fascias

Operating name	FDB	Independent co-ops
OBS!	11	—
Kvickly	57	14
Brugsen	38	231
SuperBrugsen	187	150
DagliBrugsen	74	191
Subsidiaries:		
Irma	62	
Fakta	201	
Others	68	
Totals	698	586

Source: FDB (1994).

Dansk Supermarked

Dansk Supermarked is the second largest Danish retailer and, with its Netto format, by far the most active internationally. The company was formed in 1964 as a joint private venture between AP Moeller Maritime, the shipping and industrial group, and F Salling, the owner of three department stores. For both partners, the development was seen as a strategic diversification away from static core businesses into a growth sector.

The company has clothing and shoe shops, as well as the food stores which form its basis. The latter operate in three formats, each of which is managed completely independently. These are (as of July 1994):

- Foetex supermarkets – 45 units;
- Bilka hypermarkets – 10 units;
- Netto discount stores – 183 units.

The Netto format was inspired by Aldi, but not as a direct copy. It was thought that 'a good idea could be made better' (Arnum, 1994). The first Netto store opened in a suburb of Copenhagen in 1981, and during that year a further seven were to follow. The number of units has increased as follows, an initially steady rise giving way to more rapid growth after 1987:

1982 –   15
1987 –   68
1989 – 122
1991 – 150
1992 – 160
1993 – 171
1994 (July) – 183

The size of a Netto store in Denmark tends to vary between 2,500 and 6,000 sq ft, and net margins are quoted as being between 1 and 2 per cent (although the company publishes only minimal financial data). As with other discounters, the key to its profitability lies in the very tight operational systems which are in place. All stores have EPOS, and shops run on a cash-only basis (cutting out cheque and credit card fraud, and maximising cash flow as well as speeding up the checkout operation). A high level of security is maintained to minimise theft.

Aldi

Aldi, the German company entered the Danish market in 1977, and had opened three of their limited line discount stores by the end of that year. A programme of store openings continued at an average of six to seven a year, reaching a total of 79 by 1987. Aldi had expected to show a deficit in their early years, but were reportedly still trading at a loss in 1987. It was even rumoured that they put the chain up for sale. However, their presence was maintained, and, in fact, the store opening programme accelerated. Between 1987 and 1988 another 13 units were added, and by July 1994 there were 159 in total.

When Aldi first opened in Denmark, one firm of analysts were sceptical about its likely success (Konsulentstudierejse, 1976). However, their report did include two observations which have subsequently proved highly perceptive and pertinent to the situation today:

> First, nobody in Germany believed that Aldi would be a success until it was too late. Everyone in Germany was thinking along the lines of one-stop shopping and service, taking for granted rising demand and increased spending power. Given lower growth, there will always be groups in a society with a need for lower prices and time to shop around – pensioners, for example.

> Second, it should be remembered that the tendency to trade up in retailing automatically increases costs and that creates a niche for a discounter. This poses a real threat for the existing retail trade.

10.2 THE GROWTH CONDITIONS FOR LIMITED LINE DISCOUNTERS IN DENMARK

The early scepticism about the potential for discount groceries in the Danish market has been mirrored in other countries. In Denmark it took ten years for the sector to emerge fully and the development needs to be seen within the wider context of the increasing segmentation of food retailing which both reflects and springs from changes in the broader business environment influencing both the demand for such formats and their supply.

10.2.1 Demand side factors

The three most important components of the environment to have influenced the demand for limited line discounting have been as follows.

The economy

Following a recession in the early 1980s, the Danish economy recovered strongly, and grew at between 3 and 4 per cent between 1983 and 1987. Private consumption increased in parallel. A rising public sector deficit and growing balance of payments problems led to the imposition of fiscal and credit restrictions. These produced a sudden and deep downturn in 1987 – real incomes fell by 1.7 per cent in both 1987 and 1988. A subsequent modest revival in GDP growth began in 1989, but no upturn in consumption has taken place. In 1993/94 unemployment was around 10.5 per cent of the workforce.

The recession of the late 1980s impacted on the food retail sector in two significant ways. First, and most obvious, is the sharp stimulus it gave to the expansion of the price discounting operations of Aldi, Fakta and Netto as shoppers sought to economise. Second, and perhaps paradoxically, it stimulated shop property development. House building declined sharply in the recession, and developers (and financial institutions) looked to shop property as an alternative avenue for growth. At the same time local authorities, concerned with rising unemployment, became more amenable to the granting of planning permission for retail development. They now looked upon retailer expansion as a useful means of providing job creation opportunities, and these were not resisted strongly by the independent specialist retailers who regarded such developments as essentially complementary to their own businesses.

Consumer/shopping behaviour

When food shopping, it is common for Danes to buy basic commodities at a supermarket or discounter, and to use small specialist shops for 'luxury' items. Two- or three-stop shopping is commonplace. Loyalty to the small specialist is still strong, and derives from a long tradition of small-scale, community-based retailing with strong ties of patronage which have not yet been seriously eroded by the advent of one-stop shopping. Greater use of bicycles and public transport, and concomitant lower car ownership than in much of Western Europe (305 cars per 1,000 inhabitants, compared with 435 in the UK, for example), both reflect and sustain a high weekly incidence of shopping trips by households. Surveys have shown that the Danish grocery shopper typically visits five to six different food stores (Godt, 1992).

Price-consciousness – triggered widely by the sudden increases in personal taxation in 1987 which hit the affluent shopper the hardest – remains an element of consumer behaviour, and to some extent has become 'fashionable'. This attunes with long-established consumerist attitudes which, for example, place emphasis on minimal packaging and recycling. As in Germany, there is also very limited ownership and use of international credit cards, and payment by cash or cheque remains the norm. Customers have come to expect a very competitive food market with continuous special offers, and with both branded and fresh foods subject to deep price cuts. For price/budget-conscious shoppers, the discounters also have the benefit of not providing temptations for impulse shopping, especially when children are present.

Socio-demographics

Denmark's population is static, with a marginal decline forecast for the mid-1990s. In common with other Western European countries, the population profile has been ageing, with an increase in the over 60 age group expected to be matched by a decline in the 15–24 cohort. Most significantly from the viewpoint of discount groceries is the high proportion of the population classified as either 'pensioners' (21.0 per cent), or 'students' (15.2 per cent) (Eurostat, 1991). Together they provide a large segment who are regarded as exceptionally price-conscious and, in the case of pensioners at least, have time for shopping around.

10.2.2 Supply side factors

The economic, behavioural and demographic factors which have produced demand pressures for discounting have been paralleled by a number of constraints on the development of new retail formats, resulting mainly from the politico-legal elements of the environment. Amongst the most significant have been the following.

Restrictions on the establishment of new shops

There is strict application of land use planning controls. A law restricting the number of shops that could be owned by any one retailer was repealed in 1966, but local authorities continued until the late 1980s to take negative attitudes to applications for new shops, especially hypermarkets and superstores.

Tight and strictly enforced limitations on shop opening hours

There is a standard closing time for all shops of 5.30 pm Monday to Friday, 12 pm on Saturday and no Sunday opening at all. The wish to protect shop workers from exploitation, pressure from the Lutheran Church and the political strength of the independent retail sector have all combined to ensure that operators cannot maximise the use of their physical capacity. A relaxation allowing opening on one Saturday afternoon a month has not brought the country significantly closer to UK practice, although observation suggests that enforcement *during the week* appears to have become laxer, particularly in hypermarkets (von Eyben *et al*, 1989).

Restrictions on advertising and promotion

Commercial television and radio with advertising only began in Denmark in the late 1980s. The guidelines for advertising standards are strict, and active consumer organisations are quick to contest claims they regard as exaggerated or fraudulent. Similarly, restrictions on retail promotional activity such as coupons, sample distribution and competitions are so tightly scrutinised as to make them virtually impossible to operate. Price has therefore been the only platform for promotional activity.

Social security costs

Social security costs on employers to fund the generous cradle-to-grave welfare provision are among the highest in Europe. Combined with high statutory minimum wages, applied pro rata for part-time labour, the consequences are high labour costs. Passed on to the consumer, these contribute to the high cost of living in Denmark, the third highest in Europe after Norway and Switzerland.

10.2.3 Marketing implications

The different components of the retail environment are clearly inter-related, and the impact of any one is difficult to isolate. However, in aggregate their effect on Danish food retailing in the early 1980s was to constrain, quite seriously, any one company's ability to differentiate itself other than through price-led strategies.

The specific limitations on promotion have already been noted. Variations in the retail 'Product' – the range and type of goods, service levels, opening times, etc. – were all limited by the prohibitions on large-scale shopping schemes and by the strict policy on opening hours. The large number of specialist independent shops made it difficult and risky to undertake large-scale differentiation by moving upmarket in the provision of fresh food/delicatessen items. Similarly, the ability to use location as a way of gaining competitive advantage was restricted by planning controls, the levels of car ownership, and by the provision of varied shopping down to low levels of the shopping centre hierarchy.

The focus on price as the main differentiating variable during the 1980s, and especially after 1987, favoured the limited line discount format. The overall size of the Danish market, and the locational and store size restrictions noted above, meant that high volumes with low margins were most likely to be sustained by smaller stores providing narrow ranges of basic goods. The stocking of only about 600 lines allowed maximum economies of scale in sourcing. For Aldi, the Danish shops were but an extension of their huge German operation; for Fakta, the size and resources of FDB were a major benefit. As initially the smallest of the three, Netto was perhaps the most disadvantaged in buying power to begin with, but they joined the AMS buying group, and a rapid growth in new store openings would have substantially strengthened its position. It may have also provided the additional incentive to pare costs to the minimum, and put in place the extremely tight control mechanisms which characterise the operation.

The acceptance by the Danish consumer of the limited line, no frills, discount format, and the greater price-consciousness which they have instilled amongst all income groups, may be proving the most powerful of the stimuli to the expansion of hypermarkets, where prices can be even lower than in the limited liners. For example, a recent shopping basket survey (Arnum, 1992) revealed the lowest prices for a basket of groceries to be in the Bilka hypermarket (706 Kr), followed by Netto (732 Kr) and then Foetex supermarkets (766 Kr). If the development of these continues as forecast, then a true polarisation of Danish food retailing is likely to take place. At one end, will be large hypermarkets offering a wide range of non-food items catering for car-borne, one-stop shoppers; at the other, the limited line discounters, operating at neighbourhood level and complemented by smaller, specialist shops. Within this market, the role of Aldi as a catalyst for change, and as a continuing player, is of great significance.

The relatively small size of the Danish market, the rapid growth of new stores and the need to expand to maintain and improve scale and buying economies led Netto in 1989 to consider expansion abroad. An office was opened in London to prepare the ground, and within a couple of years the company has become the most dynamic Danish retailer operating internationally.

10.3 NETTO IN THE UK

The attractions of the UK market to Netto (and a year earlier to Aldi) provide an almost mirror image of the possible reasons why Kwik Save, or any other UK grocery business, has not set up in Denmark – or probably even contemplated it. The UK provides a market of over 55 million people. By the late 1980s/early 1990s grocery retailers were making net profit margins of 6–7 per cent, providing rich potential for undercutting. The major companies had moved upmarket and closed smaller, local stores, leaving both sectoral and locational niches to be filled. Finally, for the Danes, there is a familiarity with both the English language and culture, and relatively close proximity to Denmark by sea and air.

10.3.1 Locations and formats

Netto established its first UK store in December 1990 in Halton, a suburb of Leeds. Two years later, by December 1992, there were 44 stores in operation, mainly to the east of the Pennines in an area extending from Retford (Nottinghamshire) to Bedlington (Northumberland), although recent store openings in Wallasey, Stockport, Manchester, Salford and Preston herald a westward move into Aldi's English heartland. The stores are served by newly built headquarters and a 225,000 sq ft distribution facility at South Elmsall near Doncaster. The facility has the capacity to service about 150 stores, and the option to extend capacity further if required.

The typical Netto store in the UK is closely modelled on its Danish counterpart, although the average size is larger – initially 5,000 to 8,000 sq ft, but with some new ones of up to 10,000 sq ft. Stores stock approximately 600 lines, displayed and stored within the shop in cut case displays. There is a very high level of security, including small cages for spirits at the checkouts, and sales are cash only. Together with only about four to five full-time equivalent staff, the central tenet of the business – cost cutting, high volume with low margin – is obvious.

The flat management structure of the Danish operation is replicated with a short line of command to the UK headquarters. The establishment of UK suppliers has been a priority, and although some national brands are stocked (for example, Kellogg's), Netto typically has sourced from smaller manufacturers who are not tied into an existing large store operator. They have used them to supply house brands such as Royal Ambassador, Farmers Fayre and Gillroys. The company holds out the promise of 'growing together', with access to Netto's continental markets seen as enticing bait (Gundelach, 1993).

Locationally, the choice of Yorkshire as the core from which to start the UK operation is said to have been dictated by its good motorway connections and the direct sea link to Denmark via Hull which avoids the congestion in the South East of England. In addition, the region offers good access to suppliers and to a concentration of the target population. The rapid growth in store numbers is being achieved through a combination of new site development (some in conjunction with developers of small, district centre-scale schemes), and the acquisition of existing buildings, including former supermarkets and car showrooms. The UK director has stated that the company likes to be seen as the 'neighbourhood store', and has characterised locations as 'suburban, middle market'. CIG (1992) have interpreted Netto's offer at being aimed 'squarely at C2DEs'. In broad terms, Netto's locations do coincide well with areas of the country where grocery shoppers are seen to be more price sensitive.

At the end of 1992, Netto's sales were estimated at about £125 million – 0.3 per cent of the total grocery market, and 3.1 per cent of the discount sector (compared with Aldi, 0.6 per cent and 6.5 per cent respectively), and a long way behind Kwik Save (5.4 per cent and 62 per cent), and Lo-Cost (1.1 per cent and 12.3 per cent). Netto at this stage was therefore a very small player in the UK market, as was Aldi, but their impact in raising price awareness and competition at a time of prolonged recession has been considerable (CIG, 1992).

The full extent and nature of any long-term responses by the UK discount grocers to the limited line discount operations remains to be seen, but already involves, for example, greater use of secondary brands, and deep price cutting on selected items. Similarly, the impact on the independent sector is as yet unclear, but could cause greater use of voluntary and buying groups to enable competition on price and an acceleration in the decline of the independent sector.

10.4 OVERVIEW AND CONCLUSIONS

10.4.1 Limited line discount groceries: the common features

This chapter has examined the process and impact of retail internationalisation through a case study of limited line discount operations in Danish food retailing. The role of Aldi and Netto are of special significance, the former being Denmark's largest retail 'import', the latter its principal 'export'. From a UK perspective, both companies are of special interest because of their plans in this country and the stimulus they have provided to the discount sector with a 'destabilising effect disproportionate to their numbers' (CIG, 1992).

Differences between Aldi and Netto (for example, in the use of EPOS, or the role of brands) are together much less significant than their similarities which, taken together, provide some insights into the internationalisation process in the discount grocery sector. The key points are as follows.

Taxonomy

In 1990 Treadgold placed Aldi (Albrecht Group) in his 'Cautious Internationalists' group (Treadgold 1990), characterised by high cost and high control and, at that time, concentrated internationalisation, operating in countries adjacent or close to its home. Aldi's subsequent developments in the UK, France and the USA, and plans for Italy, Spain and Eastern Europe, may warrant its reclassification as an 'Emboldened Internationalist'. CIG (1991) put them in the third of the three stages they identify in the development of international retailers – described as 'ambitious'. Netto, because of its more limited international presence at the moment, may be classified as a 'Cautious Internationalist' in Treadgold's terminology, but is already following Aldi's move out from its core. The scale and speed of its plans in the UK (and elsewhere) scarcely warrant any description other than 'ambitious'.

Organic growth

Both Aldi in Denmark and Netto in the UK have followed policies of organic growth to build up a presence. This is unusual in grocery retailing where acquisition or joint venture strategies have been more common (for instance, Sainsbury's purchase of the American chain Shaws; Tesco's acquisition of Catteau in France). The offer of a format that is distinctive within the host countries when first introduced, and which depends on tight managerial controls in combination with an organisational culture of secrecy may be the main reasons for this. The principal drawback – access to sites – is offset by the relatively small size of operating units and their neighbourhood level threshold of viability.

Private ownership

The organic entry and growth strategies of both Aldi and Netto are strongly underpinned by the ability of both companies to take a long-term perspective to development, and to be able to eschew short/medium-term profitability in return for gaining market share in the long term. The stance of banks in Germany and Denmark towards the underwriting of this approach contrasts with the inherent short-termism forced on public companies responsible to shareholders which is particularly noticeable in the UK.

Motives for internationalisation

For both Aldi moving into Denmark and Netto moving into the UK, limited opportunities for further expansion in the home market and the perception of growth potential by exploiting niches in a foreign market might be seen as the basic motives behind their moves. However, it could be argued that these are but conditions, and the motives for internationalisation stem more from managerial/entrepreneurial ambitions. Williams (1992) has drawn attention to what seems to be, for British international retailers at least, the relatively low influence of motives arising from limited domestic growth opportunities, and his analysis points to the importance of exporting retail 'know-how'. Intuitively, both Netto and Aldi seem likely to fall within his first grouping of firms by their motives, characterised as 'proactive and growth oriented'. The features of these include long-run sales growth, long-run profits, attractive current and future growth prospects in overseas markets and economies of scale.

Impact on host countries

Within Denmark, Aldi pioneered the limited line discount format and saw it taken up by its Danish competitors after some initial scepticism. Within the UK, Netto and Aldi have created much interest, again after early doubts, and although none of the major chains has yet paid them the compliment of an exact 'me-too' operation, discount formats have been introduced by Gateway, Asda and the Co-op as part of a wider process of segmentation within the UK grocery market. The catalytic effect they may be having on the lower end of the market, particularly in altering shopping behaviour among the car-owning middle classes (whose financial caution has increased markedly), could eventually prove as significant as it has been in Denmark. It could take a number of years to become widespread, but there are some early indications in areas where Aldi and Netto have been operating that the stores are used in combination with existing superstores, particularly for secondary shopping (Clarke, Bennison and Guy, 1994). To attempt to identify the discount shopper with reference only to socio-economic classifications seems far too narrow a view to take of increasingly complex shopper behaviour.

10.4.2 A wider research agenda

Four years ago, Williams (1991) noted that: 'Research and comment on Retailer Internationalisation confines itself to describing: its recent increase; underlying motivation; and profiling the major players.' While this chapter may fall to an extent within this category, its essential intention, through the case study approach, is to raise questions and help to identify areas where further research and thought on retail internationalisation could be best directed. Specific matters relating to the grocery discount sector can certainly be discerned, but it is more useful to conclude by taking a wider perspective beyond this. In looking at a particular sector in a particular country, a number of issues have been recognised. The extent to which they apply across different sectors, formats and countries, and their managerial, strategic and theoretical implications, need to be considered as appropriate themes for further research. Four main groups of topics can be identified as follows.

Motives/causes for internationalisation

The rather deterministic notion of 'push', 'pull' and 'facilitating' factors provides a framework for understanding the environmental conditions under which internationalisation may take place, but they are not in themselves its cause. Entrepreneurial flair, managerial competencies and individuals' predilections to respond to the opportunities and threats presented by the external environment seem to be at the heart of the Danish experiences in discount grocery. They have been paralleled elsewhere (for example, Lord *et al*, 1988), and, as Williams (1992) noted, are still not clearly understood.

Process and management of internationalisation

For Netto and Aldi, organic growth with tight central control has been the method of implementing internationalisation and managing its development. A number of retailers in other sectors and formats have done likewise; others have taken alternative approaches – some successfully, others less so. While the success or failure of individual companies may be relatively easy to interpret, it remains far less clear whether more general relationships do exist between performance and the development process and management of international operations.

Impact of internationalisation

The Danish example highlighted the impact that international retailers can have within their host countries, especially if they introduce or develop a distinctive format. Changes in shopping behaviour as the newcomers gain market share, and the triggering of defensive reactions by indigenous retailers are perhaps the most immediately overt consequences. However, a whole range of other, initially more subtle, changes may begin as well – for example, in supply and distribution channels, locational patterns, and management techniques and cultures – but they remain little documented or comprehended.

Conceptualisation

Finally, retail internationalisation must be seen as part of a wider process of retail change, and should not be divorced from its other elements. Conceptualisations of such change have taken various perspectives and been applied at different scales – from the individual firm through to the national and international economy. Brown (1992) has provided an excellent synthesis of alternative approaches focusing on a micro-scale perspective, and concluded that each of the main conceptual traditions – neoclassical, behavioural and structuralist – offered 'ample opportunity for additional academic endeavour'. Such a conclusion could equally be applied to the other end of the scale of locational decision-making – internationalisation – where, with the notable exception of Wrigley's (1993) work, retail-specific interpretations of the changes taking place are rare.

REVIEW QUESTIONS

1. Why do you think Aldi and Netto entered the British market? What is likely to have motivated their managers to do so?

2. From your own experience, do you believe that shoppers see marked differences in the way Netto, Aldi and Kwik Save operate?

3. From the analysis of factors contributing to the success of limited range discounters in Denmark, what differences in the British market might increase or decrease their market potential in Britain?

4. Since the case study was written, what developments have there been at Netto and why?

5. Since the case study was written what developments have there been in the discount grocery market both nationally and internationally and why?

REFERENCES

Arnum, S (1992) 'Dansk Supermarked skaerper priskrig', *Jyllands-Posten*, 13 December 1992.
Arnum, S (1994) 'Skaberen af et begreb'. *Jyllands-Posten*, 12 July 1994.
Berry, C and Holmes, S (1993) *Discount Grocery Retailing – Fashion or Philosophy?*, IGD Publications, Watford.
Brown, S (1992) *Retail Location: A Micro-Scale Perspective*, Avebury, Aldershot.
Clarke, I, Bennison, D and Guy, C (1994) 'The dynamics of UK grocery retailing at the local scale', *International Journal of Retail and Distribution Management* 22(6), 11–20.
CIG (1990) *Retailing in Europe: Denmark*, Corporate Intelligence Group, London.
CIG (1991) *Cross-Border Retailing in Europe*, Corporate Intelligence Group, London.
CIG (1992) *Discount Food Retailing in the UK*, Corporate Intelligence Group, London.
CIG (1993) *Discount Food Retailers in Europe*, Corporate Intelligence Group, London.
Danmarks Statistik (1994) *Statistisk tiaarsoversigt 1993*, Copenhagen.
Eurostat (1991) *Dansk Media Index*, Copenhagen.
FDB (1994) *Annual Report and Accounts 1993*, FDB, Albertslund.
Gill, J and Johnson, P (1991) *Research Methods for Managers*, Paul Chapman, London.
Godt, M (1992) *Forbrugerejede Butikker i Danmark*, FDB, Albertslund.
Gundelach, H (1993) 'Netto', paper given to IGD Conference, *Discount Retailing: Recession Phenomenon or Structural Change?*, 22 April, 1993.
Hartvig-Larsen, H and Bahr, H (1992) 'Detailhandelsprognosen', *Jyllands-Posten*, 12 November 1992.
Konsulentstudierejse (1976) *Discount – og Lavprisbutikker i Vesteuropa*, Copenhagen.
Lord, D, Moran, W, Parker, T and Sparks, L (1988) 'Retailing on three continents: the discount food store operations of Albert Gubay', *International Journal of Retailing*, 3(3), 3–53.
Politiken Weekly (1993), 'Oproret ulmer i Brugserne', 15 September 1993, p.12.
Treadgold, A (1990) 'The developing internationalisation of retailing', *International Journal of Retail and Distribution Management*, 18(2), 4–11.
Von Eyben, W E, Gulmann, C and Norgaard, J (1989) 'Butikstid Lovbekendtgorelse No.558', in *Karnovs Lovsamling*, 3 (12).
Williams, D E (1991) 'Differential firm advantages and retailer internationalization', *International Journal of Retail and Distribution Management*, 19(4), 3–12.
Williams, D E (1992) 'Motives for retailer internationalization: their impact, structure and implications', *Journal of Marketing Management*, 8, 269–285.
Wrigley, N (1993) 'Retail concentration and the internationalisation of British grocery retailing', in Bromley, R D F and Thomas, C J (eds.) *Retail Change: Contemporary Issues*, UCL Press, London.

CHAPTER 11

Market innovation and internationalisation: The success of Toys 'R' Us

Gary Davies and Nitin Sanghavi

INTRODUCTION

One way to ensure success in business is to offer the public something new, something unique. One way of explaining the success or failure of retail businesses, as they seek to become international by entering foreign markets, is to examine whether the retailer's business has something new to offer in other markets. If the retailer is seen as innovative, in that no one is selling the same products or that no one is offering the same service, then the retailer has a greater chance of success than if there are already one or more similar retailers established in the marketplace.

In this chapter we examine one particular retailer, Toys 'R' Us, as an example of a novel retail format known generally as the category killer. Toys 'R' Us is an example of a retailer which has been successful in a number of countries even though what it sells is available from many other established retailers. We appraise the retailer using empirical data to understand more about what a category killer offers to explain its success in the British market. We examine how the concept could be applied to other product areas. Finally, we appraise the concept in the context of market innovation theory to understand more about why certain retailers can be successful internationally.

11.1 TOY RETAILING AND TOYS 'R' US

Toys 'R' Us is probably the world's largest toy specialist. It is based in the USA but trades worldwide. By 1992 it had 39 outlets in Britain, the context for our analysis. The typical store is comparatively large, some four to five thousand square metres in size. Ninety-seven per cent of its 30,000 product items are toys. According to EIU (1992): 'There is no doubt that more lines of toys are displayed in greater depth than in any other toy chain.'

Its first British store opened in 1985 but by 1992 Toys 'R' Us had become the country's largest toy retailer. The next two largest were Argos and Woolworth, neither of whom specialise in toys. The largest specialist apart from Toys 'R' Us in 1992 was Beatties with 69, comparatively small, outlets. Mail order was an important channel for toys accounting for 28 per cent of sales (Euromonitor, 1990). Other multiples included Children's World and Toy & Hobby, both trading from large stores and, superficially at least, in a similar way to Toys 'R' Us. Independent toy retailers were still important in the market although many only focused on toys in the last quarter of the year when sales boomed in the run up to Christmas.

Toy purchasers tend to be adults, particularly parents, but the real customer is the child. Brand names appear to be highly important (Zimmerman, 1992). Unlike most other British retail sectors the penetration of own-brand products is insignificant. The name of the toy is often synonymous with the brand (Monopoly, Lego) and although there are some well-established lines a feature of the market is the rapid growth and decline of highly publicised product lines (Care Bears, Cabbage Patch dolls). A retailer's ability to offer competitive prices appears to be an important factor but mothers tend not to do price comparison shopping, even though the price of many toys is high. They appear more concerned with wide aisles for pushchairs and in-stock availability (EIU, 1992).

Toys 'R' Us claim 'low' or 'everyday low' prices (Chanil, 1991; Loeb, 1990). They offer a price pledge to assure shoppers they cannot buy cheaper elsewhere. Their cost structure would be lower than that for their high street specialist competitors due to their out of town locations. Their high market share would generate favourable terms from suppliers (Neff, 1991). Staff costs in specialist stores and department stores would be higher. Toys 'R' Us would therefore enjoy a cost advantage that it might be able to use to keep its selling prices below those of its competition.

Price and range (choice) appeared to us therefore to be the two most likely sources of competitive advantage to explain the Toys 'R' Us success in the marketplace. To appraise both a survey was conducted comparing 12 toy retailers in one city, Manchester, during the last quarter of 1992.

11.2 EMPIRICAL RESEARCH

A sample of 14 toys were selected to assess relative price and availability. One of these, racing sets, was selected to check for depth of range within one type of toy. The 12 retail outlets surveyed were: four specialist toy retailers – Toys 'R' Us, Children's World, Toy & Hobby, Beatties; three department stores: Lewis's, Debenhams, Kendals; three catalogue retailers: Argos, Argos Superstore, Index; and two mail-order catalogues were examined – Kays and Littlewoods. Figure 11.1 sets out the entire range and selling prices available in each case of racing sets. Figure 11.2 sets out the individual prices and total for the basket of items for each outlet. Where no data is shown the retailer or catalogue did not offer the product. For the shopping basket a comparison is made for the total of the selling prices of the products available in each retailer with the total for just those products in Toys 'R' Us.

11.2.1 Range comparisons

Fifty-seven different racing sets were identified in the 12 outlets. The widest range by far (35 out of 57) was stocked by Toys 'R' Us. Some of the products in Littlewoods and Index were unbranded so the range advantage on branded merchandise for Toys 'R' Us was in practice even higher (35 out of 52). The next widest range of racing sets was offered by Beatties with 15. Of the 57 sets only 22 were stocked by more than one retailer. Toys 'R' Us stocked 13 sets that were not available at any other outlet.

The entire shopping basket of 14 toys was stocked by Toys 'R' Us. Argos Superstore and Index carried almost the same range. Toy & Hobby carried only six of the items.

11.2.2 Price comparisons

The prices charged for the toys varied. In two cases the same lowest price was charged for the racing sets in more than one outlet. Of the other 20 cases, Toys 'R' Us offered the lowest price in ten cases and Toy & Hobby in four cases. However, the price advantage in Toys 'R' Us was often very small (in one case a penny on an item retailing at £199.97) and never higher than 6.0 per cent on an item selling in only one other outlet (a Kays catalogue at £79.99). The typical price advantage for Toys 'R' Us was less than 0.1 per cent.

In the basket of toys, Toys 'R' Us was the price leader on eight toys, on one item by 12 per cent but normally by 0.1 per cent or less. The prices in the two Argos stores were the same and they are not considered separately in this part of the study. The basket prices were calculated excluding the relatively expensive Renegade Jeep as it was only available in four outlets. The price advantage for Toys 'R' Us calculated by comparing only those toys on sale in both outlets ranged from 0.08 per cent to over 30 per cent. The mail order catalogue retailers appeared relatively expensive, as was one department store, Kendals, part of the House of Fraser Group and often referred to as the 'Harrods of the North'.

11.2.3 Measures of advantage

Toys 'R' Us was not always the cheapest place to buy toys nor did it always carry every toy in the range. The racing sets they did not stock included those from several brand leaders such as Tyco and Scalextric. The price

Name	Toys 'R' Us	Children's World	Toy & Hobby	Beatties	Lewis's	Debenhams	Kendals	Argos	Argos Superstore	Index	Kays	Littlewoods
Blazing Ferraris	9.99											
Bullet Car	19.96											
Canyon of Doom	54.87		49.99								59.99	
Computer Challenge	74.97			52.99						48.99		
Corkscrew Challenge												
Daredevil Rally	49.99			44.98				49.99	49.99			
Earthquake Alley	39.99											
Ferrari F40	59.97											
Formula One Challenge		49.99										
Formula One Duel	29.97	32.99		29.99								
Formula Sport											16.99	
Highway Patrol											26.99	
Index												
No name										14.99		
No name										29.99		
Jump Challenge	29.97											
Littlewoods												
No name												59.99
No name												14.99
No name												39.99
Midnight Marathon	41.97			43.99								
M'way Loop Express		19.99									69.99	
Nipco Road Chaser			29.99									
P924 Challenge			29.99									
Porsche 930												
Quadruple Loop Shoot			59.99									
Race in a Case	63.87									47.50		
Scalextric												
Alpine Rallye	59.97											
Ascot				79.99								
The Derby	124.97											
Ford Cosworth		59.99										
Formula One	84.97			79.98			82.99	79.99	79.99	79.95		103.48

Fig. 11.1 Racing set comparison

Name	Toys 'R' Us	Children's World	Toy & Hobby	Beatties	Lewis's	Debenhams	Kendals	Argos	Argos Superstore	Index	Kays	Littlewoods
Grand Prix	46.97								46.99			
Isle of Man	63.99											
Le Mans 24 hr	79.87			79.98	79.99	79.99		79.99	79.99			
Mighty Metro	34.99	34.50			34.50		34.99	34.50	34.50	34.50		
Night Stage				54.98								
Ninja Turtles				54.98								
Pole Position	74.97										79.99	
Porsche Power	49.94					49.99	52.99	49.99	49.99	49.95		64.99
Rally Cross	59.97											
Rallye Sprint	44.87			44.99		39.99						
Road Racing	62.47			62.98	62.99		65.99	62.99	62.99	62.50		79.99
Speedway 500	44.87			39.99							59.99	
World Championship	199.97			199.98								
World Sports											99.99	
Sky Fighter	64.87		59.99							59.99	59.99	59.99
Speedloop											39.99	
Stock Car Challenge	14.99		12.99									
Super Slalom	74.99											
Super Sport	79.99											
Tyco												
Grand Prix	64.97		64.99		69.99			64.99	64.99			
Miami Police					49.95							
Monaco	43.94			39.98						39.95		
Monte Carlo	53.97				49.99							
Nigel Mansell	24.97		24.99	24.98	24.99	24.99		24.99	24.99			
Team Challenge	64.99											
World Champion								74.99	74.99			
Wild Thing and Bandit	29.97		29.99									
Number of sets	35	5	10	15	7	4	4	9	10	10	10	7
Number of unique sets	13	3	2	3	1	0	0	1	1	3	5	3
Number of sets price:												
Winner or leader	11	0	5	1	1	1	0	0	0	3	0	1

Fig. 11.1 (continued)

Item	Toys 'R' Us	Children's World	Toy & Hobby	Beatties	Lewis's	Debenhams	Kendals	Argos Superstore	Index	Kays	Littlewoods
Matchbox – 30 Piece Carry Case	14.97		19.99	19.99		19.99		16.99			19.99
Duplo #2376	11.24	11.99	11.25		11.25	12.99	16.50	11.25	11.25		
Tiny Tears	16.74	16.75	19.99	18.99	16.75	17.99	23.99	16.75	16.95		24.99
Cabbage Patch Kids	32.99	32.99	32.99	*32.98		34.99	59.99	32.99	32.99	39.99	39.99
Party Lights Sindy	13.94	13.49		13.98	12.99			13.99	13.99	16.99	16.99
Dream Ballet Sindy	13.94			13.99	13.99	14.99	17.99	13.99	13.99		
Roller Blade Barbie	10.37	9.99		10.99	10.49	10.99	13.99	10.49	10.45	17.99	
Sparkle Eyes Barbie	11.97	12.49		12.99	12.49	12.99	15.99	12.49	12.45	18.99	16.99
Lego Basic 365	15.97		15.99			19.99	18.99		15.99	24.99	22.99
Meccano Junior Set B	15.97	16.99		16.98			19.99	15.99	15.99		21.99
Monopoly	8.94	9.25	9.50	*9.98	9.25	9.99	9.99	9.25	9.25	13.99	
Magic Copier	16.97	16.89		16.98		16.99		16.89		24.99	
Crayola Deluxe Case	10.78	10.99		10.98				10.50	10.50	16.99	16.99
Renegade Jeep	289.87	265.00						295.00	295.00		
Total price of stocked toys		**151.82**	**109.71**	**178.83**	**87.21**	**171.90**	**197.42**	**181.57**	**163.80**	**174.92**	**180.92**
Same toys at Toys 'R' Us		**141.91**	**100.85**	**167.58**	**87.14**	**154.10**	**138.13**	**178.82**	**162.85**	**121.93**	**133.33**
Difference (Renegade Jeep not included)		−1.26%	−8.08%	−6.29%	−0.08%	−10.35%	−30.03%	−1.51%	−0.58%	−30.29%	−26.30%

*In catalogue but not in stock

Fig. 11.2 Toy basket comparisons

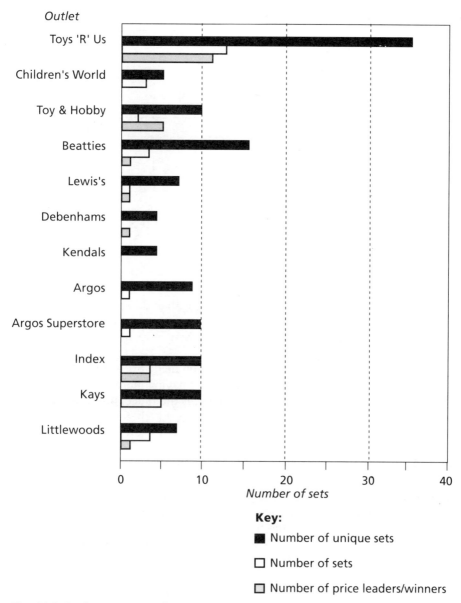

Fig. 11.3 Racing set comparison

advantage of shopping at Toys 'R' Us appears likely to be small; however, it was rare to find the same product on sale elsewhere at a much lower price. The same price pledge to refund any difference between their prices and lower prices elsewhere was given by a number or retailers, including Beatties who were often relatively expensive.

Figures 11.3, 11.4 and 11.5 show the empirical results in graphical form.

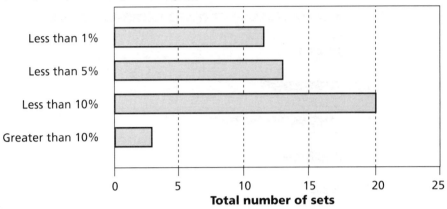

% difference from next cheapest

Total number of sets = 23

Fig. 11.4 Racing set difference

Toys 'R' Us offer a lower price to the customer than do some other outlets, notably the mail order catalogues. While their range is not always complete Figure 11.3 demonstrates what is probably their most notable advantage, choice and availability.

The Toys 'R' Us formula appears to rely upon being price competitive and by offering the shopper some assurance of not paying more than they need. The main benefit of shopping there, however, is the range, providing a wide choice if not a total guarantee of availability.

11.3 APPRAISING TOYS 'R' US AS AN INNOVATION

A number of models or theories have been proposed to explain the rise and fall of different retail formats over time. The most important to date have been the 'wheel of retailing', the 'retail accordion' and the 'retail life-cycle', (Brown, 1990). The wheel theory suggests that all new retail concepts begin as low cost and low price. Over time the retailer 'trades up' by enhancing service and ambience thus making itself vulnerable to newer, low-cost formats (McNair, 1958). The accordion theory suggests that domination by retailers offering a wide assortment of different product types alternates with domination by specialists who focus on retailing one product type (Hollander, 1966). Davidson *et al* (1976) argue that retailers follow a life cycle, similar to that of a product life-cycle, with the stages of birth, growth, maturity and decline. Imitators enter the same market during the growth stage, creating competition and, ultimately, reducing profitability.

Both the wheel and the accordion theories can be used to explain (in part) the success of Toys 'R' Us. Its scale of operation and out-of-town operation

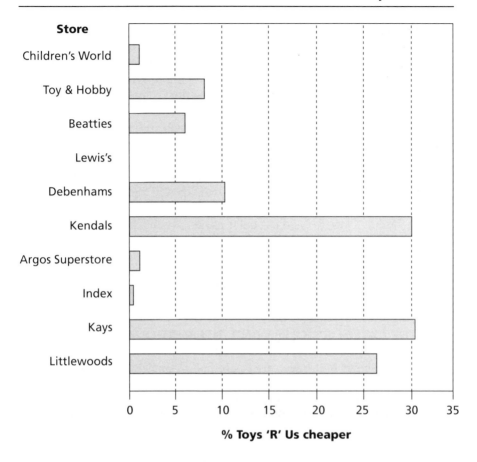

% Toys 'R' Us cheaper

Prices compared for stocked toys

Fig. 11.5 Toy basket price comparison

imply lower costs, the basis of the wheel model, but Toys 'R' Us does not use any cost advantage it may have to offer significantly lower prices. It is possible that its prices are so low that other retailers with higher costs will find it impossible to compete profitably, will be unable to justify further investment and will eventually exit from the market, but the retailer is not using low price as its main marketing platform. The wheel theory does not therefore offer a complete explanation. The accordion theory explains another aspect of Toys 'R' Us success in that it is more focused on toys than are department stores, catalogue shops or variety chain stores. The theory implies that such generalist retailers can respond or that the specialist will broaden out into allied product areas thus diffusing its specialist appeal. It is too early to say whether either will occur. The accordion theory also cannot offer a complete explanation for the success of Toys 'R' Us.

One of the authors has suggested a different approach to understanding successful innovation (Davies, 1992). It is similar in some ways to the life-cycle model in that it explains the decline of a retail format first by the attraction of imitators and then by the introduction of another innovation. It explains the bases for innovation as whether shoppers perceive either the products the retailer offers as different and better or the process of shopping the retailer offers as different and better. Thus retailers such as Benetton or Body Shop succeed mainly because their products are innovative while grocery superstores such as Sainsbury and Tesco succeeded because they offered a better shopping process (the one-stop shop). A better product is one which suits the needs of the customer better than other options. A better retail process is one which offers advantages to the shopper, usually a time or cost saving.

In the case of Toys 'R' Us the retailer has no product advantage to offer to the shopper but it does offer a significant process advantage. The process advantage is that it saves the shopper time. The product range is not 100 per cent but it is wider and deeper than elsewhere. The shopper is given a guarantee that there is no benefit to be gained on price by shopping around.

11.4 THE CATEGORY KILLER AND INTERNATIONALISATION

Our analysis shows that lower prices are not an explanation for the success of the category killer in the context of Toys 'R' Us success in entering the British market. It offers the shopper benefits of saved time and its would-be imitators such as Children's World do not carry the range needed to challenge its advantage. This view of the advantages of the category killer format differs from that given elsewhere (Goldman Sachs, 1992; Ishii, 1993) when low prices is given as the main competitive advantage. It also allows us to identify where else the format is likely to succeed.

One feature of the toy market is the low level of own-brand penetration. We think this is significant. Where own-brand is important, no category killer would be able to carry all possible product lines as retailers are unlikely to license the use of their name to a competitor. Product sectors such as clothing are unlikely to be susceptible to the category killer format as it will be impossible, due to the higher penetration of own-brand, for one retailer to claim that the shopper can see everything on sale in the sector under one roof. The category killer has to be able to offer virtually all brands for sale at one time. Markets containing strong own-brands are less likely to be susceptible to a category killer.

The second feature of the category killer is a cost structure which allows it to offer prices not significantly below those of competitors but still marginally below so that no competitor can attract shoppers by discounting. The third and final feature of a category killer is the sale of one type of comparison good. The label category killer is sometimes used to refer to retailers of assortments such as electrical superstores or to DIY retailers. We feel the label should be applied more narrowly. People rarely shop for brown goods and white goods on the same shopping trip. People rarely comparison shop for standard DIY products.

There are, therefore, a limited number of market opportunities for the category killer format to exploit. These may include individual electrical products, e.g. personal computers, televisions, car radios etc.; sportswear; types of car, e.g. all makes of 4-wheel drive or family compacts; and books.

CONCLUSION

The category killer has been hailed as a significant market innovation. Potentially it could be as important a retail format as the self-service super-market, the hypermarket, the limited range discounter or the department store have been at different stages in the evolution of retailing. The ability of any one retailer to develop internationally depends upon whether it can achieve a competitive advantage in a new market, one containing estab-lished players. Having a different retail format is one way of achieving com-petitive advantage and this chapter has sought to clarify the nature of the advantage for the category killer.

The format has clear advantages for certain types of retail business. Those who have such a format could benefit from internationalisation. Those who operate in markets without such a format and in product markets where the format is appropriate are vulnerable to market entry by such a retailer.

REVIEW QUESTIONS

1. Do you agree with the authors' view as to what is a 'category killer' or would you apply the label to other types of retailer?

2. If Toys 'R' Us entered a country in which you operated a traditional toy retail business, how would you respond?

3. Would the Toys 'R' Us formula work in every country in the world?

4. Describe what a category killer retailer would be like in product areas other than toys.

REFERENCES

Brown, S (1990) 'Innovation and evolution in UK retailing: the retail warehouse', *European Journal of Marketing*, 24(9), 39–54.
Chanil, D (1991) 'The game plan for toys', *Discount Merchandiser*, 31(2), 56.
Davidson, W R, Bates, A D and Bass, S J (1976) 'The retail life cycle', *Harvard Business Review*, 54, November/December, 89–96.

Davies, G (1992) 'Innovation in retailing', *Creativity and Innovation Management,* 1(4), 230.

EIU (1992) 'Toys overview; Toys; Part 14, EIU', *Retail Business,* 417, November, 16.

Euromonitor (1990), 'Toys and Games', *Market Research Europe,* XXIV, March, 19.

Goldman Sachs (1992) *Low Cost Formats Versus High Margin Retailers,* London.

Hollander, S C (1966) 'Notes on the retail accordion', *Journal of Retailing,* 42(2), 24.

Ishii, H (1993) 'Retailing in Japan: the price revolution, category killers and survival strategies', *NRI,* Winter, 20–33.

Loeb, W (1990) 'New realities for retailing in the next decade', *Retail Control,* 58(8), 3.

McNair, M P (1958) 'Significant trends and developments in the post war period', in *Competitive Distribution in a Free High Level Economy,* University of Pittsburgh Press.

Neff, R (1991) 'Guess who's selling Barbies in Japan now?', *Business Week,* Issue 3243, 9 December, p 72.

Zimmerman, R M (1992) 'Today's children make shopping more than child's play', *Retail Control,* 60(1), 21.

CHAPTER 12

The regulation of retail internationalisation: examples from the Pacific Asia region

Keri Davies

INTRODUCTION

The aim of this chapter is to examine in detail an area of study which most work on retail internationalisation tends to take for granted: the influence of state controls (at both the national and local levels) on retail development. Western analysts, used to studying Europe and the USA, tend to assume that any market can be entered. They use their experience to predict the level of inter-firm competition which will ensue, with some allowance for the effect of local regulations, land-use planning and zoning regulations on retail development. However, study of the Pacific Asia region shows that retail internationalisation has by no means been guaranteed as many countries have erected barriers to exclude or modify foreign retail operations. By studying this region we can learn a lot more about the process of retail internationalisation and, it is believed, cast new light on the assumptions which have guided study of the field for so long.

To aid in this work, the chapter is divided into three parts, following the structure of the discussion on the global space-economy and transnational corporations (TNCs) employed by Dicken (1994). The first part deals with firm–firm competition. It is argued here that this sphere has tended to dominate discussions of retail internationalisation in recent years, linked as it is to discussions of corporate and marketing strategy. The nub of the argument, however, is to show that this competition has a spatial component and that, increasingly, it crosses national boundaries. In so doing, inter-firm competition is increasingly subject to different regulative regimes and to competition between states.

The second section of the chapter deals with state–state interaction, or what Dicken calls the 'competition state'. Increasingly, international relations in trade are subject to regional or even global negotiations over tariff barriers, product quotas and free trade. We will consider some of the state–state interactions which have affected the trading environment for retailers within the Pacific Asia region.

Finally, we will consider interactions between firms and states. These interactions take two particular forms: the granting or refusal of access to markets, and the rules of operation which pertain within markets. These will be examined using examples from Pacific Asia to show how firms are affected by decisions made by states but also to show how firms can attempt to modify the regulatory environments within which they operate.

12.1 FIRM–FIRM COMPETITION

If we consider all sizes of retail organisations and all types of activity, the volume of international activity in retailing is high and likely to become increasingly important in years to come (Burt, 1993; Davies, 1994a). As a result, there is a growing body of literature on the subject of retail internationalisation – the vast bulk of which is concerned with internationalisation as a form of firm–firm competition. Whether setting forth push-pull factors (Kacker, 1985; Alexander, 1990), differential firm advantages (Williams, 1991) or the eclectic paradigm of internationalisation (Dunning, 1988), the models are built around the identification of factors which enhance or detract from an industry or firm's competitive position. This is made particularly clear by recent efforts (Porter, 1990; Dunning, 1993) to link the eclectic paradigm, which outlines the national factors providing the context for the activities of firms, with the value chain (Porter, 1985), which helps to determine the form of the moves taken by any individual firm.

12.1.1 Extending the value chain

The concept of the value chain is particularly important here; it is also known by the terms 'filiere' (Walker, 1988) and 'production chain' (Dicken, 1994) with some modifications to the basic idea. The core of the value chain is a transactionally linked sequence of functions, each stage of which is presumed to 'add value'. A number of authors have applied the concept to retailing, rather than allowing it to be confined to manufacturing (McGee, 1987; Channon, 1988). This has required some modification to allow for the different activities carried out by retailers compared to manufacturers.

Retailers, like producers before them, are now extending their value chains across national borders to a considerable degree. For example, Dawson (1994) stressed the importance of sourcing and buying networks in an international context, both as a means of controlling the cost structure within the value chain and as a means of differentiating the output from the chain. Where in the past they have been content to purchase fully-finished products manufactured abroad, they are now much more likely to be involved in establishing manufacturing facilities for specific products (for

example, Yaohan (food), Benetton (clothing) and Le Saunda (shoes) all man-
ufacture products in China); in designing products (for example, Daiei); in
the conditions experienced by the manufacturing workforce (for example,
Marks & Spencer); or in deals for the exchange of products (for example,
those Wal-Mart has established with Ito-Yokado and Yaohan). The Japanese
supermarket chain Seiyu has established an international buying group, the
Asian Retail Affiliates Network (ARAN), involving companies in several
countries including Hong Kong, Taiwan and Indonesia. Other Japanese companies, such as Isetan and Jusco, use their overseas branches to source products for the store network, including the Japanese parent. Through these
activities, retailers are seeking to squeeze extra value out of their existing
networks and to enhance their competitiveness, even if this sometimes
means collaboration with firms which may become competitors in the
future.

This kind of perspective necessitates a reconsideration of what we mean
by retail internationalisation. We have moved on from the mere consideration of overseas moves to look at the rationale behind those moves (Burt,
1993). The dichotomy between 'multinational' and 'global' retailing as set
out by Salmon and Tordjman (1989) had a lot to do with the form of management control and tailoring of the retail offering to local needs and local
economies and cultures. Yet, as Dawson (1994) amongst others has pointed
out, we need to put aside the notion that retail internationalisation is just
about retailers opening stores overseas (even though this will remain the
core of many retailers' operations). We are now beginning to realise that
retail internationalisation can be expressed in many ways, such as:

- *retail organisation* including wholly-owned companies, joint ventures,
  franchising, licensing and agents (see, for example, the discussion of activity in China in Davies, 1994b);
- *retail formats* such as fixed stores, retail counters, mail-order and catalogue sales, direct mail and home shopping – including services which
  operate across national borders as well as foreign-owned services aimed
  at the host country's domestic market;
- *support operations* including product sourcing (possibly even involving
  manufacturing in the host country), distribution, information technology
  systems, advertising and promotion, HRM policies, etc.;
- *retail networking* including formal organisations (such as the Inter-
  continental Group of Department Stores (IGDS) or international buying
  groups (Clarke-Hill and Robinson, 1992), as well as less formal lobbying
  and pressure groups often based around single issues.

Acceptance of the coexistence of these categories also forces us to aban-
don some of the more stereotypical views of stages or the temporal process
of retail internationalisation. We are moving from studies of purely foreign
direct investment (FDI) to see that there are other modes of retail activity,
including collaborative and network ventures (Burt, 1991), which really

takes us back to much of the pioneering work of Hollander (1970). However, even this is not enough. Dicken and Thrift (1992) have argued that studies should consider more than just the regulation of the value chain through the transactional costs of exchange between each element of the chain. Recognition must be accorded also to the complex and dynamic sets or networks of interrelationships between firms which have different degrees of power or influence. Dicken reminds us that these relationships may come about more by chance than strategic planning!

> The clear message is that transnational reality is one of a spectrum of forms of . . . organization, a diversity of developmental trajectories in which consciously planned global operations exist side-by-side with firms that have internationalized in an unplanned, often adventitious way. (Dicken, 1994: 111.)

12.1.2 The firm and its environments

We need to use these insights in two particular ways. First, we can stress the embeddedness of the individual firm in a strategic sense in its competitive environment. Companies' efforts to manage their value chains may lead them to consider many different ways of extracting value from their activities. Some of these, as for example the development of large infrastructural projects in distribution or information technology, may lead them to collaborate rather than compete with other firms (in the same or related areas of business). In his description of the production chain (his version of the value chain), Dicken (1994: 103–105) also adds the relationships between the firm and the financial system and the firm and the means of regulation, coordination and control. For example, Yaohan's development in East Asia has been facilitated by its astute use of different resources and financial regimes. It has been able to use funds from its Japanese subsidiary and from listing its Hong Kong subsidiaries on the local stock exchange in order to expand into the People's Republic of China (Davies, 1994b). These sources of funds have provided it with a distinct competitive advantage over some of its rivals now, although they also impose some constraints on future behaviour.

Secondly, we must re-evaluate the importance of the firm's links within particular social and cultural environments. Whilst the nature of retail markets has, arguably, forced researchers to look at the difference between countries, too much research plays down the role of the institutional environment, particularly the role of governments. Or, as Brahm (1993: 11) puts it:

> The assumption of decontextualized market characteristics of traditional strategy content research renders it ill-equipped to analyze some of the most important issues that arise in international competition.

The aim of this brief introduction to firm–firm competition has been to highlight not just the volume of international activity in retailing, but also its diversity. What has also been made clear is that firm–firm competition does not exist in a vacuum. We need now to turn to look at the two other parts of the framework proposed above, namely state–state and firm–state relations. The discussion will allow us to begin to address the three questions posed by Brahm (1993: 10–11) for future research on international competition:

- How does a firm's embeddedness within a societal social system affect its behaviour in domestic markets?
- How does a firm's national institutional environment affect its competitive conduct in international markets?
- What is the relationship between corporate strategy and the evolution of the world trading system?

12.2 STATE–STATE INTERACTION

Dicken's (1994) approach is to argue that states in the contemporary global economy face shifts in the global marketplace and that as they strive to develop strategies to create competitive advantage, so they start to take on some of the characteristics of firms.

> Both are, in effect, locked in competitive struggles to capture global market shares. Specifically, states compete to enhance their international trading position and to capture as large a share as possible of the gains from trade. They compete to attract productive investment to build up their national production base, which, in turn, enhances their competitive position. In particular, states strive to create, capture, and maintain the higher value-adding elements of the production chain. (Dicken, 1994: 112.)

Many of these arguments are particularly relevant in the Pacific Asia region where, in many countries, the state regulation of economic activity is supplemented by state direction of the economy. The economy itself is largely in private ownership and firms are in competition, but the state intervenes in the context of an explicit set of national economic and social goals. A high priority is placed on industrial policy and on promoting a structure that enhances the nation's economic competitiveness (Dicken, 1994: 114). A similar argument is presented in a recent report by the World Bank (1993), which seeks to identify the factors which have underpinned past economic growth in East Asia (particularly Japan, the Republic of Korea, the Republic of China and Singapore) and to see if they can be applied to other developing countries, such as the People's Republic of China and Vietnam.

Dicken uses a deliberately simple typology of state economic-political systems in which he identifies four main groupings. The Pacific Asian states, bearing the characteristics set out above, he terms 'plan rational'. Within his scenario, their main competitors are seen as 'market rational' states, such as the United States and United Kingdom, which provide the environment within which private companies operate but which leave investment, production and distributive decisions as the preserve of those companies. Whilst these 'pen pictures' include a number of generalisations, Dicken argues that 'it is not unreasonable to regard many of the current politico-economic tensions in the global economy as a reflection of a clash between competition states occupying different positions within the market-rational/plan-rational space' (Dicken, 1994: 113).

We can use this framework to examine a number of major international efforts made to remove market barriers and to open up Pacific Asian economies to foreign investment in general. These have included GATT, American 'Super 301' actions, the Structural Impediment Initiative involving the USA and Japan, and the establishment of an ASEAN Free Trade Area. Whilst their main thrust has been to open up freer trade in manufacturing and some service industries, notably banking, they have had an effect on the development of the retail sector.

It is implicit in this framework that these 'agreements' are negotiated between states and do not spring fully formed into the trade arena. For example, in early 1994, Mickey Kantor, the United States Trade Representative and the person charged with negotiating on the USA's behalf with other states, stressed that trade must be a 'two-way street', and that there can be no 'something for nothing' (Kantor, 1994). He stated his belief that if the USA's trading partners are to enjoy the benefits of the global trading system, they must accept the responsibilities of building markets that are 'comparably open'. In addition, he echoed President Clinton's resolve that USA trade policy is 'inextricably linked' to the country's three-fold domestic economic objectives of creating jobs, fostering growth and making the USA more competitive.

12.2.1 General Agreement on Tariffs and Trade (GATT)

GATT is a forum for the resolution of multilateral trade negotiations. The Uruguay Round of the GATT negotiations which ended in December 1993 took seven years to complete. Member states then had to endorse the agreement by the end of 1994; part of the agreement was for a new body, the World Trade Organisation, to come into being at the start of 1995 to oversee future developments. Multilateral negotiations provide a forum for issues that a government believes to be too large and potentially sensitive to be dealt with through unilateral or bilateral action, such as the Japanese border protection regime for rice (Porges, 1991). The multilateral context also makes it possible for each participant to pool interests with other countries. It should be noted, however, that changes made multilaterally in GATT will affect the rules for later bilateral relations as well.

The Uruguay Round raised a number of new issues affecting international trade. Of these, of particular concern to the retail sector have been Trade Related Investment Measures and the desire to include services within the round (GATT, 1991).

Trade Related Investment Measures (TRIMs)

In recent years, economists have been much exercised by the notion of Trade Related Investment Measures or TRIMs. These refer to various regulations and requirements imposed on foreign investors in host countries that directly or indirectly impinge on international trade flows, including bans on operating in selected sectors or the use of foreign labour, controls on the export of currency and requirements to re-export finished goods (Ariff, 1989). Such restrictions tend to deny foreign companies access to the host country's domestic market and to subsidise exports. TRIMs have not been included in GATT to date as it is difficult to legislate for such a wide range of interventions and because they have been viewed as being directed at the home market, and thus being part of a country's industrial or regional policy (Greenaway, 1991: 145).

Table 12.1 A classification of trade related investment measures

Input trims	Output trims
Commodity-based:	
Local content requirements	Export performance requirements
Trade balancing requirements	Trade balacing requirements
Laws of similars	Export controls
Limitations on imports	Market reserve policy
Foreign exchange requirements	Product mandating
Licensing requirements	
Factor-based:	
Local content requirements	Technology transfer
Local equity requirements	Earnings remittance limits
Expatriate quotas	
Local hiring targets	
National participation in management	
R&D requirements	
Restrictions on foreign ownership	
Technology transfer	
Earnings remittance limits	

Source: Greenaway (1991: 148).

Greenaway (1991) provides a simple classification of TRIMs (Table 12.1) which distinguishes between measures which primarily affect host country imports (for example, local content requirements), measures which primarily affect host country exports (for example, minimum export requirements) and measures whose primary effects are various (such as local equity requirements). He also distinguishes between measures aimed at the product or commodity itself and those aimed at the factors used in its production and sale. Many of the controls are aimed at manufacturing industries or any industry which targets the host country's domestic market and thus are not specific to the retail sector. However, the framework provided allows us to place the concerns of foreign retailers and investors in perspective with regard to the similar issues facing manufacturers and the other service sectors.

For retailing, the input TRIMs are far more important than the output TRIMs and the great bulk of the controls are actually factor-based input TRIMs, such as restrictions on equity participation, local content requirements, the exclusion of foreign managers and limits on the remittance of earnings out of the host country. The usage of such TRIMs by countries to help manage their economies varies significantly. The aim has been, first, to divert funds towards the manufacturing sectors in order to boost economic growth and exports and, second, as disposable income grows, to protect domestic firms (including retailers) until they have been able to adapt to the changed conditions. Davies (1993) provides a fuller description of the forms of TRIMs applied to the retail sector by Asian countries.

GATT and services

The USA in particular is believed to want to see GATT reflect the changes which have been taking place within its own economy. As the relative importance of manufacturing has declined, so services such as banking, insurance and retailing have become more important as potential sources of overseas earnings. Identifying quite what is meant by a 'service' has generated a substantial volume of literature (see, for example, Koekkoek, 1988, and Balasubramanyam, 1991). However, the stance taken by the USA in the Structural Impediments Initiative talks with Japan (see section 12.2.3) made it clear that the retail sector is one of the areas where pressure will be exerted to remove barriers to investment.

A key to much of the argument has been the need for most services to be produced and consumed within the same host economy, unlike the products of manufacturing investment which can be exported for sale. Barriers to involvement in the service industries are therefore much more closely interleaved with other domestic policies, including efforts to redistribute income, as in Malaysia (Jesudason, 1989). Any limitations on such policies would entail a substantial sacrifice of national sovereignty relative to that previously deemed acceptable by GATT signatories (McCulloch, 1990: 339). The United Nations and the World Bank have also been arguing very strongly that developing countries should not be afraid of liberalising their service sectors (United Nations, 1994). They believe that opening domestic markets to foreign service providers (particularly, but not exclusively, banks) is a major way to ensure increased efficiency in the provision of services and, by fostering competition, tends to enhance the efficiency of domestic firms. Where states are still concerned about foreign domination of an economically important sector, it is argued that they should consider allowing joint ventures in preference to outright prohibition of market access.

12.2.2 'Super 301' actions

Whereas GATT is avowedly an effort to promote a free trade regime, many commentators have argued that there has been a demand in recent years, particularly in the United States, for a shift away from 'free' trade toward 'fair' trade – 'fairness' being defined by the United States itself (Dicken, 1994: 113). The United States has been involved in a number of attempts to establish bilateral agreements, some of which would appear to run counter to the aims of the multilateral GATT negotiations. The United States has offered some 'carrots' in terms of access to their market but it has also relied to a large degree on the 'sticks' of tariff barriers, withdrawal of Most Favoured Nation status and 'Super 301'.

Based around Section 301 of the Omnibus Trade and Competitiveness Act of 1988, the so-called 'Super 301' was a broad, systematic approach to opening up foreign markets by challenging their governments to eliminate various impediments to market access (Russell, 1989; Porges, 1991). The United States Trade Representative (USTR) was required to identify priority countries with significant trade barriers in the years 1989 and 1990 and to negotiate for their removal under the threat of trade retaliations. Possible US reprisals included the suspension or withdrawal of benefits under a trade agreement being violated and the imposition of tariffs of up to 100 per cent and other import restrictions on the goods of the offending country (Svernlöv, 1992).

Many Asian countries are said to believe that once the GATT accord is signed, they will be under constant threat from the USA's Section 301 trade laws (*The New Straits Times*, 2 November 1992: F19). In 1989 the USTR invoked Super 301 for the first time and named Japan, India and Brazil as 'unfair traders' and South Korea, Taiwan and Thailand were among eight countries put on a 'watch list' as a result of their claimed failure to protect US patents and copyrights. None of the actions led to the imposition of sanctions but they stimulated negotiations between the USA and the states involved. The naming of Japan certainly aided the outcome of the SII talks and both South Korea and Taiwan subsequently made significant concessions in terms of lowering quotas, cutting tariffs and opening market sectors, including retailing, in order to prevent retaliatory measures coming into play. In October 1991 an investigation began into China on the grounds of import prohibitions, technical barriers and a failure to publish the relevant laws and regulations pertaining to importing (Barale, 1991: 18).

Whilst Super 301 fell into abeyance at the end of 1991, this did not prevent the United States from pursuing bilateral actions against other states under the original Section 301 legislation (which is often perceived as less threatening than the Super 301 provisions). In March 1993, the USTR forced the Republic of Korea to comply with bilateral Telecommunications Agreements and, later in the same year, Brazil, India, Hungary, Thailand and Taiwan were identified as priority foreign countries on the USTR's watch list. However, the most protracted set of bilateral negotiations on managed trade have continued to be those between the USA and Japan. When Japan's progress towards market opening was deemed once again to be too slow, President Clinton reactivated the Super 301 trade provision in March 1994. This time, however, the Japanese government has been much more aggressive. It has complained about unfair treatment from America in trying to push through unilateral deals and it has received support from Australia and Europe. When a partial settlement of the 14-month long dispute was reached in early October 1994 it came as a welcome relief for both sides and highlighted the need for some other means of resolving future conflicts (*Financial Times*, 3 October 1994: 1).

12.2.3 Structural Impediments Initiative (SII)

Beginning in September 1989, the governments of the USA and Japan spent almost a year trying to identify and solve structural problems in both countries that were felt to be impeding trade and causing trade imbalances (Brooks, 1993). The final SII report, issued in June 1990, was not intended to be an end in itself but to represent a commitment to an ongoing process. A number of follow-up meetings have been held and the first annual review was issued in May 1991.

Under SII the USA committed itself to increase its low saving rate, to shrink its budget deficit, to improve corporate competitiveness, to promote research and development and to promote exports. The Japanese were committed to undertake structural reforms or adjustment in six areas: savings and investment patterns, land policy, the distribution system, exclusionary business practices, relations among corporate groupings in *keiretsu* (vertically organized distribution channels with dedicated outlets) and pricing mechanisms. In terms of the distribution issues, the Japanese government passed amendments to the Large-Scale Retail Law in May 1991, making it easier to open large retail stores and shortening the period before approval for a new development is granted (Brooks, 1993). But, as Porges (1991) notes, the SII negotiations were unlikely ever by themselves to be sufficient to bring the government to disrupt *keiretsu* arrangements or loosen distribution channels.

Japan has tried to shift some of the burden implied by the bilateral SII negotiations by lobbying the OECD to take on the same role on a multilateral basis. The reported rationale has been to make the advantages of SII available to other nations but it is also true that Japan is less likely to be forced to make concessions under a multilateral process than the current bilateral system (Rowley, 1990). The USA has shown some signs of wanting to undertake SII-style negotiations with other major Asian trading partners, such as South Korea, but this has been seen by the Koreans as more of a threat than an opportunity.

12.2.4 ASEAN Free Trade Area (AFTA)

The ASEAN group of Malaysia, Brunei, Indonesia, Singapore, Thailand and the Philippines has agreed to establish a Free Trade Area which will come into existence in 2003. In 1993, the countries began to implement a series of tariff cuts as means of opening up each other's markets and to create an enlarged 'single market' which, it is hoped, will attract manufacturing and service investment. In addition, trade flows between ASEAN members and other Asian countries are increasing rapidly and this is providing pressure for cuts in tariffs and TRIMs. The ASEAN members have found it more difficult to agree on a proposal to turn the larger Asia-Pacific Economic Cooperation (APEC) group, to which they belong, into a free trade zone by the year 2020. Their fears focus on the larger APEC members, the USA and Japan, which might try to use the proposal to their own advantage, opening up regional markets faster than is planned currently (Lim, 1994; *Financial Times*, 26 September 1994: 6).

The removal of the barriers is unlikely to affect retailing in the short term but the process is being kept under review by the various national associations. The Thai Retailers' Association has been particularly concerned about the likely effect on small retailers of the expansion of foreign retailers, either direct into Thailand or from regional bases in Singapore or Malaysia.

12.3 FIRM–STATE INTERACTION

The third element in our framework represents the interaction between retail firms and states. These may not be straightforward 'because the actual processes and forms of firm–state interactions at an international scale are deeply intertwined with firm–firm and, especially, state–state interactions' (Dicken, 1994: 117). The relationships between international firms and nation-states are a complex mixture of conflict and collaboration. Firms are seeking to allocate and reallocate resources between locations, according to their own internally generated criteria and without (necessarily) any regard for local needs and local economies (see, for example, Jenkins, 1987). Bartu (1993) even goes so far as to argue that Japan's multinational companies are building an 'economic empire' in Asia. At the same time the individual state wishes to maximise its share of value-added activity. Dicken also argues that firm–state interactions tend to differ according to whether the relationship is between a firm and its home country government or a host country government.

> This does not imply that the former relations are necessarily harmonious and the latter necessarily conflictual. Indeed, many bitter disputes between firms and states have occurred where a state fears that its 'domestic' firms are shifting operations overseas or, conversely, where firms allege that their home country government provides inadequate support against external competition. (Dicken, 1994: 117.)

In terms of retail internationalisation, the two most critical aspects of state regulatory policy are, first, access to markets and/or resources and, second, rules of operation for firms operating within particular national (or suprana-tional) jurisdictions (Dicken, 1992: 304–305). As Dicken (1994: 119) points out, whilst an obvious assumption would be that TNCs will invariably seek the removal of all regulatory barriers constraining their activities, the posi-tion is not necessarily quite as simple as this. Many manufacturing and ser-vice companies may take advantage of regulatory differences between states by shifting activities between locations, as states strive to outbid their rivals to capture or retain a particular activity. The notion of bargaining between firms and states is an important one which will be expanded upon below, but arguments about what is happening in manufacturing are not terribly relevant to retailing in this case. Most retailers require a strong presence in local (domestic) markets and this reduces their bargaining power in these positions. Only some more specialised services, such as the order receiving and processing departments of a mail-order operation, are likely to be moveable between countries according to labour costs or government incen-tives.

Whilst Dicken refers to bargaining between firms and states primarily in the sense of negotiations over locations, we need to be clear that this bar-gaining or negotiation can go much deeper and affect the forms of the rules and regulations applied (Thrift, 1994) and even the acceptance of the initial premise that TNCs or international retailers are a problem to be addressed by the state. The following discussion is based on an acceptance of the notion that the 'diffusion of administrative structures and models of decision making is mediated through the cultures of society and inherited modes of formal decision-making . . .' (Clarke, 1992: 623).

> Law is *not* constructed in some ontologically privileged domain; it is necessarily a social and political construct. If we then accept the reasonable contention that soci-ety and state are, in part, geographically constructed and mediated it follows that we are obliged to recognise the interpenetration of space and law. (Blomley, 1989: 514.)

Two particular issues follow from this position. First, and most obviously, there can be a spatial differentiation of regulation within and between nation states. Since rules such as those governing investment by firms con-stitute the environments for capital accumulation, they can produce quite different patterns of economic behaviour within and across national bound-aries (Christopherson, 1993: 274).

Secondly, social conflicts are often mediated within the locale. These con-flicts often reflect – and are mediated by – locally specific definitions and disparities of legal (and thus social) relations. Whereas the first point argues that laws and rules may vary in geographical space, this point argues that the social acceptance of the ideas of rules or of a specific rule, may also vary through space. This is implicit in examples such as:

- local interpretations of national laws, which take into account local needs and power groupings, e.g. the decisions made by two local authorities in Taiwan to close two Makro stores for alleged violations of zoning regulations more than three years after they opened (local news reports say that Makro fell victim to political wrangling over whether Taipei or Kaohsiung should host the 2002 Asian Games (*Asian Retailer,* August 1994: 10)!);
- the erection of barriers to entry in retailing, as in other industries, can come in response to social and political pressures, e.g. exclusion at the local scale as with the application of the Large Scale Retail Law in Japan, or at the national level as with the Negative Lists of the Philippines and Indonesia;
- the disdain felt by some in senior positions in developing countries for 'Western' laws, such as the copyright laws, which are felt to perpetuate power and wealth inequalities and which are only enforced under the threat of retaliatory actions.

The TNC, represented here by retailers internationalising their operations, throw these issues into harsh relief but they may also represent industry's response to the problems raised.

> ... the corporation's chief importance lies in its ability to amass and wield *social power* in directed ways ... this may well be one of the critical reasons why large corporations exist. They are able to mobilize cognitive, cultural, social and political resources in a search for security *as well* as profit. These resources enable them to 'bend' their environments in numerous ways to their product and comparative advantage. They are able to bring influence to bear on other firms, on states, on markets, on cities, and so on and, in these ways, to make a significant local difference. Seen in this way, the large corporation is not just an interest, it is also a cause. (Dicken and Thrift, 1992: 283.)

The remainder of this analysis of firm–state interactions is constructed around the two categories identified above, namely access to markets and rules of operation within a market.

12.3.1 Access to markets

The problems facing foreign producers and overseas retailers hoping to gain access to the Japanese market have been well documented (Batzer and Laumer, 1989). The difficulties Toys 'R' Us have had in obtaining locations in Japan and the alleged use of the Large-Scale Retail Law to slow the pace of development are the most recent manifestations of the trend. However, Japan is merely the best known of a number of countries in Pacific Asia which have closed their retail markets to outside influence and investment at various times since 1945, using tariff barriers and TRIMs. A fuller description of the actual policies pursued can be found in Davies (1993). We are more concerned here with the rationale behind the policies which have been put forward.

The reasons for raising trade and investment barriers have been manifold, ranging from Communism in the PRC, North Korea and Vietnam, through efforts to offset the entrepreneurial advantages of the ethnic Chinese in Malaysia and Indonesia (Jesudason, 1990), to the development strategies of South Korea and Taiwan which have followed Japan in trying to slow foreign investment during the growth phase of local companies and industries (Schlossstein, 1991). Only in Thailand and the small island states of Hong Kong and Singapore (Davies, 1994a) have governments followed policies which have kept their economies relatively open to investment by foreign retailers over any long period of time.

Trade barriers and controls over foreign investment are used by many states for a variety of reasons. For developing countries, such as the majority of those in Pacific Asia, they are often seen as a means of avoiding foreign control and domination of their economies. This rationale, based as it is upon the acquisition or retention of essential manufacturing skills and export capacity, is difficult to sustain when discussing the retail trade. It is now widely recognised that the exclusionary policies which have been followed by many Asian countries at one time or another have contained a very large political element. The small shop or independent retail sector often makes up a substantial share of domestic GDP and local employment; if they are organised for particular single-issue causes they represent significant economic and political clout. For example, along with farmers, small shopkeepers received a disproportionate amount of attention from Japan's LDP governments in the decades between 1960 and 1990 and, as such, helped to keep the LDP in power throughout that period.

However, we must not forget that foreign industrialists may have a similar lobbying role to play in their home countries when those countries are seeking to reduce other states' trade barriers. The American retailer, Toys 'R' Us, featured heavily in American complaints about the Large-Scale Retail Law during the SII talks with Japan. Similar influences were seen when, in April 1987, the United States House of Representatives voted on an amendment to the Omnibus Trade Act of 1988 (described above) put down by the Democrat Congressman, Richard Gephardt. This amendment would have 'required countries with a large trade surplus with the US and with a history of "unfair" trading practices to either voluntarily cut their surpluses by ten per cent annually until a bilateral trade balance was achieved, or to be assigned tariffs or quotas aimed at the same result' (Wade and Gates, 1990: 285).

Although the Amendment narrowly passed in the House of Representatives by 218 votes to 214, it did not survive the legislative process because of opposition from the President and the Senate. In their analysis of the pattern of voting in the Amendment, Wade and Gates argued that this was one of the few occasions in recent US history when the issue of protectionism was posed squarely and seriously as a matter of national policy. The vote showed the importance of regional and district influences on national policies towards trade and, by implication, the role of industry lobbying at the local level. Similar local commercial interests have been identified as a cause of many of the delays in the ratification of the GATT deal by the American state during 1994 (Keatley, 1994).

Whilst the threat of domination of the retail industry might not carry the same implied economic threat as the domination of, for example, a domestic automobile industry, there is a second, newer argument which is also relevant here. It concerns the belief that increasingly goods and services are being produced and sold according to their symbolic values rather than their 'use' values (see the articles in Shields (1992a) for a summary of this approach). Whilst nobody argues seriously that there is as yet a global culture, there is a global set (or an attempt to establish one) of shared values based on shared product consumption. Coca-Cola, Levi's, Nike and MTV are amongst the often quoted examples of this tendency – although the success of Sony, BMW, Benetton and Swatch suggests that it is not just a case of American cultural imperialism. Just as transnational corporations have led nations to look to protect their domestic industries, so transnational products and services have led them to worry about the preservation of their cultures and traditions.

Increasingly, international retailers are likely to be seen as part of this 'problem' too. First, they may be setting up shops in foreign countries where they use global brands as part of their image creation and marketing strategy (and for some their own brand names are achieving global recognition too). Secondly, and following on from the first point, as their procurement policies are international so they may run counter to the espoused economic policies of many countries, particularly in the developing world where 'buy local' policies aim to aid domestic producers and limit foreign exchange difficulties. Finally, retailers are transferring shopping environments across national boundaries; not just store types but shopping malls and centres and with them the associated locational and land-use forms (off-centre, lots of car parking) and consumer trends (greater mobility, leisure shopping). Over and above the customer's complaint that 'everywhere looks the same', the physical and symbolic experiences of shopping get to be standardised too (Shields, 1992b).

There is, however, one qualification which needs to be made. It is easy to focus overmuch on those controls which have diverted or slowed investment by retailers from one country in the economy of another. We should also be aware that some governments have imposed controls over 'outward' investment by retailers, either by limiting foreign exchange transactions or by placing some countries off-limits. For example, Tsay (1993) reports that outward investment was illegal for Taiwanese firms for many years as the government tried to focus efforts on the domestic economy. Equally, the trade embargo imposed on Vietnam by the US government means that American retailers are forbidden to enter or invest in that country. So, we need to allow not just for the greater openness of some markets, such as

Hong Kong and Singapore, to inward investment but also to note that the greater involvement of retailers from these countries in overseas ventures also reflects particular investment regimes at home.

12.3.2 Rules of operation within a market

Once retailers are accorded the right to enter a new market, they are subject to local rules of operation. Local rules which affect retail operations abound – see, for example, the studies of the effects of land-use planning policies on retail location in Singapore (Yeung and Yeh, 1971; Sim and Choo, 1993). Pertinent literature which covers examples from outside the Pacific Asia region includes Blomley (1989) who provides a critique of the analysis of Belgian retailing undertaken by Dawson (1982) to show the interrelationship between retailers and the construction and application of the law. In addition, the effects of financial market regulation on retail forms and retail location are also only just beginning to be addressed – see Christopherson (1993) for a study of variations within just one country, the USA, and Wrigley (1992) for a comparison of the USA and the UK.

Marsden and Wrigley (forthcoming) have shown that we must also distinguish between public interest regulation and private interest regulation. The latter is where the state empowers particular private sectional interests to act on its behalf and to regulate the activities of other sets of actors in the system. They use the example of the largest British food retailers to show how these companies have wielded power over manufacturers and other suppliers, speeding up the rate at which change has taken place. By subtle use of new product strategies and by enforcing existing environmental and hygiene regulations, for example, they have been both more successful and they have changed public perceptions of what to expect from the food industry. Successive governments have allowed these retailers to exercise their growing power precisely because they are seen as acting in concert with government policy.

> Our analysis of retailing, the food system, and the regulatory state in the UK suggests that corporate reorganisation – particularly in a sector such as retailing in which the boundaries of competition and accumulation are constantly being tested but in which the regulatory state has become critically dependent upon the economic dominance of major corporations – needs contingent state practices to help construct and legitimate on a continuous basis these conditions at national and international levels. The ability of state practices to retain a certain amount of adaptability, creativity and capacity for action in these circumstances reinforces a variable and contingent interpretation of the nature of the state. (Marsden and Wrigley, forthcoming.)

We need to take these considerations into account when looking at the changing nature of the regulation of the retail industry in Pacific Asia. As the use of TRIMs to control retail operations has declined in the region, so many countries have begun to follow the lead of Japan, Singapore and Hong Kong, which do not have any formal controls over imports and investment by foreign firms. Instead, they have sometimes used systems of regulations and domestic policies which can slow the rate of change and have the same effect of excluding outsiders. For Japan, for example, Brooks (1993: 244–45) has listed the following controls:

- the Large-Scale Retail Law which regulates store location and operations;
- *keiretsu* or vertically organised distribution channels which allow manufacturers in certain consumer goods industries to sell their products in dedicated outlets, allowing them to control supply and price at the retail level;
- a lack of transparency in traditional business practices, such as rebates, returned goods and even quoted prices;
- regulations preventing the use of discounts as a market entry stratagem.

Controls over land and land use are common in many countries. In Singapore, sites for new developments in the suburban housing estates were, until recently, strictly controlled by a government agency, preventing new developments of the type which would appeal to foreign retailers (Davies, 1994a). South Korean legislation prevents foreign nationals or companies from owning real estate for retail use, forcing them to rent and leaving them with higher overheads. This policy is to be removed by the year 2000 but many of the best sites will have gone by then. Similarly, the Malaysian state of Johor has recently announced guidelines on the foreign ownership of property, which will prevent foreigners buying small shops and which will increase the cost of those properties they are eligible to buy (*The New Straits Times*, 30 January 1993: 10; *The New Straits Times*, 6 February 1993: 20).

Many of these controls on land use have been imposed because the state (either central or local) has to provide permission for development to go ahead and it is often placed under severe pressure by local companies and, in particular, by the political clout wielded by the independent retail sector because of its sheer size. In others, the problem lies with the property or land owners who may not view retailing as a particularly lucrative land use, or with the legal system which does not provide adequate safeguards with regard to land ownership.

CONCLUSIONS

This chapter has sought to illustrate the effect of regulatory environments upon the development of retail internationalisation. As retailers expand, not just by opening stores but by extending their value chains across national borders, so they enter new regulatory environments. The range of regulatory environments in the Pacific Asia region helps to illustrate the issues involved very clearly. We need to go beyond consideration of just firm–firm competition to look at state–state and firm–state interactions if we are to understand the current position and future developments in international retailing.

REVIEW QUESTIONS

1. Outline the features of the value chain concept as it is applied to retailing. How can a firm use the internationalisation of its value chain to support its strategic objectives?

2. Many countries in Pacific Asia have erected trade barriers against foreign goods and foreign companies. Describe the types of trade barriers which affect retailers and show their likely effect.

3. What role has the government of the United States of America played in the opening up of markets in Pacific Asia? What are the likely future effects of such policies for the retail sector?

REFERENCES

Alexander, N (1990) 'Retailers and international markets: motives for expansion', *International Marketing Review,* 7(4), 75–85.

Ariff, M (1989) 'TRIMS: a north–south divide or a non-issue?', *The World Economy,* 12(3), 347–360.

Balasubramanyam, V N (1991) 'International Trade in Services: The Real Issues', in: Greenaway, D, Hine, R C, O'Brien, A P and Thornton, R J (eds.), *Global Protectionism,* Macmillan, London, Chapter 6.

Barale, L A (1991) 'Section 301 Investigations: Using US Laws to Address China's Unfair Trade Practices', *East Asian Executive Reports,* 13(10), 9 and 18–21.

Bartu, F (1993) *The Ugly Japanese: Nippon's Economic Empire in Asia,* Yenbooks, Tokyo.

Batzer, E and Laumer, H (1989) *Marketing Strategies and Distribution Channels for Foreign Companies in Japan,* Westview Press, Boulder, Colorado.

Blomley, N K (1989) 'Text and context: rethinking the law-space nexus', *Progress in Human Geography,* 13(4), 512–534.

Brahm, R (1993) 'Globalization and strategy content research: critical reflections and new directions', *Advances in Strategic Management,* 9, 3–21.

Brooks, W L (1993) 'MITI's distribution policy and US–Japan structural talks', in Czinkota, M R and Kotabe, M (eds.), *The Japanese Distribution System: Opportunities and Obstacles. Structures and Practices,* Probus, Chicago, Chapter 16.

Burt, S (1991) 'Trends in the internationalization of grocery retailing: the European experience', *International Review of Retail, Distribution and Consumer Research,* 1(4), 487–515.

Burt, S (1993) 'Temporal trends in the internationalization of British retailing', The *International Review of Retail, Distribution and Consumer Research,* 3(4), 391–410.

Channon, D (1988) 'Case Study on "Kwik Save Discount"', in Johnson, G and Scholes, K, *Exploring Corporate Strategy,* 2nd edn, Prentice-Hall, Hemel Hempstead, 92.

Christopherson, S (1993) 'Market rules and territorial outcomes: the case of the United States', *International Journal of Urban and Regional Research,* 17, 274–288.

Clark, G L (1992) ' "Real" regulation: the administrative state', *Environment and Planning A*, 24(5), 615–627.

Clarke-Hill, F M and Robinson, T M (1992) 'Co-operation as a competitive strategy in European retailing', *European Business and Economic Development*, 1(2), 1–6.

Davies, K (1993) 'Trade barriers in East and South-East Asia: the implications for retailers', *International Review of Retail, Distribution and Consumer Research*, 3(4), 345–365.

Davies, K (1994a) 'The implications of foreign investment in the retail sector: the example of Singapore', *The Developing Economies*, 22(3), 299–330.

Davies, K (1994b) 'Foreign investment in the retail sector of the People's Republic of China', *Columbia Journal of World Business*, Winter, 29(3), 56–69.

Dawson, J A (1982) 'A note on the law of 29 June 1975 to control large scale retail development in Belgium', *Environment and Planning A*, 14, 291–296.

Dawson, J A (1994) 'Internationalization of retail operations', *Journal of Marketing Management*, 10, 267–282.

Dicken, P (1992) 'International production in a volatile regulatory environment: the influence of national regulatory policies on the spatial strategies of transnational corporations', *Geoforum*, 23(3), 303–336.

Dicken, P (1994) 'Global–local tensions: firms and states in the global space-economy', *Economic Geography*, 70, 101–128.

Dicken, P and Thrift N (1992) 'The organization of production and the production of organization: why business enterprises matter in the study of geographical industrialization', *Transactions of the Institute of British Geographers*, N S, 17(3), 279–291.

Dunning, J H (1988) 'The eclectic paradigm of international production: a restatement and some possible extensions', *Journal of International Business Studies*, 19(1), 1–31.

Dunning, J (1993) *The Globalization of Business*, Routledge, London.

GATT (1991) *Draft Final Act Embodying the Results of the Uruguay Round of Multilateral Trade Negotiations. Annex II: Trade in Services*, GATT Secretariat, Geneva.

Greenaway, D (1991) 'Why are we negotiating on TRIMS?', in Greenaway, D, Hine, R C, O'Brien, A P and Thornton, R J (eds.), *Global Protectionism*, Macmillan, London, Chapter 7.

Hollander, S C (1970) *Multinational Retailing*, MSU International Business and Economic Studies, Michigan State University, East Lansing.

Jenkins, R (1987) *Transnational Corporations and Uneven Development: The Internationalization of Capital and the Third World*, Methuen, London.

Jesudason, J V (1990) *Ethnicity and the Economy. The State, Chinese Business, and Multinationals in Malaysia*, Oxford University Press, Singapore.

Kacker, M (1985) *Transatlantic Trends in Retailing: Takeovers and Flows of Know-How*, Quorum, London.

Kantor, M (1994) *Press Release for Publication of the USTR 1994 Trade Policy Agenda and the 1993 Annual Report*, Office of the USTR, Washington DC, 8 March.

Keatley, R (1994) 'Rules to make GATT into US law clash with pact's principles', *Asian Wall Street Journal*, 19–20 August, p 5.

Koekkoek, K A (1988) 'Trade in services, the developing countries and the Uruguay Round', *The World Economy*, 11(12), 151–155.

Lim, H S (1994) *Japan's Role in ASEAN. Issues and Prospects*, Times Academic Press, Singapore.

Marsden, T and Wrigley, N (forthcoming) 'Retailing, the food system and the regulatory state', in Wrigley, N and Lowe, M S (eds.), *Retailing, Consumption and Capital: Towards the New Retail Geography*, Longman, London, Chapter 2.

McCulloch, R (1990) 'Services and the Uruguay Round', *The World Economy*, 13(3), 329–348.

McGee, J (1987) 'Retailer Strategies in the UK', in Johnson, G (ed.), *Business Strategy and Retailing*, John Wiley & Sons, Chichester, Chapter 6.

Porges, A (1991) 'US–Japan trade negotiations: paradigms lost', in Krugman, P (ed.), *Trade with Japan. Has the Door Opened Wider?* University of Chicago Press, Chicago, Chapter 10.

Porter, M E (1985) *Competitive Advantage. Creating and Sustaining Superior Performance*, Free Press, New York.

Porter, M E (1990) *The Competitive Advantage of Nations*, Macmillan, London.

Rowley, A (1990) 'Shuffling the deck', *Far Eastern Economic Review*, 19 July, p 92.

Russell, H (1989) 'Overview of Amendments in the 1988 Omnibus Trade Bill: Sections 301, "Super 301" and 337', *BYU Law Review*, Issue 1989(2), 729–744.

Salmon, W J and Tordjman A (1989) 'The internationalization of retailing', *International Journal of Retailing*, 4(2), 3–16.

Schlossstein, S (1991) *Asia's New Little Dragons. The Dynamic Emergence of Indonesia, Thailand and Malaysia*, Contemporary Books, Chicago.

Shields, R (ed.) (1992a) *Lifestyle Shopping. The Subject of Consumption*, Routledge, London.

Shields, R (1992b) 'Spaces for the subject of consumption', in Shields, R (ed.), *Lifestyle Shopping. The Subject of Consumption*, Routledge, London, Chapter 1.

Sim, L L and Choo, S (1993) *The Changing Face of Retail Development and Planning in Singapore*, School of Building and Estate Management, National University of Singapore, Singapore.

Svernlöv, C (1992) 'Super 301: gone but not forgotten', *Journal of World Trade*, 26(3), 125–132.

Thrift, N (1994) 'Globalization regulation, urbanisation: the case of the Netherlands', *Urban Studies*, 31(3), 365–380.

Tsay, C-L (1993) 'Industrial restructuring and international competition in Taiwan', *Environment and Planning A*, 25, 111–120.

United Nations Conference on Trade and Development and the World Bank (1994) *Liberalising International Transactions in Services: A Handbook*, United Nations Publications, Geneva.

Wade, L L and Gates, J B (1990) 'A new tariff map of the United States (House of Representatives)', *Political Geography Quarterly*, 9(3), 284–304.

Walker, R (1988) 'The geographical organization of production-systems', *Environment and Planning D*, 6(4), 377–408.

Williams, D E (1991) 'Differential firm advantages and retail internationalization', *International Journal of Retail and Distribution Management*, 19(4), 3–12.

World Bank (1993) *The East Asian Miracle. Economic Growth and Public Policy*, Oxford University Press, Oxford.

Wrigley, N (1992) 'Antitrust regulation and the restructuring of grocery retailing in Britain and the USA', *Environment and Planning A*, 24(5), 722–749.

Yeung, Y M and Yeh, S K (1971) 'Commercial patterns in Singapore's public housing estates', *Journal of Tropical Geography*, 23, 73–86.

CHAPTER 13

Directions for further development and research

Gary Davies

INTRODUCTION

The purpose of this final chapter is to reflect upon what the previous chapters have or have not achieved in developing and communicating our understanding of international retailing. The chapters are based largely on papers delivered at a series of research seminars sponsored by the Economic and Social Research Council (ESRC). The main purpose of the seminar series was to promote discussion and debate among those involved in research into 'retailing'.

The context for much of this research is an explosion of interest in the subject area in Britain during the 1980s. Degrees in retailing at undergraduate level were established at Manchester and Bournemouth Polytechnics, at Surrey, Loughborough and Ulster Universities and at Dundee IHE. An MBA in retailing was begun at Stirling University. Chairs were created in seven centres. Research groups emerged at three British universities. New academic journals were launched. Similar developments began elsewhere in the world. Why?

One answer is that retailing as a business activity has changed. Power has moved down the supply chain from producer to retailer. Retail businesses have become larger and more structured. They have become significant employers of graduates. Higher education has responded to these developments, yet retailing is still far from being seen even in Britain as an academic subject area on a par with, for example, marketing.

One reason for this is the lack of a coherent framework for the study of retailing. The focus for most research into the area is to study the practice of retailing. The intellectual challenge for academics and students is to make orderly sense of what practitioners are doing, to explain and understand what is happening. Many of the preceding chapters present analyses of particular phenomena that are current issues in the retail sector. As such they provide explanations which should be useful to those reading them. One way of categorising such research is to label it as 'advanced market research', the gathering of facts and their interpretation for the benefit of others.

The problem with such an approach is that the results of such work become dated. Look back on similar work conducted in the 1950s and 1960s and very little, if any, is of use today. Academic research should be capable of more than this. Ideally it should also be concerned with developing theory that is not only useful in providing an understanding of what is happening in retailing today but which will provide a similar understanding twenty years hence.

A criticism of the papers presented at the seminars referred to earlier was that all too few were 'theoretically grounded', that is to say few began by referring to established theory on business (in this case on internationalisation). Worse, those who were in the audience listening to the papers being presented were clearly less interested in the papers that did adopt a theoretically grounded approach. Theory can be dull, unfathomable and complex. What happened yesterday in the fast-moving business of retailing is by contrast, exciting and stimulating stuff.

13.1 APPROPRIATE THEORY

Retailing does not have some theory that is specific to it. The most obvious area is that of store location where a number of mathematical models have been developed and used to great effect. The study of marketing channels promised to provide a not too dissimilar framework but has failed to give us more than some useful concepts such as power, leadership and conflict. The study of supply chains offers a development from the marketing channels and logistics literatures that can aid our understanding of retail business.

Beyond these three areas it is difficult to think of much theory that is in any way specific to retailing. If none exists or can be created, then the alternative is to borrow theory from other more established subject areas. Marketing has evolved as a business discipline by borrowing from other social sciences. So should retailing.

There exists a substantial body of research into international business. Much of it concerns manufacturing industry but many of the ideas it contains could be transferred into a retailing context. Internationalisation of business is seen as a multi-stage process explaining the extent, form and choice of location for international production. It is useful to explain the behaviour of multinational firms who have experience in many countries and regions of the world (Johannson and Vahlne, 1990). Such work sees internationalisation as being influenced by many behavioural concepts such as the psychic distance between the home and target market. Such ideas help explain why businesses enter one market rather than another when logic would predict they would act differently. Internationalisation is seen as involving a number of stages. The classification of such stages varies between authors and some may be more relevant than others in a retail context.

A second area of theory involves identifying the characteristics of the management of international firms compared to those who define their boundaries of operation within a domestic market (Barker and Kaynak, 1992; Dichtl *et al*, 1990; Karafakioglu and Harcar, 1990). Such managers are, not surprisingly, more likely to believe that there is greater profit in exporting, but the decision-makers in exporting firms are also found to have different personalities, for example in one such study they were found to be more aggressive and dynamic (Bilkey and Tesar, 1977).

A more controversial topic in the international business literature concerns any relationship between the size of the business and its propensity to export. Most studies find a positive relationship (Bonaccorsi, 1992; Calof, 1994). There is a similar lack of agreement as to the effect of the age of the organisation (Kirpalani and MacIntosh, 1980; Ogram, 1982).

Retail business is often criticised for having a short-term perspective in its strategic planning. The importance and consistency of long-term market strategy is a factor correlated with success in exporting (Bourantas and Halikias, 1991). Information on and knowledge about foreign markets is often a barrier to internationalisation (Samlee and Walters, 1990).

There are a number of strategic options which have been compared in studies of internationalisation, particularly diversification versus concentration (Lee and Yang, 1990; Katsikeas and Morgan, 1994).

13.2   FURTHER RESEARCH

These are just some of the well established lines of research within the broader field of the internationalisation of business, which are often valid irrespective of the type of business being examined. They raise a number of research questions such as these:

- Why do certain retailers become international while other, similar, retailers continue to operate domestically? Can we identify which strategy is to be preferred?
- Are some retailers constrained from becoming international because of the orientation of their senior managers? What training or development needs might this imply?
- How should retailers seek to internationalise? Is concentration on fewer markets the most preferable option or should retailers seek to enter as many markets as they can?

There is still room for much of the phenomenological and comparative research that is typical of much of current research into retailing. There is certainly a parochial need to develop retail-specific theory so as to develop retailing as a subject area. But there is no mileage in reinventing the wheel (no, not the wheel of retailing – that is one theory that will continue to absorb our thinking). There are other wheels, well developed outside of the retail sphere, that could inform retail research and study and short-circuit much current research where similar work has been conducted in other industries.

REFERENCES

Barker, T and Kaynak, E (1992) 'An empirical investigation of the differences between initiating and continuing exporters', *European Journal of Marketing*, 26(3), 27–36.

Bilkey, W J and Tesar, G (1977) 'The export behaviour of smaller-sized Wisconsin manufacturing firms', *Journal of International Business Studies*, 8(1), 93–98.

Bonaccorsi, A (1992) 'On the relationship between firm size and export intensity', *Journal of International Business Studies*, 23(4), 605–635.

Bourantas, D and Halikias, J (1991) 'Discriminating variables between systematic and non-systematic exporting manufacturing firms in Greece', *Journal of Global Marketing*, 4(2), 21–38.

Calof, J L (1994) 'The relationship between firm size and export behaviour revisited', *Journal of International Business Studies*, 25(2), 367–387.

Dichtl, E, Koeglmayr, H-G and Mueller, S (1990) 'International orientation as a precondition for export success', *Journal of International Business Studies*, 21(1), 23–40.

Johannson, J and Vahlne, J E (1990) 'The mechanism of internationalisation', *International Marketing Review*, 17(4), 11–24.

Karafakioglu, M and Harcar, T D (1990) 'Internal determinants affecting interest in exporting: an empirical analysis of Turkish nonexporting companies', *European Journal of Global Marketing*, 3(4) 99–111.

Katsikeas, C S and Morgan, R E (1994) 'Differences in perceptions of exporting problems based on firm size and export market experience', *European Journal of Marketing*, 28(5), 17–35.

Kirplani, V H and MacIntosh, N B (1980) 'Internal marketing effectiveness of technology-oriented small firms', *Journal of International Business Studies*, 11, 81–90.

Lee, C S and Yang, Y S (1990) 'Impact of export market expansion strategy on export performance', *International Marketing Review*, 7(4), 41–51.

Ogram, E W Jr (1982) 'Exporters and non-exporters: a profile of small manufacturing firms in Georgia, in Czinkota, M R and Tesar, G (eds.), *Export Management: An International Context*, New York, pp 70–84.

Samlee, S and Walters, P G P (1990) 'Rectifying strategic gaps in export management', *Journal of Global Marketing*, 4(1), 7–37.

INDEX

N.B. Numbers in **bold type** indicate a table or figure.